To Dearest J.

DAVID BOWIE

Theatre of Music

Robert Matthew-Walker

May the light of youth shine perpetually through those eyes + radiate with vigour from that complexion ---

Yours, Maris

© Robert Matthew-Walker 1985

All rights reserved. No part of this publication may be reproduced, stored in a retrieval system, or transmitted, in any form or by any means, electronic, mechanical, photocopying, recording or otherwise, without prior permission of The Kensal Press.

British Library Catalogue in Publication Data.

Matthew-Walker, Robert
  David Bowie: theatre of music.
  1. Bowie, David
  I. Title
  784.5'0092'4   ML420.B754

ISBN 0-946041-34-2

Published by The Kensal Press
Kensal House, Abbotsbrook, Bourne End, Buckinghamshire.
Second impression 1986

Typeset by Sprint Productions, Beckenham, Kent.

Printed and bound in Great Britain by
Hollen Street Press Ltd, Slough.

Preface

Popular music is many things, and resists attempts to classify and define it. It may, intentionally or otherwise, be neither – paradoxically – popular, nor a branch of art – which it rarely aspires to – although of course it can be both, as well as other things. What cannot be denied is that it is music, and it is in musical terms that it should, in the last analysis, be considered.

It is therefore in these terms that I have attempted, within this book, to describe what I believe to be the important features of David Bowie's musical work. It should be apparent, however, even to the most cursory observer, that the visual presentation of popular music has, in recent years, assumed very great importance; in Bowie's case, this has been an integral feature of his creativity from the very beginning. His music is often conceived in strongly visual terms, and is frequently thus presented. Consequently, the sub-title 'theatre of music' is particularly appropriate for this artist's work. But no matter how strong the visual element, no matter how splendid the spectacle, the value of Bowie's musical creativity has to rest upon the quality of his music. I make no apology, therefore, for discussing Bowie's primarily in terms of his music, and making the theatrical aspect secondary; after all, the most beautifully produced new opera means nothing if the music is of indifferent quality, and certainly will have no future. It is in detailed musical terms that the majority of the analyses in this book have been written, but not so that the interested reader need find himself adrift.

Of the small number of popular 'rock' artists who arose in the 1960s and who have demonstrated lasting qualities, Bowie's output and influence have possibly been more diverse than that of any other. Bowie's variety has often encompassed work which is peripheral to the main thrust of his artistic life; therefore, I make no apology for concentrating almost exclusively upon his albums, which are the main artistic statements a musician can make. I have not interrupted the flow of Bowie's creativity, for example in discussing the Trilogy, to consider in chronological order a release (in that case, the 'Stage' double-album) of little artistic value, but the Discography in Appendix 1 contains comments on those albums which are not analysed in the main body of the book.

In recent years, Bowie's career as an actor has developed considerably, and any book about his music subtitled 'theatre of music' would be incomplete without a discussion of his acting. As a writer on music, I am quite unqualified to discuss this aspect, and so I am very grateful that Curtis Hutchinson, assistant editor of *Films and Filming*, has contributed what seems to me to be an excellent analysis of Bowie as actor.

As I believe an artist's work can be better appreciated once an outline of his life has also been grasped, the first part of this book is biographical, but the reader looking for salacious details will be disappointed. In the first place, such indiscretions as David Bowie may have committed are the province of the detailed biographer; and, in the second place, are of no consequence to the commentator on his music, for such details cannot alter his work. In just the same way, the private details of Tchaikovsky's or Wagner's lives tell us nothing regarding the former's Fourth Symphony or the latter's *Ring* cycle; I have concerned myself with setting out the known facts of Bowie's life as straightforwardly as possible, giving the framework against which the subsequent parts of the book can be set.

If art has any value, this can best be appreciated by reference to the art itself, and not by special pleading on the part of the artist. Even the most fanciful post hoc reasoning will not create on artistic silk purse from a basic sow's ear. An artist is not necessarily the best person to appreciate all the qualities in his own work. This is not to say that the artist's comments are invariably worthless; in Bowie's case, that of an intelligent and perspicacious creator, such views would indeed be valuable. But as he has often been as enigmatic and silent as on other occasions forthcoming in his comments, it is better to treat his stated opinions with caution, and to rely mainly upon our own observations and analyses.

Apart from Curtis Hutchinson, who has helped in various ways, I wish to thank a number of people for their help during the writing of this book. First, Betty Millan and Georgina Shomroni of the Kensal

Press for their infinite patience and understanding; secondly, my ex-colleagues at RCA, particularly Madeleine Kasket, Shaun Greenfield, Tommy Loftus, George Lukan, Ken Glauncy; and Rodney Burbeck, James Greet and Modwenna Chamberlain. Thanks should also be extended to those who have supplied photographs and given permission for their reproduction. Finally, I must thank my wife for her support and forbearance during the writing of this book.

R.M.-W. London July 1985

Contents

Preface
Illustrations

Part I   The Man
1	Origins	3
2	The Growth of the Artist	10
3	At the Crossroads	18
4	Virginibus Puerisque	23
5	The View from the Top	34
6	Apotheosis	43

Part II   The Music
7	The Early Years 1964–69	57
8	The Stardust Years 1970–72	71
9	After Stardust 1973–76	96
10	The Trilogy 1977–79	110
11	Into the Eighties	126

Part III   The Artist
12	Bowie as Producer	143
13	Bowie as Actor *by Curtis Hutchinson*	149
14	Conclusion: Theatre of Music	163

Appendix 1   Select Discography 169
Appendix 2   Filmography 185
Select Bibliography 189
Index of Music and Album Titles 191
Index of Persons 195

Illustrations

Frontispiece: David Bowie. *Photograph: London Features International.*
David Bowie in 1971.
1972 in the Ziggy period.
As Ziggy Stardust 1973.
Live on stage, during the Ziggy Stardust era. *Photograph: London Features International.*
David Bowie in 1973.
Live on stage c. 1974.
Live c. 1975. *Photograph: Andy Kent.*
David Bowie with Bing Crosby, on Crosby's television show, December 1977.
As Paul von Przygodsky in the Leguan film production 'Just a Gigolo' (1978).
As Major Jack Celliers in the Nagisa Oshima film 'Merry Christmas Mr. Lawrence' 1983. *Photograph: Palace Pictures.*
As 'The Shark' in 'Yellowbeard' (1983). *Photograph: Rank Films.*
David Bowie with Catherine Deneuve in 'The Hunger' (1983). *Photograph: MGM/UA Entertainment Co.*
In 'Jazzin' for Blue Jean' (1984).
Portrait from 'Jazzin' for Blue Jean' (1984).
Hamlet. *Photograph: London Features International.*
Live in the Eighties. *Photograph: David Redfern.*
David Bowie as Colin Morris and Michelle Pfeiffer as Diana in Universal Pictures 'Into the Night' (1985). *Photograph: Universal City Studios.*

PART I
THE MAN

CHAPTER ONE

Origins

At the time of David Robert Jones's birth, on January 8th 1947 at 40 Stansfield Road, Brixton, London SW9, that suburb of London was very different from what it became a few years later. To most people today Brixton means an area of high immigration, but to the immediate post-war inhabitants it retained, apart from the obvious scars of the bombing, a large part of its traditional character. Brixton developed, as did most suburbs of London, in the second half of the nineteenth century, and was notable for its high incidence of housing for the prosperous middle class, from which David Jones's father, Haywood Stenton, had come. It would not be true to describe the boy's father as retaining much of his middle class background, for in the years before World War II he had lost a reasonably substantial legacy on a business venture in London. The business venture was a small drinking club, hardly the sort of investment one would have expected the son of a Doncaster shoe manufacturer to consider making with his legacy of £2,000. Apparently the failure of this drinking club told heavily on Haywood; shortly afterwards he took a job with Dr Barnardo's Homes at Stepney Causeway, an organization for which he worked until his death in 1969.

David's father had been born in 1912 and so was eligible for call-up into the armed forces following the outbreak of World War II. He did not wait, however, for he joined the Army as a volunteer soon after war was declared. His wife Hilda was unable to have children. But in 1941 his daughter, Annette, was born, to a nurse with whom Haywood had developed a liaison. The child, however, was brought up by Haywood's wife. During the war Haywood Jones served in the Eighth Army in north Africa and after demobilization he returned to his job with the Homes.

War changes many people, and the marriage between Haywood and

Hilda had been fractured by their separation. In 1946, whist working for Dr Barnardos, he often visited their Home at Tunbridge Wells, and it was there that he met a waitress, Margaret Burns, known as Peggy, and shortly afterwards they fell in love. Peggy and Haywood lived together for a time in North London and after a while they bought a house in Stansfield Road, Brixton. At this time Peggy was expecting Haywood's child and the parents were waiting for the divorce from Hilda which finally became absolute in 1947. Peggy had two previous children. The first, a son Terence, was born in 1937 and a daughter Myra Ann in 1943. In both cases she had been let down by the fathers and had not married either of them. Terence lived with his mother's parents and Myra was adopted as a baby, so when David was born his mother was experiencing day to day life with a man for the first time. She stipulated that Terry should come to live with her and Haywood after their marriage, which occurred on 12th September 1947. They had no more children, so David was their only child, but in Terry he effectively had an older brother. His father's work was centred mainly at Dr Barnardo's near Kings Cross and his mother took part-time work in a local Brixton cinema.

The two boys, apart from the nine-year difference in their ages, got on very well and indeed Terry was an important influence on David. While Terry attended the Henry Thornton Grammar School in Clapham, David's first schooling was in Streatham Hill, South Lambeth, but in the summer of 1955 both boys were sent to Haywood's brother's farmhouse in Yorkshire where they lived for two years. During that time David attended boarding school near Doncaster and his first musical impressions were of a cousin dancing to Elvis Presley's "Hound Dog". By all accounts the first record David owned was "Blueberry Hill" by Fats Domino but the most important influence on the young boy of the first wave of the new Rock and Roll stars was Little Richard, whose "Ready Teddy" and "Rip It Up" were favourite songs.

In the summer of 1957 the boys returned to the London area to a new home which their parents had bought in Sundridge Park near Bromley. This was just on the boundaries of London and Kent. Their parents had been living there for some months to prepare for the boys' return and this little terraced house in Plaistow Grove remained David's home for the next twelve years. Plaistow Grove adjoins Sundridge Park station and is behind the Crown public house in Plaistow Lane. David finished his junior schooling at Burnt Ash Junior Mixed School in

Rangefield Road close by. In September 1958 David began his secondary schooling at Bromley Technical High School, Keston, an all-boys school. For a short time David sang in the choir of St Mary's church where another member of the choir was George Underwood. They had met in 1957 whilst enrolling in the cubs of the Eighteenth Bromley Scouts. Both boys went to Bromley Technical High School and became life-long friends. This did not prevent them falling out on occasion and a fight between them in which George got the better of David affected the loser's right eye so much that David was taken to Farnborough Hospital where both eyes were operated upon. David remained in hospital for three months, but before this his musical ability had already begun to show itself.

His mother had bought him a saxophone for Christmas at the end of 1959 following his obsession with a plastic model on which he taught himself sufficiently well to have learnt by heart a song by Little Richard. In 1960, when he was thirteen, David arranged lessons from the saxophonist Ronnie Ross who lived in Orpington a few miles away. He had also been strumming a ukelele but the saxophone was his first instrumental love. By 1962 David was proficient enough to be able to think of forming his own group and they played at the school Parent Teachers' Association fête during that summer, a few months after the fight with George Underwood. As was the custom of the day, the five members of the band went to the expense of having identical suits made. By this time David's older brother had introduced him to the work of jazz musicians John Coltrane and Eric Dolphy as well as the writings of the American Beat Generation. A teacher on the staff of Bromley Technical High School was a Mr Frampton who organised a concert to raise money for a proposed sports pavilion. Three bands appeared at the concert, one being David's band, the Kon-Rads, another George and the Dragons (founded by George Underwood), but the top billing went to the Little Ravens, in which group Mr Frampton's son Peter played. There were two performances and the appeal for money was successful, for the pavilion which was built as a result of this concert still stands. Peter Frampton later recalled that by this time David had become the hero of the school: "David brought the house down", he said. It is significant that the previous Christmas (1962) the Kon-Rads sent out a Christmas card in their own name on which David signed himself Dave J.

In July 1963 David left school with GCE 'O' levels in Art and

Woodwork. He had little idea apparently of what he wanted to do apart from a vague notion of becoming a commercial artist which indeed he could have achieved through his first job, a visualiser at a commercial art company, which he started the moment he left school. He did not stay there long, however, as the pull of music was too strong. In the evenings he played saxophone and this took its inevitable toll on his energy in the shape of continuous late nights. Less than six months later David quit his job and decided to attempt to become a full-time musician. A chance meeting with three aspiring fellow musicians in a barber's shop in Bromley, whilst waiting for their hair to be styled, led to talking and the decision to form themselves into a band. They were known as the King Bees and specialised in rhythm and blues.

This was the first and most important change of direction in David's early life, for the music they played was some way from the jazz which David had previously attempted. In April 1964, after they had been playing together for several months, they took the surprising step of writing directly to John Bloom, a popular millionaire who had made a fortune from revitalising the Rolls Razor company by providing cheap and serviceable washing machines. The letter asked for financial help for the band. Bloom must have been impressed by their initiative for he passed the letter on to his friend Leslie Conn who was in the music business. Conn contacted David and engaged the King Bees to play at a wedding anniversary party in Soho. Although they were paid £100 for the gig their style of music did not really appeal to the guests for they were asked to stop after only two numbers.

Conn, however was sufficiently impressed with them to get them a contract with Decca who issued a single on the Vocalion label of "Liza Jane" and "Louie, Louie, Go Home" in June 1964. On the strength of their record they were able to appear at the Marquee Club and the Roundhouse as well as a number of universities. Although the King Bees went on to make at least one more record on the Coral label, this was with George Underwood, who had replaced David, for by this time he had joined his next band, the Manish Boys, whilst remaining on good terms with Conn, particularly as he had engineered David's first television appearance to promote the Vocalion single. Unfortunately, the record, although it had been featured on the television show "Juke Box Jury", was not a hit and listening to it today one can understand why. It was during the time that David was managed by Leslie Conn that he met Marc Bolan and the two struck up a friendship which lasted until Bolan's untimely death in 1977.

David's new group, the Manish Boys, originally came from Maidstone where they were known locally as Band Seven. It is uncertain how David met this band or under what circumstances they changed their name, but they were a seven-piece outfit of which David was clearly the leader. The style of music they played was greatly influenced by Georgie Fame and Zoot Money's Big Roll Band with a greater emphasis on the rockjazz organ character of both groups. They built up an impressive local following and created considerable publicity for themselves by wearing their hair very long. This was before long hair as such became fashionable, and cashing in on their hair David founded the International League for the Preservation of Animal Filament (i.e. long hair). On the strength of this David appeared with other members of the Manish Boys and the King Bees on BBC1 television in November 1964, interviewed by Cliff Michelmore, defending their flowing locks.

Because of their local success they were able to engage the interest of Shel Talmy, a noted record producer, who agreed to record them. They recorded two songs, "I Pity The Fool" and "Take My Tip". Apparently Talmy intended to get a single issued on Decca, but for reasons which are not clear it was never released. Talmy must have had faith in David's ability as a songwriter for he introduced "Take My Tip" to the singer Kenny Miller who recorded it, the disc being issued in 1965 on EMI's Stateside label. This was the first song by David that had been recorded by any artist.

Two months later the Manish Boys single was finally released on the Parlophone label. The billing on the label somewhat upset David who imagined the band would by billed as 'Davy Jones (by which name he had now come to be known) and the Manish Boys', but his name was omitted as top billing. Three days after the record was released Les Conn had arranged for the group to appear in the new BBC2 television programme "Gadzooks! It's all happening" but the length of David's hair caused some consternation to the producer Barry Langford who demanded that it be shortened. This was a heaven-sent publicity opportunity which Conn used to the full, persuading fans to picket the BBC studios with placards, as the group's appearance would not take place on the live show without them previously having had a haircut. A compromise was effected when David agreed to a trim. However, the resultant publicity did not help the sales of this second single on which David sang, and it flopped badly.

The group supported Gerry and the Pacemakers, the Kinks and Gene Pitney on tour but the lack of success and a certain amount of tension within the band – probably coupled with inordinate delay in the release of the single – led them to split up by the end of March. Immediately afterwards David joined forces with The Lower Third. They originally came from Margate and were a five-piece group, but in the month of David's split from the Manish Boys three of the members had travelled to London. They were loooking for a singer to join them and David attended the audition and got the job, although he placed as much faith in his ability as a saxophonist as in his ability as a singer. They got on very well and stayed together for almost a year during which time thir reputation increased enormously.

This reputation grew through hard work. Davy Jones and the Lower Third played their first gigs together in towns on the south coast of England, particularly Bournemouth, in June and July 1965. They supported Johnny Kidd and the Pirates (whose big hit "Shakin' All Over" became one of the most important British ethnic rock singles) in the Isle of Wight, at Ventnor. In the following month the first single by Davy Jones (and the Lower Third) was issued, also produced by Shel Talmy, on the Parlophone label. Both songs were composed by David and were "You've Got A Habit Of Leaving" and "Baby Loves That Way". By all accounts the press cover obtained for the release of this single marked a distinct advance over that accorded David's previous releases, but once again there was a series of internal disagreements. These were not too serious in themselves but probably arose from the fact that the band was not credited on the label. They led, however, to disastrous consequences. Talmy severed his connections with the group. The lack of success for this single was in part, perhaps, the result. Some impact was made by the disc, because towards the end of 1965 the influential record executive, composer and producer, Tony Hatch, signed David and the band to Pye Records.

The following year David and Hatch intended to collaborate on a musical called "Kids on the Roof" along the lines of Lionel Bart's "Oliver". This never materialised but apparently a number of ideas led to a planned television series called "Peacock's Farm", concerning the adventures of a young man who ran a fashionable boutique. Once again this project came to nothing, but these ideas surfaced later on David's album for the Decca Deram label, "David Bowie".

Prior to this David and the band were working reasonably frequently, particularly at the Marquee Club in London's Wardour Street. A result of their appearances at the club was that they came to the attention, through a mutual acquaintance, of Kenneth Pitt who first saw them at one of their live Sunday afternoon appearances. Pitt was sufficiently impressed to seek a meeting in which it was agreed that he should become David's manager.

Ralph Horton had been looking after David's affairs and was responsible for the change in David's appearance. Gone now was the long hair of previous months, to be replaced by a more fashionable style, accompanied by a change to a more modern style of dress. At the end of 1965, in fact on New Year's Eve, Davy Jones and the Lower Third played their first (and as it transpired, their last) date outside the British Isles when they appeared at the Golfe-Drouot Club in Paris, with The Crazy World Of Arthur Brown.

It was also David's last appearance under his own name.

CHAPTER TWO

The Growth of the Artist

Tony Hatch had not been idle; David and the band had recorded their first Pye single featuring two songs by David, "Can't Help Thinking About Me" and "And I Say To Myself". Kenneth Pitt, although he was not yet officially David's manager (and did not so become until a few months later) cabled David from New York that he had seen a new American group, which had been formed for a television series, called The Monkees. One of the members of this band was an English actor called Davy Jones and it was quite clear that if, as seemed likely, the series was to be shown in England there would be considerable confusion between David Jones and Davy Jones. A change of name therefore was demanded and immediately David changed his professional name to David Bowie.

One may speculate fruitlessly as to why this particular name was chosen. It may have been, as some have suggested, that it was because of David's fascination for the American Jim Bowie, the inventor of the Bowie knife, an instrument with a distinctively shaped blade. It may equally have been because David felt a name was required which would be familiar internationally. Jim Bowie was a famous figure, but most importantly, perhaps, it was because the name was unique in the world of entertainment. There could be no confusion in the future. Whatever the reason, it proved to be a brilliantly successful choice, and the first single to be released under the new Pye contract, issued by the company on 14th January 1966, also marked the debût of David Bowie's name on a record label.

This record did much better than any of David's previous singles and within a month of its release it had entered the *Melody Maker*'s Top Fifty charts (albeit at number forty-five). In spite of this, and further press coverage in the shape of his first press interviews, for *Disc and Music Echo*, the single failed to capture the public's imagination, although a contributory factor could have been that Pye's promotion department was being worked very hard at the time with no less than seven singles in the top Fifty. As is so often the case, the demands of constant live appearances and the necessity of being immediately available for media interviews meant that David and the band had virtually no time they could call their own. With the failure of this first Pye single the Lower Third disbanded late in February 1966 after an extensive tour.

Almost immediately David got together a new band, The Buzz, with whom he appeared on the brilliant live television show "Ready, Steady, Go!" performing "Can't Help Thinking About Me". Significantly, in view of one of David's later creations, he appeared on this show wearing an all-white suit. This was on 4th March, and three days later David and the Buzz were in the Pye recording studios putting down David's next single, a coupling of "Do Anything You Say" and "Good Morning Girl". This was his first release as a solo artist, for The Buzz were regarded as no more than session musicians for this purpose and were paid the standard rate of £9 each with no rights to royalties. Sadly, this record did even worse than the previous single and the lack of success possibly caused Pye to have second thoughts as to the wisdom of their signing. David, however, together with The Buzz, continued touring and had built up a small but ardent coterie of fans. They travelled to Scotland early in April and a fortnight later the singer signed a five-year contract with Pitt.

The following month the first David Bowie and the Lower Third single was released in the United States by Warner Bros., by which time Pye seem to have indicated a growing uncertainty as to the likelihood of their continuing to record David. In the summer of 1966 his regular appearances at the Marquee Club had become known as the "Bowie Showboat", and the pirate radio station, Radio London, had been sufficiently taken with them to sponsor six Sunday afternoon shows which were broadcast in August.

With such a respected figure as Kenneth Pitt working with them, together with the records, live appearances and broadcasts, it may seem strange in retrospect that Bowie had not achieved any real success by then on a national scale. The essential reason for this, as anyone can tell who listens to the recorded matter released during this time, was that Bowie's music lacked quality, originality and distinctiveness. Ralph Horton was still working with the band, but Pye's decision to drop

David must have come as a serious blow. Or so it would seem; in fact Pitt's inability to break his artist into the charts in any meaningful way meant that the time was ripe for a fresh approach.

Towards the end of 1966 the Decca company, having achieved world fame for turning down The Beatles, but redeeming themselves somewhat by signing The Rolling Stones, was starting a new contemporary label called Deram. In spite of the lack of commercial success David had experienced in 1966, he continued to compose, and by September of that year had written enough songs to make an album. Thanks to Pitt's brilliant negotiating skills Decca were persuaded to issue a contract for David to make an album on the Deram label, which must have come as a considerable boost to David's self confidence.

With the Decca contract safely assured Pitt travelled to America in an attempt to sign David's publishing rights to an international company. According to Pitt he actually succeeded in doing this, obtaining an undertaking that the company would pay David a considerable advance in royalties, but while he was in America – and subsequently in Australia – Ralph Horton had secured a contract with Essex music which David had signed, and which offered an advance against royalties substantially less than that which Pitt had negotiated in New York. Pitt intended to keep the announcement of his successful negotiations a secret until he returned, but on his arrival back in Britain, doubtlessly shocked and disappointed that a far less attractive contract had already been signed in his absence, he decided not to tell David, fearing that he would only cause great disappointment at a crucial stage in his career. One should not be too hard on those responsible for signing the contract with Essex Music: it was dated 7th December 1966, five days after David's single for Deram had been released, a coupling of "Rubber Band" and "London Boys". Clearly, with a new single out on a new label, some sort of publishing deal was essential, although in retrospect, of course, one can only wonder What Might Have Been.

During the early weeks of 1967 preparations were well advanced for the first album, which was virtually completed by the end of February. On 14th April, Decca issued the second single of two more Bowie songs, "The Laughing Gnome" and "The Gospel According to Tony Day" which is interesting if only for having backing vocals supported in part by Kenneth Pitt. Pitt must have had some success during his American visit outside of the abortive publishing deal, for the resultant "David Bowie" album was first released in the USA in April, two months before its initial release in Britain. However, the U.S. version omitted two tracks which subsequently appeared on Decca LP. They were "We Are Hungry Men" and "Maids Of Bond Street".

Significantly, Bowie appeared to be the first British artist to issue an album without having first had a hit single, and a few weeks prior to the U.K. release of the album Bowie was introduced to a man who had considerable influence on his future career, Tony Visconti. Tony and David took to each other immediately and became close friends. Tony Hall, a Decca executive who had been most enthusiastic about David's potential and who had used his influence within the company to great effect on Bowie's behalf, left Decca around 1967, with the result that one of the main driving forces within the company, whose influence could have been very important, was not available at the crucial time of the release of the album. Pitt became alarmed at the consequent lack of interest he felt was being shown to the release of the LP and the second single, and wrote to the company expressing his unease, but his letter appeared to have little effect. As a result of Hall leaving the company, and possibly also the wide-ranging nature of David's material, the album did not do at all well, although it received some reasonably significant airplay as well as some effective press notices. One of the comments most frequently expressed concerning the album was of an apparent similarity David had to the English actor-singer Anthony Newley, but in truth this was merely superficial. Occasionally one could note a connecting tone between the two, but in retrospect there really is no comparison. In many ways Bowie's first LP was artistically a success, and almost twenty years later it can still be listened to for enjoyment and interest, although occasionally one has to use a certain amount of indulgence.

The following month (July) the third Decca single was issued, of one song taken from the album, "Love You Till Tuesday", and "Did You Ever Have A Dream?", a new version of the song "When I Live My Dreams", which closed side one of the original LP. This proved to be David's biggest Deram single so far and his growing importance as a songwriter is shown by the fact that the British MOR singer, Ronnie Hilton, recorded "The Laughing Gnome" for HMV a month or two earlier.

It says much for Bowie's inner strength of character that far from sitting back and basking in the achievement of having had an album issued at last, he continued exploring and experimenting with artistic possibilities, for shortly after moving from his home in Sundridge Park to a spare room at Kenneth Pitt's West End flat at the height of the early 'flower power' movement, he began to study Buddhism on an occasional basis. This was not because of any growing religious conviction, but simply because of the undoubted benefits in terms of mental clarity that the religion offers. Furthermore, at around this time David came under the influence (which has since been disputed in terms of length and importance) of Lindsay Kemp, who claimed to be descended from William Kemp, a sixteenth-century pierrot figure who appeared with Shakespeare at the Globe Theatre on Bankside. Kemp also undertook what was called "Kemp's Nine Daies Wonder", when he danced from London to Norwich in nine days.

Lindsay Kemp had become known as a highly talented and respected mime artist and it was doubtless this aspect of his work that attracted Bowie to him, for there had been in Bowie's stage work from the previous two or three years a growing element of theatricality in terms of presentation. One can make too much of it at this stage of Bowie's career: but a historic streak was clearly already there. He showed an interest in it and a desire for it. David obviously felt the need for what might at first have seemed a surprising move and within a few months of study David appeared with Kemp's company in a mime production, "Pierrot-In-Turquoise". David made his first appearance in the role on 28th December 1967 in Oxford, with subsequent appearances the following month in Cumberland, and in March over an eleven-day period in the show's brief run at the Mercury Theatre, Notting Hill Gate, concluding with performances at the Intimate Theatre in Palmers Green.

In the last four months of 1967, while it was obvious the Decca album was unlikely to become a major commercial success, some idea of Bowie's importance as a songwriter can be obtained from the fact that songs by him were recorded by a growing number of singers and groups. In November he appeared on Dutch television for the first time and a week before Christmas sang five songs on the BBC radio show "Top Gear". For this engagement David was accompanied by an orchestra conducted by Tony Visconti. Within the first week of 1968, and just before his twenty-first birthday, David auditioned for BBC television for a play, "The Pistol Shot". The part was a non-speaking small rôle but at least David was successful and the play was recorded, for later transmission towards the end of January, at the BBC Television Centre in Shepherd's Bush, London.

"The Pistol Shot" was shown on 30th January; another member of the cast was Hermione Farthingale, a young lady for whom David clearly developed a strong attraction as the two lived together for a while. Nor is this the full extent of Bowie's activities at this time. He was engaged by Essex Music to write the English lyrics for a number of foreign songs, which because of the company's international connections were continually being received. The impact in America of the "David Bowie" LP had also not been as successful as the record company had hoped, but this was not due to any lack of enthusiasm or promotional expertise on the part of those working on it. The first printed book of music by Bowie was issued in America by the U.S. affiliates of Essex Music some months after the release of the album. When all this activity is taken into account it is clear that David had a great many lines to hang on to to compensate for the lack of commercial success of his current material. For someone with a certain belief in himself, such as he had, it was clearly only a matter of time before the longed-for breakthrough arrived.

Still, an artist needs more than a belief in himself to survive, and Kenneth Pitt was anxious to ensure some regular, if not greater, income for David. He suggested that he adapt his music and presentation with a view to breaking into the lucrative cabaret market: in retrospect, a surprising decision but really nothing more than an extension of the work David had undertaken with the Kemp company. Although "Pierrot-In-Turquoise" was a mime production, he had sung several songs in the course of each performance and it surely did not need much imagination to see that this approach might very well be adapted for cabaret performances. It did not lead to successful results, at least in commercial terms, although he had undertaken a mime engagement at the Royal Festival Hall in June 1968 as part of a more traditional rock concert in which Marc Bolan and other artists appeared too. The audience was not enthusiastic.

By this time David had been offered the chance, through an affiliate company of Essex Music, to write the English words to a French song, "Ronnie d'Habitude" by Claude François. David's lyric was called "Even A Fool Learns To Love" of which he made a demo recording by the simple expedient of overdubbing himself on the François single. Nothing came of this, either, and a few weeks later the Frank Sinatra version of the Paul Anka lyric, "My Way", was released to the same tune.

Following this David formed a new multi-media group, Feathers, made up of David, Hermione and John Hutchinson. This also was not a commercial success: although recordings were made, none was issued commercially. The group did not last many months, their last appearance being on 8th February 1969. Curiously enough, this performance was actually preserved on celluloid as part of a much larger film which had been suggested to Pitt by a German television producer. The idea behind the film was to showcase David's many talents and specifically to utilise songs from the Decca LP. Although filming began in February 1969 in Greenwich, south-east London, before the film had been completed the German interest had evaporated and the sponsors withdrew their financial commitment. This left Pitt having to put £7,000 of his own money into the venture to ensure that the film was completed. Significantly the film included a new song specially written for the project, "Space Oddity". This was inspired by Stanley Kubrick's *2001: A Space Oddyssey*, a remarkable film of considerable impact and influence. David's film has never been shown in its entirety, although various segments of it have, and it was many months before "Space Oddity" was released on disc. A more significant appearance on celluloid, however, simply because it *was* shown, was undertaken by David towards the end of 1968 when he appeared in the film version of Leslie Thomas's *The Virgin Soldiers* as an extra.

The new year 1969 dawned with continuing disappointments, particularly the abortive television film, and yet with the continuing belief of David and Kenneth Pitt in the ultimate success of their work. An insignificant but curious aspect of David's career on film at this time was his appearance in a Lyons' Maid Ice Cream television commercial. This was to launch a new brand of ice cream, "Luv", and although the commercial was shown, and was by all accounts a good piece of work, the ill luck that seemed to have dogged Bowie's efforts up to that time (with one or two notable exceptions) even affected the success of this new confection, for "Luv" did not catch on.

At around this time David and Hermione split up and Pitt's disenchantment with Decca led him to seek a new record company for his artist. At the same time Pitt was successful in arranging for David to appear in *The Image*, a film directed by Michael Armstrong, in which Bowie appears as the image of the title as "The Boy", whose physical appearance fascinates an aspiring painter. Prior to making *The Image* Michael Armstrong indicated to David that he wished him to write the music for what would have been his first feature film, "A Floral Tale". This was never made although David did write seven pieces of music for it which have never been released. During the early part of 1969 David additionally played support gigs to Marc Bolan's Tyrannosaurus Rex, as a one-man mime show.

Shortly afterwards he met Mary-Angela Barnet at a press reception at the Speakeasy venue in London, held to promote the group King Crimson.

CHAPTER THREE

At the Crossroads

Mary-Angela Barnet was born in the late summer of 1949 on the island of Cyprus. At the time her father ran the mill for a mining company at Xeros, having served with the American army during World War II, where he had risen to the rank of Colonel. Angela (the name by which she is best known) was the second of two children; her brother Milton John was sixteen years old when she was born. Her mother, Helena Marie, was of Polish extraction, although her father, as indeed her mother, was American, his parents having been British. After schooling in Cyprus, later at Clarens near Montreux, and Connecticut, Angela found her way to London where her mother initially accompanied her as chaperone. Angela enrolled at a secretarial college in Oxford Street for a shorthand-typing course, following which she applied for a place at Kingston Polytechnic to read for a degree in Economics with an alternative Higher National Diploma in Business Studies. This was in 1968, and during her first year at the Polytechnic she shared a bed-sit in Surbiton. Unfortunately she had not pursued her studies assiduously and she was shaken to learn that the Polytechnic staff refused to let her take her finals because her lecture attendances had been insufficient. Rather than return to her parents she resolved to stay in London and took a job with the Travel Club in Sussex Gardens, sharing a flat above the premises.

It was while she was working at the Club one day that Calvin Mark Lee came in and struck up a friendship for her. At this time she had vague notions of becoming an actress and hoped that Lee, who worked for Mercury Records, might be able to further her interest in this direction. One evening early in 1969, Bowie's group Feathers was playing at the Roundhouse as a support act to The Who and The Scaffold. This was the first time Angela saw Bowie and she was immediately captured by his charismatic personality on stage. After the show she was briefly introduced to him and following the proper introduction by Lee at the Speakeasy the three of them, Angela, David, and Lee had dinner.

Lee would have known of David in any event, owing to his position in an important record company, but concurrently with this meeting Kenneth Pitt was pursuing negotiations with Mercury Records in an attempt to get David signed to that company. He was successful and in the middle of 1969 the contract was finalised. Mercury Records in the UK was handled by the Dutch giant Philips but it was an independent organisation in the US and it was through the parent American company that Pitt managed to get David signed. The first project under this new deal, potentially the most exciting that David had had with a record company up to that time, was a new recording of "Space Oddity" coupled with "Wild Eyed Boy From Freecloud". This was recorded on 20th June with Rick Wakeman and Herbie Flowers as well as Paul Buckmaster among the backing musicians. With the imminent launch of the American Apollo space mission, a successful attempt to land men on the moon scheduled for the third week in July, there was considerable urgency to get this single released during the month of the moonshot.

It was in fact issued in the UK on 11th July by Philips and marked David's first important success. After a great deal of hard work the single entered the charts two months later. The record was also released in America at the same time but apart from creating a certain amount of media interest the single was by no means as successful in that country. While "Space Oddity" was creating interest, David and Kenneth Pitt flew to Malta where David participated in the Maltese Song Festival. This was not regarded as a particularly important engagement but it did provide an important break from the hectic schedule, as well as affording a few days in the sun. David, who sang "When I Live My Dream" to an orchestral accompaniment by Norrie Paramor, was awarded second prize and following this success the party flew to Rome *en route* to Monsummano-Terme where the organisers of the Malta Festival had arranged to hold a repeat competition. Some time before David told Kenneth Pitt that Angela might be joining them there. In the weeks following their meeting in London Angela and David had fallen in love, and it was appropriate that she should spend time with him on her way to join her parents in Cyprus for a short holiday. This second festival, *Carasello Internazionale Del Disco*, had not been as well organised as the first in Malta: when it was discovered that the members of the backing band could not read music the arranged performances had to be abandoned. In their place an impromptu concert was given, at David's instigation, and many of the personnel associated with the event were anxious that David should receive an award for his efforts to save the situation. According to Kenneth Pitt, it was suggested that David be awarded a special prize entitled "Best Produced Record". David and Kenneth returned to London, the former clutching his award, and Angela left for Cyprus.

During this time of the growing relationship between Angela and David they had moved into a large house in Beckenham where, close by, The Three Tuns public house permitted him to use a large spare back room to play in. There he created the Beckenham Arts Lab. David had definite ideas about how this organisation should work. He particularly wanted it to be devoted to those popular arts which were then termed 'underground'. The phrase was frequently used at the time, referring to those popular artistic manifestations, particularly music, which lacked commercial success but were notable for the fierce dedication of the frequently anarchist people who created them. On the day of David and Kenneth's return to London, Sunday 3rd August, he went to the Arts Lab that evening to perform. He would have been in high spirits following his Mediterranean success and the sales of "Space Oddity", but this evaporated when he was horrified to learn at the end of his performance that his father Haywood was seriously ill. He travelled immediately to his parents' home and it was there that his father died several days later, but not before David had shown him the award he had gained in Italy.

David, with Pitt's assistance, attended to the administration of his father's estate. It was decided that that the house should be sold, and so it was a few months later. The following weeks were hectic. With "Space Oddity" steadily moving up the charts Pitt was able to get David an appearance on the BBC television show "Top Of The Pops", which coincided with the usual press interest which attends the first important hit by an artist. The success of the single now assured, plans were advanced in the Philips organisation for the release of the first album under David's new contract, which was scheduled for 14th November. The album was entitled "David Bowie" and featured nine songs, all composed by David and recorded at the Trident Studios in London. A few weeks previously David had appeared on tour with Humble Pie, a new band managed by Andrew Loog Oldham, who at that time also handled The Rolling Stones, but his appearances were not uniformly successful. However, around the time of the album's release he undertook another tour in Scotland followed by an appearance at the Purcell Room, part of the South Bank complex, an event which had a number of backstage problems. These were not communicated to the enthusiastic audience, but someone omitted to ask the Press 'en bloc', the only reference appearing in 'The Observer' by Tony Palmer, who had been invited by Kenneth Pitt, with the result that this appearance, which by all accounts was sensational, went almost unreported.

An interesting spin-off from the Beckenham Arts lab was the 'Free Festival' which David organised at the near-by Croydon Road Recreation Ground. David later said of this, "It was a very unusual kind of festival because it was all local people . . . the idea was just to get people from the area who never got the chance to be seen by more than a hundred people . . . the enthusiasm was tremendous." Indeed this was a very successful event of its kind for over 5,000 people turned up and David performed with a few musicians for 90 minutes, being praised by the Mayor and the local Superintendent of Police for the excellent way in which it had been organised. Although David never repeated this experience, its success obviously meant a great deal to him for he commemorated the occasion in a song, "Memory Of A Free Festival", which was later released as a single. During the month of October, which saw "Space Oddity" approaching the zenith of its popularity, David and Angela had moved from the place they shared after his father's death to a much larger building in Southend Road, Beckenham. A number of friends joined them in this Victorian town house and perhaps for the first time in his life David found himself in a domestic environment which suited his lifestyle and encouraged his creativity.

The following month David received his first British accolade, the Ivor Novello Award, from the Songwriters' Guild of Great Britain for what was termed the most original song of the year: "Space Oddity". And on the last day of that month he was presented to HRH Princess Margaret at a charity concert at the London Palladium. His relationship with Angela had developed further and by the end of the year they had decided to marry as soon as was practible.

In America, the Mercury Corporation had been disappointed at the initial lack of success of "Space Oddity" but towards the end of October they released the single again, servicing national and local disc-jockeys and the Press. Unfortunately the message contained in the song, that of an astronaut who is unable to return to earth, caused considerable resentment and led to the song not being selected for airplay by many stations. As a result "Space Oddity" failed to take off at its second attempt in the US. In Europe, however, the success of "Space Oddity" gathered pace, and David travelled to Berlin (for the first time) to appear on television, and later to Zurich, where he appeared on the Swiss television programme "Hits A Go Go".

By the end of the year the single had virtually dropped from the charts in the U.K. but it had sold over 100,000 copies and had guaranteed a ready acceptance for the new album. At long last, Bowie had arrived.

CHAPTER FOUR

Virginibus Puerisque

1970 dawned with David's career seemingly set fair for continued success. A follow-up single to "Space Oddity" now became necessary and it was decided that a new song "The Prettiest Star" would be it, coupled with a new recording (with Decca's permission) of a song originally written for them, "London Bye Ta Ta". These were recorded with some doubt as to which would be the 'A' side. Before these problems were resolved David had been voted 'Brightest Hope' in the *Disc and Music Echo* readers' poll and he received the award in the second week of February.

    David also decided to form a more permanent backing group and put together a band called The Hype which included Tony Visconti on bass and John Cambridge on drums. They appeared on 3rd February at the Marquee Club where they shared both the billing and the drummer (Cambridge) with another band, Junior's Eyes, which were about to split up. In the audience was a young guitarist, Mick Ronson, who agreed to join The Hype and live in David's house in Beckenham. Within a few days he appeared with David in the new line-up but Philips had meanwhile scheduled the release of the new single in early March when "London Bye Ta Ta" was replaced by another song, "Conversation Piece". The success of David on the Philips label had caused Decca to reactivate their Bowie material and on the same day that saw the release of the new single Decca reissued the first LP including some previously unreleased material, in their "World Of" series of budget records. These releases should have guaranteed adequate exposure for the new single, and this is indeed what it obtained, but it was not translated into chart success. Not for the first time in the music business, and certainly not for the last, did a follow-up single to a previous hit fail to achieve the hoped-for repeat success. At this time David and The Hype were performing relatively frequently, and in March he and Angela married. On the twentieth of that month they were pronounced man and wife at Bromley Registry Office in Beckenham Lane. Angela's description in her autobiography of their adventures the night before makes startling reading, but for whatever reason they were both late for their marriage, arriving half-an-hour after the prearranged time. Bowie's mother and a few close friends were there, including some local press photographers, without whose presence the marriage of this unconventional pair would have gone unrecorded for posterity. After the ceremony the friends repaired to the Swan and Mitre public house across the road for a few drinks, and later celebrated with a party at their house in Southend Road.

There is no doubt that David and Angela were very much in love and although to all intents and purposes very little changed in their lifestyle (after all they had been living together for several months) the fact of being married may well have marked a watershed in his life and in his relationships with other people: a few weeks after his wedding David sent Kenneth Pitt a letter indicating that he no longer wanted him to act as his personal manager. A meeting a few days later between Kenneth, David and Tony Defries, a solicitor representing David, closed Kenneth Pitt's association with the artist whose career he had done so much to nurture. Although the break was obviously a sad occasion it did not lead to ill feeling. Originally David wanted Defries to handle his financial affairs, but within a short while he had become the man responsible for almost every aspect of David's career and business dealings. Shortly afterwards the song written to commemorate the Free Festival was issued as David's third single for Mercury and on it David's new drummer, Woody Woodmansey, made his first appearance on a Bowie record. Almost immediately David and his fellow musicians started work on what was to be his last album for Mercury, "The Man Who Sold The World". This took a considerable amount of time and the result was an album of outstanding merit and originality.

David's spasmodic European success with "Space Oddity" led to the suggestion that the song might stand a better chance in some countries if David re-released it in a foreign language. Italian words with the title "Ragazzo Solo, Ragazza Sola", became David's first recording of any of his songs in a foreign language, but in spite of this effort and the issue of a cover version by an Italian band, the song did not do well in Italy. "The Man Who Sold The World" album was first released in the United States, a reminder that he was still signed to Mercury Records in that country. Indeed, personnel changes within the Philips company and the lack of success of his last two singles probably led the company to postpone releasing this album at the time. Eventually, however, it was released in Britain in April 1971 but by this time David had undertaken his first American visit, planned to promote the U.S. issue of the new album and the release in December 1970 in America of a single from it, "All The Madmen". However, in America the record did not do particularly well, for he was unable to perform in that country as his work permit was not granted in time. He managed to circumvent this problem on one or two occasions by appearing at colleges under the guise of 'discussion'. His inability to perform live did not prevent him from undertaking interviews for the press and radio, and he caused a furore by appearing in several dresses designed for him by the British couturier Mr Fish. He also let slip several (probably well-chosen) remarks as to his sexual ambiguity. This got him notorious publicity as well as an altercation with a Texan who threatened him with a rifle. Although the American trip did not last very long David travelled widely, from New York to San Francisco, and on to Hollywood. In spite of his change of image, Bowie's songwriting efforts were now universally noted, and a song of his, "Oh You Pretty Things", was handed to the famous record producer Micky Most, before David left for the States, and was chosen as Peter Noone's next single, becoming a sizeable hit. On the single David played piano. The Philips Company in England must have been aware of the impact David's visit had made on the media in America, and with commendable courage they issued "The Man Who Sold The World" album in April, with a picture of David wearing one of his now-famous dresses reclining on a sofa. The earlier American issue showed a cartoon drawing of a cowboy, a much less controversial picture.

This exciting period for David was made more so by the birth of his son, Duncan Zowie Haywood Bowie, in Bromley Hospital on 28th May and weighing in at 8lbs 8oz. David was not present at the birth but later that day, delighted with the news, he wrote the song "Kooks", in memory of the event, which he performed for the first time on the John Peel BBC Radio One show In Concert a few days later. Also on the show George Underwood performed a song that David had written especially for him. As George was a Bob Dylan enthusiast (rather more so than David) the number was titled "Song For Bob Dylan". A few days before Zowie's birth David stalled his car outside Lewisham Police Station whilst driving to London. In an attempt to crank the engine into life he forgot that he had left the car in gear. The vehicle lurched forward and the starting handle badly gashed his leg. The result was a week's stay in Lewisham Hospital. This respite brought an opportunity to develop a new friendship: a few weeks before the birth of his son he met an art student and dress designer, Freddi Buretti, who with David's encouragement set out to become a singer. Buretti adopted the professional name of Rudi Valentino and used his appearances for showing his clothes designs. David wrote and produced a single for Rudi on the B & C label but this died a death.

The critical reaction to "The Man Who Sold The World" was generally very favourable. The album's sexual undertones could not be ignored. Meanwhile, Tony Defries was seeking a change of record label. In 1971 CBS's managing director in London, the American Ken Glancy, was on the point of joining RCA. After clandestine negotiations he joined the company that summer and soon began making a number of personnel changes at RCA's London offices in Curzon Street. He managed to get Olav Wyper, Geoff Hannington and Ralph Mace to join RCA, all of whom had worked with varying degrees of involvement with David during their days at Philips. Both RCA and CBS had expressed interest in signing David, and RCA's Artist and Repertoire head, Dennis Katz, had been enormously impressed with four newly-recorded songs of David's which it was planned would form the basis of his next album. Glancy's change of company reinforced the importance of the signing RCA made at this time. Perhaps aware of these changes, David, as far as the public was concerned, kept somewhat out of the limelight. He appeared at the Glastonbury Fayre at dawn on 20th June playing acoustic guitar and harmonica, in keeping with the hippy style of the event. His set at Glastonbury was recorded live by Jake Riviera but has remained unissued. However, a memento of his appearance can be heard on the boxed set of three albums entitled "Revelations – A Musical Anthology for Glastonbury Fayre". This was issued on Revelation Records at a price of £3.99 for the set but the sole Bowie track, "Supermen", was recorded at Trident Studios in London and is not taken from the live appearance.

Under the new regime at RCA, which immediately began to show considerable success with regard to chart positions, the new album from David became an urgent project. The four songs which Katz had approved were added to five others and the resultant "Hunky Dory" was released in December. By this time David had come under the spell of Andy Warhol, whose theatrical show, "Pork", had opened in London in August 1971. Several members of the relatively unknown cast of this astonishing evening in the theatre saw David appearing in London and made themselves known to him.

With his interest in the stage, and more especially the extravagant style of direction at that time, David can hardly have been unaware of "Pork". Apart from his natural delight at the rapport between himself and members of the show he was deeply impressed when he visited the production a few days later. There is no doubt that the outrageous and iconoclastic nature both of Warhol as a media artist and the startling originality of the production itself (nothing had been seen like it in London for a very long time) had a profound effect on Bowie, who with his own attempts at shocking the press in America some months previously found in the cast of "Pork" several kindred spirits. After the show closed on 28th August, following a run of almost four weeks, several members of the cast joined Tony Defries's Mainman organisation.

With the members of the cast notorious fron their appearances in "Pork", and also very much in tune with David's aims, coupled with the outstanding press work at RCA by Rodney Burbeck (another Glancy appointee) by far the greatest amount of media interest and coverage for David so far was engendered by the "Hunky Dory" album. "Hunky Dory" was actually first issued in the States in November, following a visit to New York by David, Angela and Tony Defries to sign officially the new RCA contract. During his New York visit he saw RCA's Elvis Presley live at a concert at Madison Square Gardens, but he did not meet the superstar. David did meet for the first time both Lou Reed and Iggy Pop, at the RCA building on the Avenue of the Americas, as well as Andy Warhol. At this latter meeting David played Warhol a song he had written, inspired by him, but initially conversation was virtually non-existent. Eventually the ice was broken but, although they spoke at length, by all accounts David left the Warhol Factory little the wiser. Soon afterwards, following a visit to Cyprus to see Angela's parents with several friends, the aeroplane on which they were returning hit extensive turbulence. The unnerving experience of this storm, easily understood by all those who have undergone similar flights, caused David to vow never to fly again.

At the turn of the year Burbeck had obviously done his job well, for the media interest in Bowie was considerable. It may have been that the "Hunky Dory" album, as has been suggested, was a result of the impressions David gained during his first American trip. Now that he was signed to an American company, such American connections as the album possesses did his career in that country no harm at all. One of the more surprising revelations from the many interviews David gave at Burbeck's behest was his revelation that he was bi-sexual, which was probably nothing more than the truth. His life-style and marriage to Angela had certainly been unconventional, and whatever sexual inclinations he may have had mattered little to his wife. The result of this revelation was sensational. Never before had a rock artist, and a married one with a child at that, come out in this way. Such a statement would have been unthinkable in public even a few years before, but the liberalisation of recent British legislation covering sexual behaviour and the coincidental rise of the Gay Liberation Movement meant his admission came at a time, calculated or not, when it worked to his advantage.

With the immense interest in him and his new album it was now easier for Defries to fix up his first major British tour. From that time on, during the whole of 1972, David found himself working with greater regularity and with a greater armada of fans than he ever had before. During this hectic activity, and doubtless inspired by the growing success which his work seemed to be attracting, David had not been idle in the studios. The British tour had been carefully planned with regard to the presentation of the music on stage. David, as well as the group, dressed in startling attire, as remarkable as his dresses had been, but reflecting the pan-sexual nature of his material and lifestyle. Here at last was a charismatic character with whom all segments of his growing audiences could relate. It was an astonishing achievement and laid the ground more securely than anything he had ever done for the massive and instantaneous success of his new album "The Rise And Fall of Ziggy Stardust And The Spiders From Mars". The fire had already been lit and RCA were shrewdly adding fuel to it in the shape of two singles issued during the first five months of 1972. The second of these had as its 'A' side "Starman" which was taken from the forthcoming "Ziggy Stardust" album.

On this album Bowie created the most successful of his early alter-egos. Ziggy Stardust, as we shall see, was another-worldly character,

brilliantly chosen for his total ambiguity. For many people Ziggy *was* Bowie and vice-versa and it may well have been that Bowie himself began to think that the character he had evolved and created (containing within it strands from his early mime experience and experiment with appearance and dress) had combined with the surrealist influence of Warhol and the challenging nature of the early Gay Movement. Indeed, it would have been difficult, if not impossible, for David not to have thought this, and it would have been intriguing for him to let the character of Ziggy take over and direct his actions to see where they led.

The advance orders for the Ziggy Stardust album were enormous: sales in the first week were 8,000, a large figure at that time. Bowie had at last achieved the massive breakthrough for which he had struggled so long and so hard. Whatever David may have felt about the character of Ziggy he was still able, between engagements, to live his life with Angela and Zowie in Beckenham, but a curious later comment by David probably indicates the true nature of the character he created when he said that he had packaged a "totally credible rock-star – much better than any sort of Monkees fabrication". It may well have been that having had to change his name because of the earlier success of the American television group, he secretly harboured a desire to create his own fabrication, i.e. Ziggy, which would trump the success enjoyed by the Monkees. Some idea of the extent of his impact in the summer of 1972 can be gauged by the fact that over 1,000 people were unable to get in to his Croydon appearance in June. The following month David and the Spiders (the new name for his backing group) played at a concert in aid of Friends of the Earth at London's Royal Festival Hall, a concert in which Lou Reed made his U.K. debut. At this time David's stage appearances were remarkable for his wearing what can only be described as a white satin space suit so skin-tight that many must have wondered how he got into it.

His command over his audience was complete; it was by no means unusual at this time for him to give surprisingly restrained performances. Often ignoring his most famous songs, as though tantalising the audience, playing with their expectations, he was still able to convey, through this very restraint, an electrifying stage presence that was invariably rewarded with a standing ovation.

On September 1st RCA in England issued his new single, perhaps the most explicit up to that time in terms of sexual ambiguity, "John I'm Only Dancing". It is one of his very best songs of this period and achieved a high chart position in Britain. Soon after this CBS released an LP by Mott the Hoople called "Mott The Hoople" containing the song "All The Young Dudes", written and produced by David. As a result of his unnerving flying experience the previous year David was determined not to travel by air to America for his first tour of the United States. He sailed on the liner *Queen Elizabeth II* and arrived in New York in late September. His appearances were spread over three months during which time he and his group travelled everywhere by chartered Greyhound bus. The tour was phenomenonally successful and enabled Defries to use his recently established Mainman organisation in New York to look after David's interests in the States and to monitor the support given his appearances by RCA. David was in great demand for concert engagements press as well as radio and television interviews. On 28th September he appeard at Carnegie Hall, New York, a debut which was an extraordinary occasion in itself as well as being an outstanding success.

This American tour became a classic of its kind. In the first place Defries was shrewd enough to get RCA to underwrite it, and secondly he had the good sense to persuade RCA in America to fly a contingent of U.S. pressman to see David's astounding Ziggy Stardust performances live in Britain and to meet him as well. From the moment David arrived in America for the start of this tour he already had all the press of any significance on his side. As an equally shrewd move the tour was originally not planned to last as long as it did. In case David's appearances should prove less successful than everyone hoped, Defries had not taken engagements for David for weeks after the original end of the US tour was scheduled. Consequently, with the success of the Carnegie Hall concert behind him, it was a straightforward matter to extend the tour, with David in the country seemingly carrying all before him.

RCA were not slow to capitalise on their new signing and they did all they could to support him. The result was that this tour could not have been more successfully master-minded. Whilst in America, having agreed to an extension of the tour by eight weeks, David was writing on the road, and recording in RCA's New York studios "Jean Genie". The tape was rushed to England before David had returned in time for it to be released in November of that year as his next single. Those companies who had recorded David in the past were not slow on the uptake. Pye re-released some of their material, and in America RCA, having bought from Mercury at the time of David's signing the tapes of his earlier material, re-released "The Man Who Sold The World" album. While in America David put the finishing touches to an album on CBS by Iggy Pop and the Stooges.

David returned to Britain on the ship *Ellinis* and during the voyage he composed the song "Aladdin Sane". On his arrival in England he found himself in colossal demand. He appeared on television and live in London. During his Rainbow concert on Christmas Eve the audience, pre-warned, brought along toys for orphaned children, and on Christmas Day Dr Barnardo's received the many hundreds of gifts donated by the previous night's audience. David's father would have been very proud of his son.

The new year saw David with little time to spare. He appeared in Scotland and put the finishing touches to the "Aladdin Sane" album in the week beginning 20th January. Five days later he left Southampton, sailing again on the *Queen Elizabeth II*, to commence a three-month world tour. New York was the first port of call and he stayed in the United States until mid-January although at one point early in the tour he was clearly suffering from exhaustion. He left Long Beach in California to sail to Japan, but as on his previous tour in America he composed and recorded a new song "Drive-In-Saturday". This was released in Britain just as he was arriving in Japan on 6th April, to coincide with the release of the "Aladdin Sane" album in the UK. The advance sales for this new one in his own country were well over the 100,000 mark, and the album went straight in at number one, certifying itself a gold disc on the same day. The artwork for this album's cover was more remarkable than his previous sleeves had been. On it David had subjected himself to some extraordinary multi-coloured make-up; not as was used at the time (and still is) to enhance his physical appearance but using his body in a Warhol-like manner almost as a canvas on which the make-up artist could draw. The play on words of the title "a lad insane" should have alerted Bowie's admirers to the fact that he had reached the furthest point along the road that Ziggy Stardust had taken him. From this point of introversion, paradoxically expressed in the most public manner possible, there could only come a violent reaction. But Bowie's millions of admirers were quite prepared to follow him wherever he went. The titles of some of the songs indicated this: such as "Watch That Man", "Aladdin Sane" (1913 – 1938 – 197?), "Panic In Detroit", "Cracked Actor" and "The Prettiest Star". The years shown after the title track are somewhat ambiguous, and can either have some deep-seated personal meaning or reference to public events which have not been revealed, or to nothing at all. But it is difficult not to feel in this work a touching reference to his older brother Terry who, when in his early twenties, had begun to exhibit signs of a serious mental condition. Terry committed suicide in January 1985.

All these musings, however, were swept aside at the astonishing success of this album, made more so by the fact that David was out of the country. He was on the other side of the world in Japan, where his appearances were remarkably triumphant, so much so that at his last show in Tokyo what might have been the beginnings of a riot marred his appearance, but there were no serious injuries. During his stay in Japan David managed to see several Noh dramas which created a profound impression on him. On leaving Japan he travelled to Russia and caught the Trans-Siberian Express at Vladivostok for the weeklong journey to Moscow. Whilst in the Russian capital, where he spent two days, David was able to indulge in sight-seeing before catching another train which took him through Poland and East Germany, eventually arriving in Paris. He and Angie overslept at the Hotel George V, as a result of which they missed the boat-train to London, but they managed to catch another train to Bologne where they boarded the hovercraft.

On arrival at Victoria Station he was mobbed and on the journey by road to Beckenham he found time to give a press interview. A few days later he began the UK tour at Earls Court, then a comparatively unknown venue for rock performers. The acoustics were unsuitable for David's show, and with an audience of 18,000 it was clearly asking too much for them all to be on their best behaviour. Such were the problems attendant on this performance that the show was halted several times and the second appearance, originally scheduled for some weeks later, was cancelled. Following this unsatisfactory appearance Bowie began the biggest tour he had undertaken in Britain up to that time. It covered the country and culminated in an appearance at the Hammersmith Odeon on July 3rd. RCA intended to record this show and issue it on LP, but this only appeared in 1984; at the end of his performance

David made the startling announcement that he was retiring and giving up live performances. Although for this tour the costumes had been specially designed to highlight the "Aladdin Sane" album, the spectre of Ziggy Stardust still loomed large. With his announcement that he was to quit, Bowie killed off Ziggy, who had threatened to become the monster that might destroy him.

CHAPTER FIVE

The View From The Top

There is no doubt that the world-wide tours David had undertaken, and which had been triumphantly successful, had, as is so often the case, taken their toll. With a wife and a young son he must have felt the need to break away from his peripatetic lifestyle and devote more time to them. In addition he had no doubt felt the need for a reappraisal of his musical direction. Three albums of quality had been recorded, issued and released within a very short time and the demands this placed upon his creativity, to say nothing of the demands the tours made on his physical stamina, were proving too much. It was only natural that he should have become, in a word, homesick, and as if to reinforce this view he had already planned his next album by way of diversion. His idea was to look back into the sixties and to take from that golden age of popular music songs which meant much to him, personally; he would then reinterpret them, not to recreate the sounds of the sixties, but as if to view that period through the eyes of experience. With this in mind, and having been encouraged by Marc Bolan, he travelled with Angie to France where he stayed at the Château d'Hérouville just outside Paris, where Chopin had stayed. The château had become an important recording studio, in the country away from the hurly-burly of city life. The resultant album was "Pin-Ups", a collection of British songs by various composers. Angie at that time wished to pursue a career as a model, and in fact did so with David's assistance, as well as striking out as an actress, with a number of cameo appearances on American television series. For the cover of "Pin Ups" David was photographed with the model and actress Twiggy, perhaps the most famous face of the sixties. It was originally proposed that the photograph should appear on the cover of the English edition of *Vogue* magazine, but this did not in fact happen.

Whatever new directions David's personal and artistic lives were taking as a result of this enforced break, the public acceptance of his previous work remained undimmed. All of his five LPs were in the UK album charts in the same week in July, and Decca, who had already re-issued all of his previous material (including songs never before released), took "The Laughing Gnome" and released it three weeks before RCA issued David's new recording of the sixties hit "Sorrow". To David's reported embarrassment the single became one of his biggest selling hits, but although he might have felt uneasy at this resurrection of material from six years before, it helped the public to realise that he had not always been Ziggy Stardust.

In spite of his declared intention not to perform in public he took part in an NBC television show filmed at the Marquee Club in London, called "The Midnight Special". This was a remarkable coup on RCA's part, who had been justifiably alarmed at their star's announcement of his retirement from live appearances. The NBC television network (along with CBS one of the two biggest networks in the world) is actually part of the RCA corporation. For reasons which remain unclear, this outstanding piece of cinema was not shown in the U.K. In the film, while wearing a succession of colourful costumes designed by himself and Freddi Buretti, David sang eight songs. The title of the show was "The 1980 Floor Show" which contains a verbal pun on the title of a project he was forming in his mind and which was never fully realised, a musical version of George Orwell's "Nineteen Eighty-Four".

During the previous few years David, like most rock stars, had taken a hand in the sound production of his recordings. As we have seen, this led to him being invited to produce albums on other labels for other artists. He undertook, for instance, to produce an album by "The Astronettes", but although a substantial part of this album was recorded, the project was never finished.

In the concluding months of 1973 David worked very hard on his own new album, "Diamond Dogs". In many ways this extraordinary record ties together several strands on which he had intermittently been engaged during the previous six months. After "Pin Ups" he is reported to have toyed with the idea of a similar follow-up, but this never materialised. However, "Diamond Dogs" does contain material from an earlier generation, but only as a paradoxical coda to the first song, "Future Legend". The material in question is the Rodgers and Hart song "Bewitched, Bothered And Bewildered". The other thread from his recent work is the song "1984", salvaged from the aborted musical version of Orwell's novel. While the conceptual format is readily apparent on the "Ziggy Stardust" and "Aladdin Sane" albums, with "Diamond Dogs" this is carried a stage further. On the first side of the album, for example, the cutting engineer has provided rills for only three tracks, although six songs are listed (not including "Bewitched"). On playing the album, the growing continuity of the music indicates quite clearly a development within the concept album. This should not be mistaken for an example of the old-fashioned medley in which one song follows another without a break, but, as we shall see later, the close juxtaposition of material indicates an interesting direction in album planning and layout.

A fashionable adjunct to albums by rock stars at the time was the addition of various kinds of packaging material related visually to the music contained on the album. In some ways this threatened to get out of hand and was often taken to extreme lengths. This was not the case with Bowie, although given his background and experience it was unlikely he would remain uninfluenced by this trend, and was indeed able to take from it those aspects which suited his purpose. Included with "Diamond Dogs" was a striking visual, a dream-like montage of architectural images from more than one country. These are dully perceived through an extraordinary haze which in its tonal colouration varies from the palest blue to a deeply burnished yellow. All this is used as an unusual background to a piece of free verse by Bowie entitled "Future Legend". Even without listening to the album, therefore, it is posssible to discern in the album's presentation a clear indication of temporality. Nor is this all: the cover for this album, a painting by Guy Peellaert, contains another startling visual umpact which had been such a feature of Bowie's recent work. It is best described as pop surrealism, for it depicts David's face and upper torso as part of an animal, joined to the bottom half of a dog's body. Even the shape of the hands and fingers have the appearance of paws, whilst close behind this monstrous figure are two female shapes, echoing the human-canine aspect of the front. This may not be quite as irrelevant as possibly it first appears. No one needs reminding of the warnings given to mankind of the likely effects on survivors of a future nuclear war. Mutations might be among them. With the album's glimpse into the future, Bowie has taken this mutant nightmare to a logical if frightening conclusion. At the same time Bowie's sensitive and often understated sense of humour adds the required element of levity. So the album is not all gloom and despondency.

However, the importance of this album and its music remained – in the closing weeks of 1973 – very much in the future. David's fame led to increasing pressures on him. His house in Beckenham was often under siege from fans and he decided to move with his family and some of his friends to a more central address in London. They lived for a while in a house rented to them by the actress Diana Rigg in Chelsea until they were able to move into a new home which David purchased some months later in Kensington. He had finally broken that umbilical cord, although by some accounts the change of address was not without personal problems.

Bowie's interest in producing records for other artists led to him overseeing and appearing on a single containing two songs written by him and sung by the Scottish singer Lulu, released in January 1974 on the Polydor label. The songs were "The Man Who Sold The World" and "Watch That Man", the last taken from the "Aladdin Sane" material. The following month RCA issued a new single containing a track from the forthcoming "Diamond Dogs" album, "Rebel, Rebel", and "Queen Bitch".

Mick Ronson's career as a solo artist had taken several steps forward, and a new album by Bowie's lead guitarist was released at this time by RCA. It contained several songs by David, and indeed has many qualities of its own. In the last analysis, however, Ronson did not possess David's extraordinary charisma or originality. Prior to the release of "Diamond Dogs" David travelled to New York for the first time in many months. There, after many discussions with Tony Defries, David began looking around for musicians to form a new band now that The Spiders From Mars were no more. Defries, perhaps under pressure from RCA, was anxious that David's retirement should be only temporary. He hoped that the extraordinary success of David's previous American tours was to be recaptured for a new tour of the North American continent being put together by Defries, ostensibly to promote the release of "Diamond Dogs". But during his stay in New York, while these negotiations were in hand David slipped away to black clubs and venues in Harlem, immersing himself in the then-growing influence of black soul music.

The Tamla Motown label from Detroit had become the most important soul label in the world and during the early seventies had

had some massive hits with a whole variety of singers. But the equally industrial city of Philadelphia, through the entrepreneurs Gamble and Huff, had its own soul movement, the "Philly" sound. In 1974 this label, too, was poised to make considerable inroads on the world record market, perhaps its most important act being the female trio The Three Degrees. The essential difference between Motown and Philly was that Gamble and Huff used large orchestral backing as the norm, and although Motown by this time had certainly increased the number of its backing musicians, they were never as numerous, nor was the beat of such secondary importance as on the Philadelphia label. The effect of this private influence on Bowie's music only became apparent some time later.

"Diamond Dogs" was eventually released in Britain in April 1974. Many people were startled by the extraordinary cover and not a little disconcerted by the gloomy nature of the songs it contained, but to the committed Bowie enthusiast he could do no wrong. In June 1974 David undertook what was to become the famous "Diamond Dogs" tour of America, opening on the fourteenth of that month in Montreal. The show regrettably was never seen in Britain, which was a great pity as it was the most spectacular and fully integrated of all David's stage presentations up to that time. Every conceiveable detail of lighting, choreography and stage projection of the visual impact of the by-now totally theatrical creations of David, to say nothing of the musical content, was planned to the final degree of perfection. The show contained one segment in which David appeared suspended above the audience as if on a pole, clearly anticipating Andrew Lloyd Webber's "Starlight Express" by a decade.

In America RCA had had bitter experience of Elvis Presley being unwilling to tour, and in his case it became increasingly difficult to get him to make new studio recordings as frequently as the company would have liked. Many new Presley albums at this time were live recordings, and it was a prudent move on RCA's part to get David to agree that they should record him live during this tour. Apart from virtually guaranteeing (assuming nothing went wrong) that they would have familiar material to market in the future it also gave the company a product to offer the many thousands of fans who would see him on this tour. RCA probably felt such an album was the one thing missing from his previous phenomenonally successful appearances. With this in mind, the company recorded his performances on 12th and 13th July at the

Tower theatre in Philadelphia (the home of course, of the Philly sound). Those who followed David on this tour have claimed it was a pity RCA did not record later performances by which time the artists would have been rather more into their stride. But the result is by no means unworthy of those involved, who must be commended (along with the record company) for not adding subsequent studio takes or other enhancement, with the single exception of a few backing vocals in which the microphones at the theatre had intermittently malfunctioned.

The impact of the American tour on David's creativity was tremendous. While in Philadelphia he took advantage of his stay and recorded a lot of material at the Gamble and Huff Sigma Sound Studios. This was to be yet another new departure for him, his reaction to and adoption of the essential features of soul music which he had encountered at a basic level earlier in the year in New York. A result of this increasing fascination with soul music was that the extensive "Diamond Dogs" tour underwent a number of changes as the weeks went by.

David spent the rest of 1974 in America. He had good reason to be pleased with his success there, for he had the major part of a new album ready, an acceptable and as yet unreleased live double album, and he had reached the position where it was unnecessary for him to work at such a high level of tension. This is not to say that his performances lacked electricity, but that having reached a high plateau he was now in a better position to observe the world from this elevated viewpoint. After a real break, the tour became what was known as the Soul Tour. The complicated sets were removed and replaced by a severe visual reaction against them, namely a simple white background against which (dropping the "Hallowe'en Jack" character he had assumed for the "Diamond Dogs" tour) he could appear as a different persona. In this way the new tour continued almost as a straight singing show, without elaborate production.

He had met John Lennon in America, who appeared on "Young Americans", the title-track of the album David had recorded at the Philly Studios. Lennon's contributions were recorded in New York where the album was edited and mixed, but before this David had spent some time in Los Angeles. Rumours began to circulate concerning his interest in the occult and drugs and it may have been at about this time that David decided to dispense with Defries's services as his manager. He spent Christmas in New York with his wife and son and a projected tour of Brazil was cancelled owing to unsatisfactory travel arrangements. In January 1975 David indicated to Defries that he wished their association to come to an end, but the parting from Defries was not to prove as straightforward as his previous separation from Kenneth Pitt. Eventually, after protracted negotiations, both manager and artist went their separate ways, although the link between David and Defries's Mainman organisation was kept. But it was, as can be imagined, a troubling time for Bowie.

During David's long stay in America the British RCA company had managed to persuade the BBC to do an 'Omnibus' programme on him. This contained some previously unshown material of earlier performances and was transmitted in Britain in January 1975. The following month David entered into discussions in New York with the English director Nicolas Roeg to appear in his forthcoming film "The Man Who Fell To Earth", but the negotiations were not completed until some weeks before filming began in July of that year.

Before then, in March, the "Young Americans" album had been released, affording British fans the first opportunity to come to terms with his most recent work, and most recent change of image. They had had a foretaste of this with the release in February of the title track as a single. Possibly as a result of the changes in senior personnel that were taking place in the British branch of RCA at this time, the song, which is one of Bowie's finest, did not do as well as was hoped. This disappointing lack of success, the unhappy period following David's decision to break with Defries (coupled perhaps with a degree of uncertainty about his future music) and the pre-occupation with the preparation for his first starring role for the cinema may have contributed to what became known as David's low period. This may seem somewhat surprising in retrospect, especially as six months before he had reached a postion of importance and influence. But it may be that his innate sensitivity caused him to react more deeply to events which were, after all, merely passing phases.

Decca meanwhile had decided on one more shot with their Bowie material. In a move which earned the gratitude of all Bowie enthusiasts the company issued every one of their Bowie recordings in a double album entitled "Images". In America David and Iggy Pop spent some time in a Hollywood recording studio but with little result. More significantly Pop entered a psychiatric clinic in Los Angeles as a voluntary patient. David, doubtless with the experience of his brother's illness, visited Pop in hospital incognito, and later, after Pop's return to health, Iggy claimed that David was the only visitor during his hospitalisation. Production on the film of Walter Trevis's novel "The Man Who Fell To Earth" was scheduled for eleven weeks and during this time David's lawyer, Michael Lippman, informed David that terms had been settled with Defries. Filming took place in Northern Mexico and during breaks in the shooting, possibly relieved that problems with Defries now appeared to have been settled, David's creativity began to flow more freely. In addition to several songs, some intended for the film, David also wrote a number of short stories, perhaps with an eye to future film possibilities; these have never been published. The filming did not go entirely smoothly, but this was nothing new for the film makers and eventually it was completed by September. This made a welcome relief for David, reinforced by his single "Fame", taken from the "Young Americans" album. It had reached number one in the U.S. singles charts, where it remained for four weeks.

Armed with his new songs and encouraged by his chart success David travelled to Los Angeles where he began working on his new album, "Station To Station". He appeared on television and, under increasing pressure from the British company, to say nothing of pressure from his mother, he recorded a satellite interview with the British television personality Russell Harty. A feeling of homesickness also contributed to David's decision to return to England early in the new year and in December 1975 details were announced for a European tour. He spent Christmas at the home of Keith Richard in Jamaica but was annoyed on his arrival to find that Michael Lippman had apparently omitted to make arrangements for the stay. David telephoned Lippman and for the second time within a year dispensed with his manager's services.

Perhaps in expectation of David's return, and partly as a result of the success the Decca reissues had enjoyed, the British company, under its new Australian managing director, George Lukan, re-released "Space Oddity" as a single. This was a highly successful move for it eventually reached number one in the UK single charts for the first time. But confusion arose ten days after the re-release of "Space Oddity" when the British company issued "Golden Years", a single taken from the forthcoming album "Station To Station". It was difficult for RCA's promotion staff to work on two singles by the same artist at the same time, but they did a remarkable job; "Golden Years" was another hit and reached number eight.

His return to Europe had to wait for a suitable break in a world tour that David began in February 1976, to coincide with the release of the "Station To Station" album throughout the world and reinforce his image as the 'Thin White Duke', which was the appellation given to him during his soul-influenced period. His Canadian debut at the beginning of this tour in February marked his first live appearance in America for about eighteen months. The tour, after two concerts in Canada, switched to California for a week, travelling mid-west with engagements *en route* before arriving in Cincinatti on 23rd February. Two days later he was back again, completing this extensive tour at the end of March in New York. In the middle of this month "The Man Who Fell To Earth" opened in London to a mixed reception from the critics. This was not perhaps the most fully-rounded performance that could have been imagined from Bowie but it contained examples of considerable acting ability on his part. The world tour, and the film, indicated that Bowie had reached a plateau in his career.

CHAPTER SIX

Apotheosis

The European Tour opened in Munich on 7th April, by-passing England, and a few days before, whilst visiting Russia for the second time, David was stopped at the Polish border by the Communist authorities and forced to hand over some Nazi material he had with him. Apparently he was toying with the idea of a film about aspects of the Third Reich. This project came to nothing, although a few weeks later the press, doubtless hungry for new Bowie material, attempted to blow up his interest in the subject out of all proportion. The month of April saw David and Angie staying at a house she had rented in Zurich. He stayed in Switzerland for several weeks, using this as a new base from which to continue his world tour, recommencing with appearances in Scandinavia.

His interest in producing and his close friendship with Iggy Pop led him to produce a new album for Iggy, titled "The Idiot", at the Château d'Hérouville but this was not undertaken until after his triumphantly emotional return to England in May. David appeared at the Empire Pool, Wembley, on 3rd May 1976, his first live performance in England for virtually three years. Overcome with emotion at the end of the show on his return to his native land and by the warmth of the reception accorded him, David burst into tears. He gave five further shows at Wembley, each one playing to a capacity house, the final appearance being on the day before the film went on general release in Britain. The world tour was not yet over: there were engagements in Holland and France, the last being surprisingly a comparative failure owing to a disinterested public response. Perhaps stung by the re-released Decca material the previous year David decided to put out a compilation album of his own choice; later in May the "ChangesOneBowie" album was released in England.

Bowie was disappointed that the severing of his relationship with

43

Michael Lippman had left him with a fair amount of unused material. Apparently David had understood that he was to provide the music for the Roeg film and had written a portfolio of songs for this purpose. In the event these were not used and some of them appeared on later albums. One, "TVC 15", surfaced on the "Station To Station" album. Perhaps these pressures, coupled with exhaustion after his extensive tour and his emotional return to England, tended to sap his creative strength. As if to get these depressive feelings out of his system, David put together a new album with the ominous title "Low". One of the remarkable features of this album is that for the first time in his career as a songwriter the words are almost of no importance. Indeed, here Bowie experiments with single syllables, an equivalent perhaps of the American composer John Cage's famous dictum: "I've got nothing to say but I'm saying it". There is no doubt that RCA were puzzled by this offering. As the album had been finished ahead of schedule there was no reason why it should not have been released immediately. It was delayed, however, until January 1977, hardly the best time of year for the issue of a new album from a major artist.

During the previous summer David had met Brian Eno, an immensely talented musician and record producer who had gained a considerable reputation for himself as one of the most influential and innovative masters of his craft. He worked with David and the musicians for a short while at the Château on the "Low" album, but possibly because of the less than perfect facilities there it was decided to move the production for the remainder of the album to the Hansa Studios in Berlin to edit the existing "Low" material, as well as Iggy Pop's album, with Tony Visconti. David was enthralled by Berlin and in October he moved into the Schoeneberg district. This gave him an opportunity to consider his position as a person and as an artist. His work with Eno, in whom he found a like-minded and dedicated sympathy of artistic purpose, (in spite of the puzzlement which the resultant "Low" album created and the inevitable flood of ideas and images which always attend a first stay in a new and exciting environment) enabled him, on his own admission, finally to secure his release from a growing dependence on drugs. Within this new environment 1977 proved to be another remarkable year for David. He was clearly pleased with the Iggy Pop album as he decided to go out on the road with him playing piano as he had done on the record. Many people in the audiences on the tour did not realise that it was

David Bowie as the band's pianist on stage. They appeared in England and America, to which country they travelled by air, this being David's first flight for six years, having now overcome his nervousness, and on to Canada. It was a remarkable gesture from one major artist to one of lesser stature and following the conclusion of the tour they returned to Berlin to work on a new album for Iggy. This album was "Lust For Life".

In July David attended the French premiere of "The Man Who Fell To Earth" and after the show managed to fight off a would-be mugger in the street. While in Paris David and his companion, the actress Sydne Rome, discussed a possible future film collaboration. Although they eventually worked together on the film "Just A Gigolo" this was not one of the projects they discussed.

In September David appeared at the Granada Studios in Manchester in Marc Bolan's weekly television series. David contributed a new song, "Heroes", and a duet with Bolan, although technical problems marred the proceedings. Seven days later Marc Bolan was killed in a car crash in Barnes, south-west London and David flew from Switzerland to be at the funeral four days later. This tragedy marred David's undoubted pleasure at having completed a new album in Berlin some weeks previously, "Heroes", made initially with the same line-up as "Low". This had been entirely recorded at the Hansa Studios in Berlin but, rejoining his family in Switzerland, the tapes were finally mixed in Montreux. Bowie's career was expanding on several fronts: his "Just A Gigolo" part had been confirmed, and the film was to be directed by David Hemmings, who had discussed the project with David in Switzerland. Filming was scheduled to begin early in the new year.

A completely new direction for him came out of RCA's Red Seal classical department. It is customary for classical recordings by international companies to be placed in what is affectionately known as the 'Ice Box', in which material will sometimes wait years before a suitable coupling can be found. It is common practice for an artist to record say, a Mozart piano concerto at a time when pressure of commitments prevents the recording of a companion piece to make a complete album. In such circumstances the tapes will be placed in the 'Ice Box'. At the international meeting of RCA classical staff held in London in the spring of 1977, with representatives from the European countries, Australia, Japan and the United States, discussions took place as to what might be released from the 'Ice Box'. The Philadelphia

Orchestra under its conductor Eugene Ormandy had recorded the orchestral music to Prokofiev's "Peter And The Wolf" but no narrator for the work had been found. A suggestion was made that Bowie be approached and after some initial surprise had been registered it was decided that Ralph Mace (who was then director of European Marketing and who had played at short notice on "The Man Who Sold The World" album) should approach David to sound out his reaction to the proposal. David was intrigued by the idea and readily agreed to record the text to be edited into the already-existing orchestral tape. He said he had Zowie in mind when reading the famous story. In October the "Heroes" album was released.

Those who had been puzzled by the somewhat experimental nature of much of "Low" had their belief in David as a lyricist triumphantly reinforced by this new album, "Heroes". The musical experimentation which the previous album represented is here refined in material which is more straightforward in presentation. The title track, always shown as having inverted commas, was co-written with Brian Eno. The use of quotation marks possibly implies that the "Heroes" are not to be taken too seriously.

Bowie's European sojourn led him to record the title track in both French and German as well as the original English. His adept handling of these languages was further proof of his commitment to become a truly international artist.

A few days after the tragic accidental death of Marc Bolan, David instigated a trust fund for the singer's son, Rolan, but this was marred by a second tragedy. David had agreed to appear in a television Christmas special with Bing Crosby, and in September had recorded two appearances for this purpose. In one of them they sung a duet of "The Little Drummer Boy". Sadly Bing Crosby died in October; the single of their duet was eventually released in November 1982 when it became a top ten hit.

Following the London engagements with the press at the time of the release of "Heroes", Bowie travelled to Kenya where he stayed at 'Treetops' (the place where Princess Elizabeth and the Duke of Edinburgh stayed when news came through on the morning of 6th February 1952 that her father, King George VI, had died in his sleep at Sandringham). David returned to New York and Europe and spent Christmas with his son in Switzerland, but relations between David and Angie had reached their lowest point. She was in New York at this

time, and David, clearly resentful at her absence over Christmas and the New Year, issued a statement replying to accusations by Angie that he had 'kidnapped their son'. Although this breach between them was mended by all accounts, they agreed to go their separate ways and Angie filed for divorce a little while later. Befitting their unconventional marriage, husband and wife actually celebrated the mutually agreed separation with a private dinner party.

Returning to Berlin in January 1978 David commenced filming his new feature film, *Just A Gigolo*, which was completed the following month. The shooting was not without attendant problems which were brilliantly solved by the director: David's co-star, Marlene Dietrich, refused to leave Paris, and the scenes in the film where they appear together were shot in different locations and edited to create the illusion of being in the same room.

His natural interest in the graphic arts was fired by the making of this film (and possibly by Hemmings' intriguing solution) for, immediately following the completion of the filming, David painted several pictures and made a number of woodcuts which he photographed. These remain in his private possession.

Plans were also announced for a world tour, including his first British tour for five years, but before this began he returned to Kenya for another short holiday. The tour was scheduled to begin in the United States and in March he flew to that country to prepare for the opening night at the San Diego sport arena on 29th March. Much to everyone's astonishment the show included both a resurrection of Ziggy Stardust, now an affectionate tribute to his previous alter-ego which clearly delighted his fans, as well as – naturally – more recent material. Great care went into the preparation of this show, but it gained more perhaps from understatement and suggestion than the massive production of earlier appearances. It was an enormous success and ended on 9th May in New York at Madison Square Gardens, not before his appearances in Philadelphia were recorded live for another double album. The pirating of live performances by unofficial recordists and their subsequent release on 'bootleg' albums was becoming a serious threat to record companies everywhere. RCA were anxious to avoid losing sales to illegal entrepreneurs and engaged Tony Visconti to supervise the editing and release of the "Stage" album. The tour continued in Europe later in May with appearances in Germany, Switzerland and France. Following five appearances in Scandinavia, three in Holland

Live on stage, during the Ziggy Stardust era. Photograph: London Features International.

and two in Belgium David and his entourage returned to Britain for the final stage of this part of his world tour. He appeared in Newcastle and Glasgow, at Bingley Hall in Stafford and finally at Earls Court in London.

Extensive sections of David's Earls Court appearances were recorded for a proposed film, and although the material was complete it has never been released in its entirety.

In spite of RCA's desire to release the "Stage" quickly David and his record company were in disagreement. His contract with the record company would probably have referred to "albums" or "long playing records" (with clauses covering their release in other formats), the number of albums required by the company during the period of the contract being stated as a minimum requirement. Whatever David's undertaking was to RCA in terms of the minimum number of records he should make for them, he felt that the "Stage" double album should count as two records under the contract. RCA insisted that it count as one, as the records were not sold separately and would be bought as a single purchase, The dispute was finally resolved and the release of the album could go ahead, being issued for the first time in England on 8th September

David arrived in Australia to begin the second part of his world tour early in November where he appeared throughout the month. His concerts were phenomenally successful: an estimated audience of 20,000 attended his open-air appearance in Melbourne at the cricket ground on the eighteenth. The dedication of his supporters was more remarkable when one considers that the al fresco concert took place during incessant rain. David travelled to Japan early the following month for five appearances in Osaka and Tokyo which proved as successful as his Australian concerts had been. During his visit *Just A Gigolo* was premiered in Japan.

David Hemmings had experienced problems with the finished film. The world premiere, scheduled for Berlin the previous October, had had to be postponed owing to disagreements over the translation. The initial critical reactions were far from favourable. But the result after further editing was a fascinating document. David spent Christmas with his son in Japan and returned to England for a short promotional visit in February. In March he was in New York to complete work on a new album, "Lodger", which he had recorded in the late summer and early autumn the previous year in Switzerland. Once again he had used many of his recent collaborators on this new project, and whilst in New York Bowie made a surprising debut as a string player during a recital of music by Steve Reich and Philip Glass, playing viola.

He returned to England, initially for press interviews following the British premiere of *Just A Gigolo*. The English reaction to the film was just as mixed as that on the continent. Following the demands of the world tour during most of the previous year, together with the making of the third album with Brian Eno, the first six months of 1979 saw David in a more relaxed and easy-going frame of mind than for some time. In London he was often seen around town and made himself available for radio and television interviews centred on the forthcoming release of the "Lodger" album on which he continued work after his return to New York at the end of May, when he retained the relaxed lifestyle he had followed in London.

Whilst in Switzerland he met Oona Chaplin, the widow of the great comedian and film director. Lady Chaplin was also in New York at the time of Bowie's return there and the friendship was renewed. In spite of frequently-reported social life, both in London and New York, David had found the time to make a number of promotional videos for the "Lodger" album. One of the most remarkable of these was for the song "Boys Keep Swinging" in which David appeared in drag.

Bowie was now able to range over the whole of his previous work with a sympathetic detachment that can only come with the passage of time, but probably prompted by the re-emergence of some earlier material. RCA re-issued "John I'm Only Dancing" as a single (in a somewhat confusing coupling with another performance of the same song) and he made a video of the old "Space Oddity" track. Earlier in the year, in March, EMI re-issued the four songs that David had recorded for them on the Parlophone label in 1965, and his importance and stature as one of the most influential and successful stars of his generation can be judged from the fact that a major record company considered him worthy enough to resurrect his very early material.

At the end of 1979 David was back in New York and spent Christmas in that city with his son. Whilst there he was offered the part of John Merrick in *The Elephant Man*, a dramatic version by Bernard Pomerance of the touching story of the hideously deformed Merrick. David had seen the off-Broadway production a few weeks previously and by the following February the director, Jack Hofsiss, had formally invited him to take over the role on Broadway. The same month his divorce became final and he obtained custody of Zowie.

Having accepted Hofsiss's invitation to appear in the play David was anxious to work on a new album he had in mind, as he knew he would have no time to do this once preparations for the play had commenced. In the event the album was not completed until later in the year in London. During this busy month a single of the "Alabama Song" from Kurt Weill's opera *The Rise And Fall Of The City Of Mahagonny* – written in Berlin in the late twenties to a text by Bertolt Brecht, and which had starred Weill's wife, the legendary Lotte Lenya – was released. Clearly Bowie's time in Berlin had sparked off other interests, although the song was recorded at the Mountain Studios at Montreux.

In March 1980 David accepted another unusual undertaking when he travelled to Japan to make two commercials for television, on behalf of the Takar Shuzo Company, promoting a new drink called 'Crystal Jun Rock'. The JVC (Japanese Victor Company), the equivalent in that country of RCA, took advantage of his visit to issue a new single containing "Crystal Japan", the music he had written for the television commercial. He returned to Berlin and was back in London in May attempting to complete the new "Scary Monsters" album.

Bowie was anxious that the album should be completed in London, for the John Merrick Museum, a part of the London Hospital enabled him to see for himself several of Merrick's possessions as well as the masks taken of the deformed man after his death. This was a pricelesss opportunity to get as close as possible to the part. He travelled to America to begin final preparations and saw a performance of the play in San Francisco with Philip Anglim as Merrick. Rehearsals began early in July and on the twenty-ninth 'The Elephant Man' opened with David in the title role at the Denver Center of the Performing Arts.

It was obvious that his appearance in just about anything would have guaranteed a sell-out but few of David's keenest admirers could have predicted the astonishing public and critical acclaim which attended his performances. Whatever reservations people might have had after his two less than wholly successful starring roles for the cinema, there is no doubt that his performance as John Merrick declared him to be an actor of considerable stature and ability,made all the more convincing by Bowie's appearing in the part without any makeup to give the physical appearance of Merrick. Merrick's deformities were suggested by gesture and by the actor's sheerly charismatic force of will. On 5th

August the play opened in Chicago for three weeks, and eventually on Broadway on 23rd September at the Booth Theatre. The success and acclaim from the public and the critics was, if anything, greater in New York. Capitalising on the immense media interest in his performances "Scary Monsters" was issued at the time of the Broadway premiere, but not before the single, "Ashes To Ashes", had been issued the previous month. David had prepared a remarkable video to coincide with the release of this single, and not in vain, for it became a number one hit in Britain in August. The album marked yet another change of direction, for in it David attempted – successfully – to create songs which were both commercially popular and artistically satisfying, a combination which he had not always been able to achieve in his previous work, or at least not to the same extent. Brian Eno, who had been an important collaborator on his previous three albums did not appear on this one. *The Elephant Man* ended its run on 3rd January 1981; Bowie had spent Christmas with his son and his mother, marking the first time that all three had spent Christmas together for seven years. The impact David was continuing to have on the young generation of music fans was demonstrated when he was approached in New York to appear as himself in a German film to be produced by Bernd Eichinger and Hans Wath. This was *Christiane F*, the lurid story of a young girl from a respectable middle-class Berlin family who found herself – when only fourteen years of age – caught up in the city's youth drug culture. Bowie's appearance was significant for several reasons: clearly a major star was desirable, and the selection of Bowie demonstrated his international appeal (he appears as himself in several scenes ostensibly shot during a live gig in Berlin); his own experience with drugs led him to view the story with great sympathy; and his music used in the film declared it to have a relevance to the time which no other solo artist could have fulfilled. In fact his scenes were shot in New York during the run of *The Elephant Man* and were intermixed with existing film of another live Berlin concert not of a Bowie performance. A further demonstration of David's total command of the popular music scene was the issue by the Canadian-based K-Tel company of a television-marketed compilation album entitled "The Best Of Bowie".

His success in *The Elephant Man*, although he was not seen in the role in Europe, had become international drama news, and as result BBC Television engaged David to appear in the title role of Bertolt

Brecht's play *Baal*. Preparations began in August 1981 at the Television Centre and filming was completed by the end of that month. The previous month whilst in Switzerland, David was at the Mountain Studios at Montreux, where the group Queen were recording a new album at the time. In conversation with them David and the band agreed to produce a new single together, which they would co-write and perform. This was "Under Pressure", and was released on the EMI label on 2nd November and soon afterwards it reached number one. As a result perhaps of the selection of tracks for the K-Tel album, Bowie put together a new compilation album entitled "ChangesTwoBowie".

In December *Christiane F* was released in Britain and became commercially the most successful German film ever. In spite of his success in other fields, and his growing acceptance as an actor, reinforced by the transmission of *Baal* in March 1982, 1981 was the first year in which Bowie had not issued a new album since 1970, and his absence from the recording studios continued during 1982. It was acting which now demanded most of his time, for on 1st March 1982 shooting began on *The Hunger*, his third film in a starring role, and Tony Scott's feature film debut as a director. His co-star, Catherine Deneuve, was seen with him on social occasions. The film was completed in mid-July. In it he played a character who ages 300 years, but unlike his appearance as the Elephant Man this time make-up was necessary, with all its attendant interuptions to shooting. It was also reported that earlier in July 1982 David and the tennis player John McEnroe were neighbours in rented flats in London. According to reports David was troubled by the noise coming from McEnroe's flat, a result of the tennis player's singing and guitar playing, particularly one of David's own numbers, "Rebel Rebel". David is supposed to have knocked on his neighbour's door and after introducing himself was invited in to give McEnroe guitar lessons.

Early in September he began work on another film, an Anglo-Japanese production entitled *Merry Christmas Mr Lawrence*, based on a short story by Sir Laurens van der Post. His co-star was Tom Conti and the fim was shot on location in Auckland, Tokyo and the Cook Islands. With the film completed by the middle of November David flew to New York to resume his musical career.

His contract with RCA was up for renewal and, perhaps because of his recent concentration on acting, and also because he had not produced a new album for almost two years, RCA may have had reservations about signing him, although his success in other fields was not materially affecting his record sales. Whatever the reason David accepted a new contract offer from Capitol Records in New York, the American branch of EMI. This was to last five years, and on 27th January 1983 the contract was formally signed. EMI were delighted at the coup: David's new album, "Lets's Dance", was recorded in New York with Nile Rodgers as co-producer. Shortly after the album was completed David flew to Australia for the location of promotional videos for the title track and "China Girl", a song included on the album and part-written with Iggy Pop. EMI moved fast, releasing the album in England on 14th April. Bhaskar Menon, head of the USA Capitol company who had negotiated the contract with David, must have been thrilled at the response to his judgement and financial inducement. David had received a considerable sum on signing with Capitol, but this was amply justified with EMI's announcement that the "Let's Dance" album had become their fastest selling LP for sixteen years, in fact since The Beatles' "Sergeant Pepper". The single "Let's Dance" remained at number one in Britain for a month and was a remarkably successful prelude to a new European tour which had been planned to follow the international release of the album.

This tour was called "Serious Moonlight" and reinforced Bowie's commercial success in music, making it a landmark in his continuing development. His art, on the "Let's Dance" album, has a drive, not that of a traditional hard-rocking variety, but of a purely musical forward-looking intensity. The British segment of the tour opened on 2nd June at Wembley Arena and continued in Birmingham, Milton Keynes and Edinburgh. Every ticket was sold on the day the box office opened, conclusively proving that Bowie's absence from the recording studios during the previous years had, far from causing his appeal to fade away, only increased anticipation for what everyone believed – and were proved right to believe – would be a triumphant return to the world of popular music.

The month of June 1983 saw the release of the film *The Hunger*, and whilst this came in for a certain amount of critical approbation the release of *Merry Christmas Mr Lawrence* shortly afterwards was almost universally received with acclaim, not least for Bowie's performance as one of the two prisoners who resist the attempts of their war-time Japanese guards to break their spirit.

At the beginning of 1984 Bowie had clearly reached the pinnacles of his career as a performing musician and as an actor, enabling him, perhaps for the first time in his life, to face the future secure in the knowledge of his own abilities and confident in the international acceptance by both public and critics of his artisitic work at every level. This positive, optimistic outlook can be found in most tangible terms on the "Tonight" album, released towards the end of 1984. Bowie is reported to have come to Le Studio at Morrin Heights, just outside Montreal, more fully-prepared than he had ever been. As Carlos Alomar said, "It was the first time in the eleven years that I've been with the damn man that he's brought in anything", and it is not just in his preparedness that Bowie's new-found optimism can be discerned. The material itself, with only four new Bowie songs in the eleven that make up the album (two of these co-written with Iggy Pop) has a wide-ranging coherence, a less obsessive Romanticism, a more outward-looking frame of mind. It is encouraging to experience the work of an artist with such a perspective of the world, the more so when one is aware of his previous work which has essayed the depths of despair. The touch is lighter, no less considered, more buoyant and not so overtly 'significant'. Bowie seems to be saying 'enjoy yourself' and from him, of all contemporary rock musicians, the message here – as always – has the ring of truth.

PART II
THE MUSIC

CHAPTER SEVEN

The Early Years 1964 – 1969

It is always fascinating to examine the early work of an artist who has become a major figure, not least to try and indentify those early manifestations of what we like to feel are important qualities in his later work. With some creative musicians, however, their subsequent flowering is not really foreshadowed in their youthful endeavours and a great deal of frankly unworthy material is examined, often to no avail, simply because an important artist's name is attached to it. Had the artist in question not become an important creative figure, such work would quite properly be confined to oblivion, and we would not bother with it, but such is the fascination that great artists hold for us that we rightly feel our knowledge of them would remain incomplete without examining their work in detail.

Of course, an artist as multi-faceted and chameleon-like as Bowie immediately presents us with a number of problems, the first being the sheer variety of his musical interests. On the one hand, can we take any aspect of his music as typical? Surely not, for, exceptionally among rock-oriented musicians, Bowie has the widest and most complete artistic objectivity. And, on the other, we *have* to look for representative traits in every part of his output, simply because of the same wide artistic objectivity. This is not to suggest that we give everything equal prominence – our own artistic sensibility would make that difficult, and it is manifestly absurd to try – but that we attempt to be as complete as the artist we are examining. In the second part of this book his work will be analysed in chronological order, broadly speaking of record release, for that was the order in which his career unfolded to the world. Occasionally, this leads to inconsistencies, when a record might contain the odd track which dates from a much earlier time and which it would be wrong to consider as typical of other material released later. I have not hesitated to change the chronological release format where it seemed more appropriate, in terms of Bowie's development, to do so. With that small proviso in mind, let us now turn our attention to David Bowie's musical work.

1964

LIZA JANE/LOUIE GO HOME
Recorded as Davie Jones and The King Bees
The producer of this record, Leslie Conn, was also the composer of the A-side "Liza Jane" and he was therefore responsible for the recording quality. In some ways it is this recording quality which is the least satisfactory aspect of the record. It was recorded in mono only and there is no production feel, at least by comparison with contemporary work by other artists on other labels. One assumes that the crudity of the recording is deliberate but a problem is that the music does not breathe or have any light and shade around it. In some ways it is similar to early impacted Rolling Stones records but one cannot avoid the impression that this first recording by the man who subsequently became David Bowie is poorly recorded technically. A much better effect, and a more musical one, can be obtained by turning the bass level virtually down to zero. There is a lot going on on this tape and one would like to hear the original studio masters, for when this recording is compared with re-issues of other recordings made at around the same time, one gets the distinct impression that when they were originally released restrictions of various types were imposed on them: limitations, in fact, of the state of technology in transferring recordings to disc and playing them at home. Today, those limitations can be lifted significantly and previously hidden virtues of original recordings can be better revealed and appreciated. The problem is that Decca may not think that this material is worthy of such treatment, and one would be inclined to agree with such a decision, although it is tempting to ponder on what might be.

As performances, however, although the A-side is comparatively meaningless in the larger scheme of things, it is nonetheless quite expert and effective in its own way, being above the average one used to get from comparatively sub-standard British bands of the early 1960s. The B-side is much better; at least with regard to sound and the use of sound-image. It is an ostinato-type song, of the sort that Bowie himself

David Bowie in 1973.

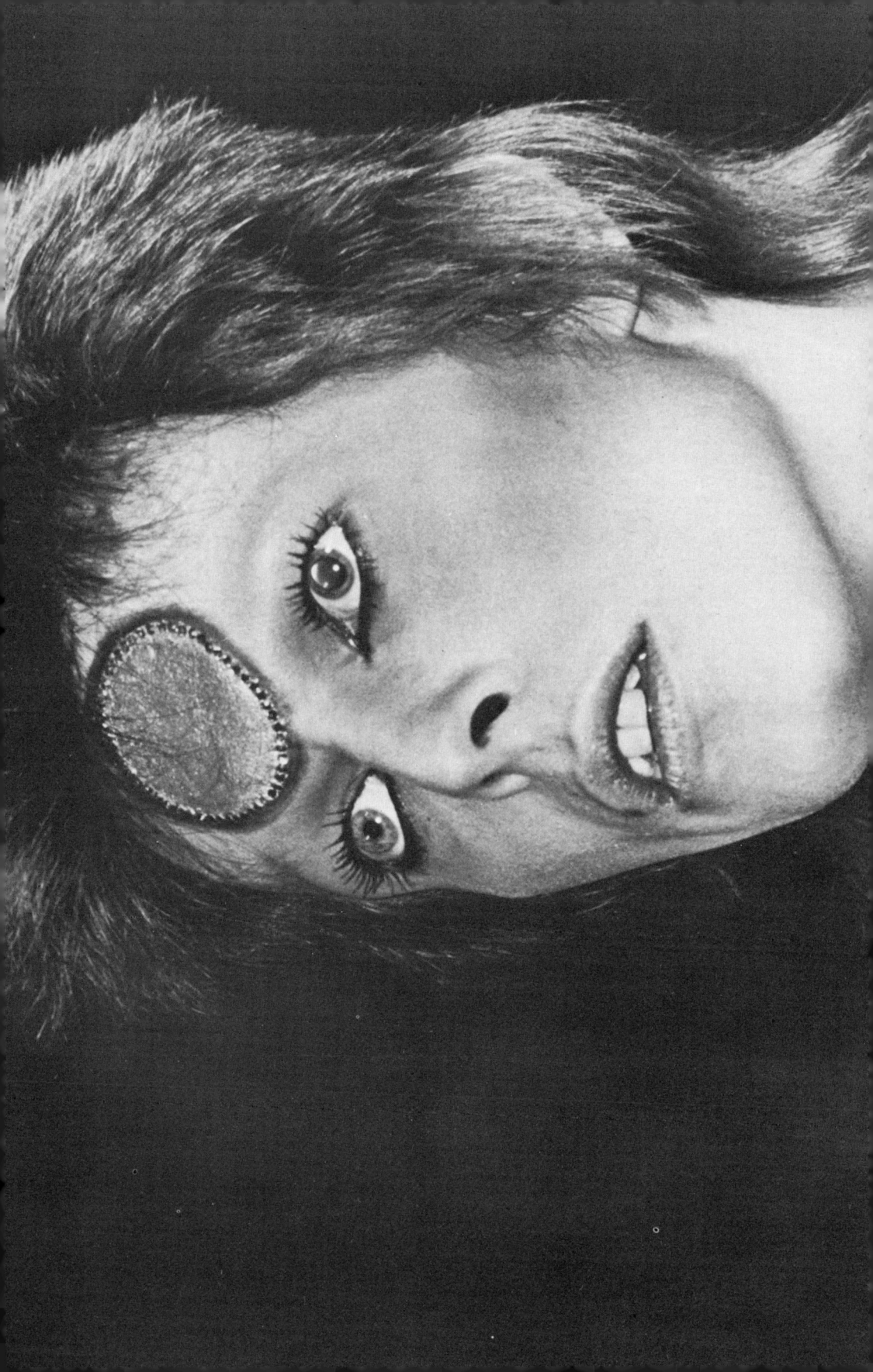

was to use later in his career, and shows a certain passing influence from the Beatles (a slight "Twist and Shout" derivation) as well as from early Rolling Stones performances. It is likely that the latter band had the more direct influence as they were based, broadly speaking, in the same area of London from which David came. In its own way, this performance of a song by Paul Revere, the American popular singer-songwriter of the period, is really very good indeed, although there is no real indication of what David Bowie was to become. It was the sort of record that a sympathetic critic might comment on at the time as being "promising". Other critics, however, might feel rather less charitable towards David's first efforts.

1965

I PITY THE FOOL/TAKE MY TIP
Recorded as The Manish Boys.
This was the only recording issued of David with The Manish Boys. On almost every level, it shows a distinct improvement over the Decca-Vocalion single. The Manish Boys appeared on the Parlophone label and the producer of this record, Shel Talmy, was also producer of early recordings by The Who, among others, and his surer touch is evident. In terms of broad repertoire, "I Pity the Fool" is not very far removed from Rolling Stones' Chicago-style influence noted on David's first single, and he turns in a fine performance of a song that was reasonably well known at the time. What is immediately noticeable is the brass section, absent from The King Bee's line-up, whose raucous timbre regularly distorts. But the drive and feeling of David's singing have a considerable cumulative effect. "Take My Tip" was the first song of his that David recorded; it is hardly a masterpiece, but is distinguished by a very good melodic line and some fine moments, as well as an overall genuine jazz flavour that is really very good indeed.

YOU'VE GOT A HABIT OF LEAVING/BABY LOVES THAT WAY
Recorded as Davy Jones and The Lower Third (only "Davey [sic] Jones" credited on label).
The Shel Talmy connection with the first Parlophone single continued with this. Although the new band had dropped brass and keyboards,

Live on stage c. 1974.

the influence here of "The Who" is unmistakeable; both songs are by David, but in the first his voice sounds different in timbre from that which we have encountered before. "Baby Loves That Way" is more recognisable in this regard but this record is the first indication we have of David's multi-vocal abilities. For all these mildly interesting points, the record is of marginal significance, and although EMI have re-leased their Parlophone recordings in latter years, none of the four performances issued by David on that label is of more than historical interest.

1966

CAN'T HELP THINKING ABOUT ME/AND I SAY TO MYSELF
This was the first of three singles David recorded under his new name of David Bowie for the Pye label produced by Tony Hatch. In terms of vocal technique and general performance, to say nothing of recording quality, this marks a considerable improvement on his previous work. On this record, perhaps for the first time on disc, Bowie seemed to have found his feet, for there is a far greater experience and expression in his singing as well as his writing. There also seems to be a definite but faint influence of the singer Spencer Davis. Bowie's music is a curious mixture of hard driving rhythm (very much in the background) with a florid and insistent bass-line, which supports a slower vocal line. The hook of the title is also quite remarkable in itself and Tony Hatch uses a wide stereo spread, placing David's voice much more forward and centrally within the stereo image than David's previous recordings for Decca and EMI. What is interesting, however, is that the locale of the songs is very much that of London. On the B-side ("And I Say to Myself") the recording balance changes dramatically. The backing instrumentalists are brought much further forward, almost in an attempt, it would seem, to squash the singer, whose close proximity to the microphone causes occasional distortion. It must be admitted that the song itself is somewhat confused, matching this constricting recording quality. The song is spoilt by irrelevant vocal backing from the band and a less than confident use of instrumentation. The words are somewhat less than coherent themselves, and it is perhaps just as well, as the song fades at the end not a moment too soon.

DO ANYTHING YOU SAY/GOOD MORNING GIRL
This is the first single that Bowie recorded solely under his own name. "Do Anything You Say" is a very strange song because it shows for the first time in his work the influence of modern classical music. Whether this is deliberate or not, there is certainly more than a hint here of the work of the Bavarian composer, Carl Orff, whose 'Carmina Burana' is occasionally recalled. The influence is doubtless a non-conscious one but Bowie attended a number of BBC Prom concerts at The Royal Albert Hall in the mid-1960's and it is likely that he first encounterd the work there. Be that as it may, the band's instrumental contribution is so interesting, with a facinating use of piano and organ, that the vocals tend to detract from this important strand of music. This time, on the other hand, Bowie should have been placed rather closer to the microphone. It was strange for Hatch not to have done this, for the result is unmistakably somewhat unmusical. Another interesting point about this song is that it shows also the early influence in Bowie's work of black singers. The rising appoggiaturas at the ends of phrases is very much endemic to black soul singers. The big influences on South London singers at the time was Spencer Davis's "Keep On Running" and early Kinks songs and these are apparent here as well. The net result is that this song has a number of less than fully-realised influences, and one gets the distinct impression that Bowie is here being crafted to satisfy some idea outside of himself, rather than contributing what is necessarily within him. In "Good Morning Girl" we encounter a marginally more (or less) interesting performance than the previous one. The song itself is very poor, without any redeeming feature, but Bowie's performance makes the most of it, duetting in scat style with the lead guitar in the manner of early Chris Farlowe, although his voice was at the opposite end of the range from Farlowe's.

I DIG EVERYTHING/I'M NOT LOSING SLEEP
This is the last of the three singles that David recorded for the Pye label. "I Dig Everything" is a much better song than either of those on his previous singles, although the recording balance is too fussy and overloaded with a shade too much echo. However, one should not make great claims for this effort; it is better only by comparison. In all other respects it is poor, and one doubts if Bowie was satisfied with it at the time. The B-side is rather more of the same. It is another poor song, overloaded with extranous and irrelevant instrumental backing

(although fashionable at the time) in what might have been a vain attempt to pump life into the cadaverous object. To compound the faults, this song is poorly recorded, with very little light and shade in the relatively thick texture. This would have turned nobody on, and it is unlikely that it ever did.

In spite of there being one or two flashes of talent on the six songs that Bowie recorded for Pye, the total result is bitterly disappointing. There can be no doubt that Pye were right to have dropped David while he remained in this particular vein, and taking his recordings on the Vocalion, Parlophone and Pye labels, the best that can be said for them as a totality is that they show a gradually evolving and multi-faceted artist. It is also true that the very multiplicity of his talents had not been fully revealed nor fully expressed in any of the songs released up to that time.

RUBBER BAND/LONDON BOYS

This was the first single released under David's new Decca contract, on the Deram label. It shows yet another aspect of his developing songwriting and performing career. The song could hardly be more different. On the one hand, "Rubber Band" (chosen as the A-side) is a strange cameo of the 1910s. The ending of National Service in 1963, and more importantly the screening of the BBC television series "The Great War" in 1964 marking the fiftieth anniversary of the outbreak of World World I, made it possible for young people to take a more critical view of the country's military history. This manifested itself in many guises, not exclusively concerned with young people, from Britten's "War Requiem" to "I Was Kaiser Bill's Batman". Appropriately enough, Bowie incorporates a brass section, but not that more properly associated with popular music of the time. The song tells of a young soldier who, on his return from the war, discovers that his girlfriend has fallen for a military bandsman. For all its charm and effectiveness, this song is very much of its time and appears very dated from a distance of twenty years. This comment is not meant as an adverse criticism, rather a statement of fact. Oddly enough, the contemporary nature of the B-side "London Boys" appears timeless by comparison. The brass section, heard in a whimsical manner on the A-side, is here used in a much more solemn fashion. Commentators are quick to point out the connection between some of Bowie's performances at this time with those of Anthony Newley, and it may well have been that Newley's transition from actor to singer intrigued David, proving to him that it was quite possible for an artist to be successful in more than one field. This, however, is a somewhat tenuous reason for the comparison which is often made. The most likely is that Bowie had, in his repertoire of different singing voices, one which sounded remarkably like that of Anthony Newley. Both were Londoners, and in the "London Boys" Bowie uses his 'nasal' tone to great effect, especially in the extended high register, when he comes over pure and strong. Indeed, so fine is this aspect of the performance that one can state that with this song for the first time in Bowie's recorded career he shows himself to be a natural and greatly gifted singer.

1967

THE LAUGHING GNOME/THE GOSPEL ACCORDING TO TONY DAY

No one could accuse Bowie of not being varied in his material. "The Laughing Gnome" is a song that he later came to feel greatly embarrassed by, although in reality any self-respecting singer-songwriter would have been pleased to have written a song that sold a quarter-of-a-million copies (as this one did, but only when it was re-released after Bowie's later success). It is, in essence, a children's song. As such it works brilliantly. It is completely un-selfconscious, without a hint of condescension – this is a remarkable achievement – being creative, intelligent and sensitive all at the same time. The use of bassoon and oboe in the instrumentation places this beyond normal rock or popular music and his performance matches the ludicrous nature of the song itself to perfection. He clearly enters into the spirit of the thing, communicating an infectious feeling of sheer happiness. The song begins with what at first appears to be a speeded-up version of the "Tennessee Waltz" but the two songs could hardly be more different and the connection (if there is one) is probably unintentional. In many ways, "The Laughing Gnome" is a truly remarkable achievement, and retains a gaiety which is quite irresistible.

With "The Gospel According to Tony Day" the oboist from side one has here become an extraordinary rock instrumentalist, joined by his fellow wind instrument, the bassoon, also from side one. It is the bassoon that intones a solemn funeral march, akin to that which begins the last movement of Shostakovitch's Fourth Symphony, creating a slow, hypnotic, black, depressive mood. The influence of Wilson Pickett is also in evidence, but the overriding impression is created by the singer, who is obsessed by the trivia of the human foibles he has seen, and encapsulates them epigrammatically. Essentially, the music remains static throughout this song, the harmonies being hardly changed, in utter contrast to the joyous bounce of "The Laughing Gnome".

"DAVID BOWIE"
Side 1: *Uncle Arthur/Sell Me A Coat/Rubber Band/Love You Til Tuesday/There is a Happy Land/We Are Hungry Men/When I Live My Dream*
Side 2: *Little Bombardier/Silly Boy Blue/Come And Buy My Toys/ Join The Gang/She's Got Medals/Maids Of Bond Street/Please Mr Gravedigger*
This was David's first album. The contract with Decca which produced it was a valuable one and in fact, during the course of the contract period, David recorded enough for two LPs with the company although not all were issued until some years later. The Deram label was concerned with artists who stood a little to one side of the mainstream of pop/rock 'n' roll of the period. But few could have imagined the range of material, and the penetrating manner of its performance, in Bowie's first LP with all 14 songs being composed by him. It is, in retrospect, a remarkable achievement for a nineteen-year-old. No one would claim that it is outstanding or meaningful in any profound sense but the very variety of the material clearly shows that here is an artist who simply refuses to be put into any kind of straitjacket. In that regard, it *is* a significant album, and will always remain so, although it contains failures as well as mistakes. The material has merit enough to demand our attention.

Throughout the varied material on the album are one or two recurring themes which are treated differently. For example, the opening song, "Uncle Arthur", and "There Is A Happy Land" are both concerned with aspects of childhood. The first is an acutely observed portrait of an increasingly familiar character, that of the little boy who won't grow up, but more properly one who is, even in adulthood, under the thumb of his mother. "There Is A Happy Land" is an observation of childhood seen from a distance. Of the two songs the first is by far the better and it must be admitted that the second is innocuous and not up to standard. For all the flashes of acute observation, such as are found in "Sell Me A Coat" and other songs, the quality of Bowie's music is highly variable. His observations of the capital city as a swinging Londoner, the second recurring theme (for example in "Maids Of Bond Street"), however sharp and to the point they may be as verse, are, in this instance, set to music of a somewhat second-hand nature. This song in particular shows an early fascination with jazz piano (significant when one considers Bowie's later development) and not at all out of sympathy with the subject-matter of the song; but the result is hardly memorable. What is more significant, however, is that Bowie was quite prepared, at this early stage in his career, to go out on a limb, musically speaking, although whether this was entirely his own idea or that of his manager at the time, Kenneth Pitt, is unclear. In any event, Bowie's natural self-confidence and inherent creativity (qualities apparent on this album) would not have permitted him to be used as the tool for someone else's ambitions. The juxtaposition of the songs on this album creates tremendous tension and drama. One almost literally does not know what is coming next. Unfortunately, Bowie is unable – at this stage in his career – to maintain our interest convincingly enough through the whole of the album's extensive playing time. But one is in no doubt as to his intentions, even if his manner of executing them is less than perfect.

Sometimes, as in "The Laughing Gnome" and more properly in "Please Mr Gravedigger" the dramatic theatricality of much of his work is already on the surface. "Please Mr Gravedigger", in the light of Bowie's future development, is of more than passing interest. He utilises such disparate elements as Musique Concréte (the use of extra-musical sounds to create a musical effect) and builds around this material the widest range of musical drama.

The other songs recorded by David at this time, but not released until some years later, ought really to be considered with those which appeared on this first album. Of these, the most outstanding is "In The Heat Of The Morning" and it is inexplicable that this was unreleased for such a long time. It may very well have been Kenneth Pitt's influence that suggested it be held in Decca's ice-box. It is a pity that "In The Heat Of The Morning" was not issued for there is a greater degree of seriousness and committedness about Bowie's performance than one finds on most of the songs on his first album. The use of tremolando strings, the easy-paced rock tempo without side- or snare- drum too much in evidence, the sudden change of key sliding down a semi-tone, the sleazy clapping, the ecstatic guitar and organ riffs – all these combine to make a musical montage of considerable power. Furthermore, it was recorded in genuine stereo which was not the case with all of David's Decca recordings.

An interesting adjunct to this album was the release of a single, one month after the album first appeared, of another version of a song contained on the album "Love You Til Tuesday", coupled with "Did You Ever Have A Dream" which was not issued on the album. The first song is very theatrical with a full wood-wind orchestral complement. It is also outstandingly well recorded but some confusion exists as to whether it was, in fact, recorded in stereo for all of its later reappearances have been reprocessed for two channels. However, the quality of the original recording is so fine that one wonders whether a stereo tape is still in the Decca vaults. Musically neither version is outstanding, making one question the validity of recording the song twice.

The remaining songs from David's period at Decca, which were also not released until 1970, are "Karma Man" and "Let Me Sleep Beside You". The first is notable for its fairground setting and because Marc Bolan played guitar on this track. The second is perhaps David's most overtly sexual song up to then.

1969

"DAVID BOWIE"
Side 1: Space Oddity/Unwashed And Somewhat Slightly Dazed/Letter To Hermione/Cygnet Committee
Side 2: Janine/An Occasional Dream/The Wild Eyed Boy From Freecloud/ God Knows I'm Good/Memory Of A Free Festival
In the first part of this book we learnt the circumstances surrounding the issue of this, David's second album, and confusingly given the same title as his Deram LP. By all accounts, this new album, on the Philips label, was not a success but it remains an astonishing achievement.

The album opens with "Space Oddity", an outstanding work approaching genius. It begins with a fade-up from silence, as if it has been going on for some time, and gradually we begin to overhear events. Harmonically the song oscillates between C major and E minor, and Bowie provides a linking thread between both keys by the use of the note D in the melody. It is clear, a few seconds into the song, that we are in an atmosphere of considerable imagination; flickering percussion patter around the left hand channel. Bowie uses the primitive electronic instrument the Stylophone on this track and such is his aural imagination that he manages to bring off the remarkable feat of convincing listeners that the instrument has some musical value. Against Bowie's depiction of an astronaut being called from ground control, a whispered count-down, from 10 to zero, adds a disembodied voice. This disembodiment is continued brilliantly when Bowie's duet with himself begins to produce a third vocal sound. This is a remarkable effect, somewhat similar to that used by Benjamin Britten in his Canticle "Abraham and Isaac", although it is to be doubted whether Bowie's experience of music extended quite that far. In any event, it is a wholly appropriate effect. As Major Tom (the astronaut) enters, Bowie uses another vocal timbre; the astronaut is now humanised although he is disoriented. As the astronaut lifts off the harmonic spectrum of the song is extended. In this way, Bowie uses purely musical language to reflect what is actually going on in the song. For example, the C major, E minor oscillation expands to F minor and F major, in which airy and light key Major Tom now sings his first descending phrase. This is the only time in the song that the music travels downwards, at the words "here am I sitting in a tin can". A sudden two-bar phrase, without voices, raises the harmonic and rhythmic tension as well as the dramatic. This is a curious, tiny interlude, difficult to justify in context but performing a useful musical function and contrasting vividly with the soft rhythmic beat that characterises this song. As the awful realisation – that the astronaut is doomed, of his own volition – is made clear, the song fades gradually away to nothing, into the space from which it came. It remains a classic rock recording (although virtually abandoning traditional elements of rock music); the whole is absolutely certain in its impact and strength. "Space Oddity" has an amazing, hypnotic power and is still capable of creating a tremendous impression. There is no denying the dramatic impact and basis of the song; it is almost theatrical, and can at one level be regarded as a kind of solo mini-opera.

The second song, "Unwashed . . .", returns us to earth. At the beginning Bowie's voice is placed further away in perspective, but again changes against the continuous driving Chicago-style rhythm repeated as an ostinato under the free-wheeling voice with its startling, deliberate images. The damaged youth's voice, independent and seemingly engaged in some serio-political-sexual struggle, is finally overpowered by the music underneath, which gradually expands at a colossal rate to become a hypnotic cocoon of sound. After "Space Oddity" the effect of this song is equally powerful although, of course, quite different in imagery and musical expression.

In great contrast, the clean, uncluttered sound of Bowie's voice begins the third song on this side, an intimate, personal letter to "Hermione". The result is a gem; a short (2′ 30″) cameo, enabling the listener to let his imagination (rather than that of the performer) meander around the image of a young man, reasonably literate, writing to a girl. The autobiographical aspect of this song is never in doubt. The singer is writing to an ex-girlfriend; she has a new man in her life but he sympathises with her because she isn't really happy with her new love. Some surprising sexual undertones are subtlely expressed. The listener may find it difficult to identify with Bowie's view, but there can be no doubt as to his phenomenal ability as a singer. His extraordinarily soft scat sounds – as Peggy Lee as maybe – are exceptional, ending this late-sixties vehicle in an air of bemused intimate indifference. Paul Simon is recalled in the "observer" nature of the frailties of human existence in this material. This is a haunting song with great quality.

With "Cygnet Committee" we come to what is without question Bowie's most remarkable creation up to then. If "Space Oddity" is a mini-opera then "Cygnet Committee" is a solo cantata of considerable power and originality. It traverses an exceptionally wide harmonic spectrum with tension and counter-tension present in every bar. It seems that there is hardly one bar in the whole of this nine-and-a-half minute work which can be said to be in any one particular key; although that is something of an exaggeration, the impression of harmonic uncertainty is unmistakeable. The harmony screams tension and drama; there is no let-up as the singer expounds his tract. The considerable ambiguity in this song would appear to be the imagined confession of a superman figure sympathetically looking down on those followers of his who – having been given free will – have merely been handed the tools by which they will fashion their own destruction. No better example of the correlation between music and meaning can be found in the phrase "and as the sparrow sings". It begins in B flat minor and then suddenly slides down a semitone to A with an added D sharp, almost tilting the music through a vast tonal spectrum dizzying the listener with richness and strangeness. Such is Bowie's power that in the concluding pages of this work the music almost takes on a modal aspect with the voice high in its register tortured between two semitones (the melodic justification for the previous harmonic slip), incessant in its demand and pity. The kind of monstrous physical assault which this song seems to depict leaves most listeners stunned. No more potent pointer to aspects of Bowie's later development can possibly be found in his work up to this time.

If the first side has been a succession of wholly original material, the second side is somewhat less so. Although there is a distinct falling-off of impact, Bowie is free to use the discoveries that proceed from giving his imagination full rein in a collection of songs which, in general, are less serious. For example, the first song, "Janine", is an innocuous piece of music redeemed by some very surprising harmonic changes and "An Occasional Dream", the next song, seems to quote from Leonard Bernstein's "Maria" (or at least evokes a fragment of it) and is a soft rock number with irregular scansion and rhythm. The soft tempo is repeated in "Wild Eyed Boy From Freecloud". It is interrupted by the singer but he is not well balanced technically as Bowie tends to fade backwards into the image. Although this may be deliberate in view of the full woodwind and "orchestral" backing, which is quite brilliantly arranged, it may very well be that this effect, if effect it is, has been carried too far. Once again, Bowie's now familiar fingerprint of the falling semitone is present. In "God Knows I'm Good" his voice takes on almost a northern accent, or that of a soft Bob Dylan. The song is a strange story of an elderly shoplifter which leaves a slightly odd taste in the mouth. In the last song on the album, "Memory Of A Free Festival", Bowie returns to aspects of his life a year or so previously. It begins as a chorale intoned behind Bowie's self-conscious spoken introduction, spoken like a hymn. He begins singing almost mezza-voce as his voice moves slowly to the right channel and then slowly to the left, the aural equivalent of scanning the horizon with dimmed eyes. A montage of simulated crowd calls coalesce into a "sing-along" phrase repeated over and over again, like the Beatles' "All You Need Is Love". But Bowie's song lacks the calibre of that of Lennon and McCartney. What it does do, in the context of this album, is to make up for the black despairing hopelessness of "Cygnet Committee", although one doubts if real happiness is intended to be conveyed by Bowie in this song.

Thus does this astonishing album end on a slightly quizzical note: one never really knows where one is with this artist. And in this LP the ambivalence is openly displayed.

CHAPTER EIGHT

The Stardust Years 1970 to 1973

As we have seen in the previous chapter, Bowie's two earlier solo albums had been mixtures of the brilliant and the mediocre. What was quite clear to the Bowie enthusiast was that the Mercury album "David Bowie" marked significant advances over the earlier Deram LP. But with "The Man Who Sold The World" and the album that succeeded it, "The Rise And Fall Of Ziggy Stardust And The Spiders From Mars", David finally arrived at the apogee of his early maturity. Both albums in their own way appear as syntheses of his various styles, although neither of them looks backward to the same degree as did the Mercury LP. Both albums, however, have become seminal influences for a whole variety of later styles – not just for Bowie himself, but also for large areas of rock music of the 1970s and beyond. In this regard, Bowie showed himself to be a true seer.

1971

"THE MAN WHO SOLD THE WORLD"
Side 1: The Width Of A Circle/All The Mad Men/Black Country Rock/ After All
Side 2: Running Gun Blues/Saviour Machine/She Shook Me Cold/The Man Who Sold The World/The Supermen
As with "Space Oddity", which began his last album with indeterminate noises, so "The Width Of A Circle", the first song on "The Man . . ." album, begins with vague mutterings of life on the left hand channel. These soon freeze into a passacaglia-like theme: insistent, like a massive pulse to which more and more strands are added; a sudden doubling of tempo introduces Bowie in his highest register with the faintest hint of Jagger's timbre. This is Bowie's alter ego, a monster, in dialogue.

The music is heavy, thick, closely-miked in its instrumentation. A young man is here, Bowie singing the "a" sound in "man" in a grossly-elongated form with the drama subsiding to the constant thick imagery of the instruments which only occasionally flicker malevolently to the surface, insistent and unyielding in their power. The words reflect the pansexuality of the original cover, which shows Bowie reclining on a chaise-longue in a dress. The young man's bisexuality is laid bare, but we never know for certain whether it is the sexuality of the artist, or that of the persona of the song. This aspect is gradually revealed through two extended verses with repetitious instrumental episodes. The image fades and we are in a different climate; momentarily less thick and absorbed, slower and more intimate but the throbbing passacaglia with constant, powerful entries, leads to a gathering of forces for the startling middle section of this composition. The effect is unfocussed; not uncertain, for the smudged outlines and blurred images are clearly intentional, as though one was watching newsreel pictures of a disaster wherein the hand-held camera-work conveys the overall horror without dwelling on individual events. In this way, the song implies many things, but essentially the acceptance, and enjoyment, of the widest experiences, making an other-worldly happening, now reflected without words in the massive final part of the song, a hard, metallic succession of concentrated guitar licks tumbling over one another as each new sensation pushes the total experience to ever-widening and barely-perceived frontiers before the final slow coda, complete with timpani, tonic and dominant.

The sexual implications of the title are here vibrantly subsumed through the musical expression of the most phantasmagorial events. This has been an astonishing opening, immediately plunging the listener into a world far removed from the everyday.

In "All The Mad Men" the succeeding extraordinary song, the words, now clear, are obviously meant to be heard. Here the singer is faintly deranged, sympathising, in his own personification of simple insanity, with "all the mad men of the world". We can all list types of people we assume to be mad, principally those we feel threatened by – if we know them well enough. Bowie's musical expression of this pervasive unnaturalness is sure. The key as published is a kind of F minor, with the by-now familiar Bowie side-stepping moves of a downward semitone, in this instance turned upside-down to G flat, then down to E flat, surrounding and trapping F minor. Another spoken idea, and the clarity of his voice (in spite of other voices surrounding it, spattering the image) demands our focusing attention. This is cushioned by a weirdly fluid tonal basis that eventually opts for a massive oscillation between B flat and A flat – the latter key seeming to exert the stronger pull although with a wildly discordant augmented fourth lacerating the tonality. With the constant repetition at the end, the "Free Festival" formula is here turned into something more frightening in its implication, as it did briefly at the end of "The Width Of A Circle". This is a world apart from the song's simple, solo acoustic guitar opening. There is a faint trace of Mediterranean influence, of child-like innocence, a half-remembered, dimly-perceived echo of "Laughing Gnome" and "Cygnet Committee" at the parlando. From a detached level the observer's own insanity is commented upon by way of a completely sane portion of the mind: dangerous matters with the "Zane" in the final phrase completed by "Open the dog" in French, looming at us from right and left stereo channels.

"Black Country Rock", the next song, begins almost as a welcome return to normalcy, but the relief is relative as we are now aware that with this artist there is no such thing. The music is programmed with computer-like precision; the bass guitar thrusting like a colossal object which, as in "The Width Of A Circle" forces itself through the very fabric of the music, like something being moved behind the folds of a curtain, so that we can hardly fail to experience a violent reaction. In some ways, "Black Country Rock" is the scherzo of this album side's four-movement symphonic piece, affording a little (but only a little) relief until the blackness returns via the pulsating instrumental coda with a sickening, doom-laden fixation in "After All".

Here is virtually all despair, the song being immensely slow in tempo, just hanging on to the 12/8 triplet rhythms of early rock ballads, so slow as to embrace finally waltz tempo in a deep heavy-beat parody. The bass-part is constantly-shifting, forever undermining the tonal basis and recalling that of the album's opening song, thus reinforcing the quasi-symphonic nature, a final touch being Bowie's voice rising for the only time in this song to the register of the opening track. Although this is not a concept album in the generally accepted sense of the term, there are clear linking threads between each of the four songs. It is certainly a conceptual side and brilliantly planned. It is important to remember that with Bowie being aware of the nightmare he has unleashed in the opening song, he now needs greater space and time to explore aspects of it. The four-movement structure has already been touched upon, but it is virtually impossible to play these songs separately. They demand to be heard in sequence when their total impact becomes the more powerful.

The public violence – indeed, the political violence – of much of western life in the late 1960s, especially the problems in the United States associated with the Vietnam war, spawned many musical treatments, although little in contemporary classical music, but "Running Gun Blues" is not really one of Bowie's better efforts (at least compared with the outstanding material on the first side of the album). One thing is certain with this artist – for all the theatricality and occasional ambiguity of his lyrics, there is no missing his central point. His subtlety is rarely so obscure as to cause confusion (the mind- and body-expanding experiences of "The Width Of A Circle" could hardly be delineated by music that did not reflect the resultant, immediately filled, fresh and uncertain territory), and Bowie knows more than most that it is no use having an idea if it cannot be properly communicated. But in the last analysis the spectacle of a gun-toting urban guerilla is only interesting in the context of this album, confining its doomed fatalistic imagery, if it does not at the same time produce a valid musical expression capable of standing on its own feet. This song fulfils its functions well enough, but not consistently so. However, after the creeping exhaustion of "After All" it comes as a welcome infusion of energy, albeit one expressing another pessimistic image: that of carnage.

"Saviour Machine" begins with a fade-up and is another fascinating glimpse into a near-future world of technological dependence; for all this the music is the most important aspect of this track – particularly the intriguing instrumental breaks. There are three of these, based on the sliding, disconcerting, semi-tonal slitherings which infect so much music on this album, making it like a musical talisman. These three episodes show Bowie's grasp of extended composition in a wholly remarkable manner. The first is almost like pleasant muzak, with light airy phrases dancing in the air, totally removed from the slow chanting of the second part of the verse, with its upward strivings. The basic fast 3/4 tempo, multi-fractioned to obtain the most from the speeding pulse, is, in the second episode, gradually undermined by tonal quicksands. Our expectations are broken, yet again, and we are made to accept in this instance that forces of darkness are more powerful

than those of light. At the very end the music attempts to rise upwards, but is dragged down at the same time (an astonishing feat of aural imagination) producing a feeling of utter hopelessness and anxiety.

From such a despairing psychological state, only a massive injection of energy can hope to redeem the situation; and "She Shook Me Cold" begins with a fierce, spasmodic rhythmic figure which soon settles uneasily into a somewhat indifferent song. Indifferent because the words are largely inaudible, the recording quality is close, hard-focused, offering no aural balm – still less escape – and, as in other songs on the album, the instrumentation assumes greater control and importance. The tonal haze is total, with the semi-tonal chromaticism sliding all over the place, just kept this side of sanity by being balanced on a single bass-note tightrope. If the title is true, the "She" offers less salvation than might have been imagined, being reduced almost to the rejection of a mother-figure, chaste, complex and ultimately, in her statuesque impassivity, unforgiving.

Unable to see a way out through virtue, or through the usual channels, the singer has to face facts; the fact of the obliterating alter-ego monster of "Width Of A Circle". He is here, now, in "The Man Who Sold The World". This masterpiece, for such it is, is possibly Bowie's most important song up to that time. The "other-worldly" nature of the title and the paradoxically clear yet unfocussed lyrics – true poetry here – demand a purely musical solution to the immense problems uncovered in the course of the album. The solution is entirely musical. The tonality is a basic D minor but approached by a circuitously unusual harmonic route: beginning in A major with a little hypnotically-repeated pulse, A-G natural-A-B flat-A, worming its way, like a gently penetrating object, through the expression of the song. It is a reassuring thing; reassuring in its familiarity and repitition but never doing quite what we think it will. The G flat is the flat seventh of A, the B flat the diminished ninth, but the tonality falls naturally, like a soft beach-ball gently borne on a mild breeze across smooth and unbroken terrain. Striking the mediant F, whose sudden natural completely negates the A major of the opening, means that in this brief opening Bowie has charted the three areas, each of equal importance and pull but cancelling each other out by way of the impulsive guitar refrain. Only one tonality can win; the question is, which one?

As the singer enters D minor seems to be the most important, reinforced by the first 6/4 bar in a 4/4 piece (the significance of which is only made apparent towards the end of the long phrase). But the singer ranges freely over all three keys, now reinforced by the fluid bass part – far removed from the semitonal slidings of previous songs and reassuring in its gentle firmness. This is indeed new territory for this album. As the song progresses, the slight tilt to the rhythmic fine tuning caused by the insertion of the 6/4 bar has to be put right; it comes with the words "died alone" through a 2/4 bar insertion, restoring the rhythmic equilibrium, and not a moment too soon, for the music slips into a completely new tonal region, C major, but felt as the dominant force of F, in which key the bass confirms its importance by a series of rising scales, measured and purposeful, which eventually fall onto D flat, enharmonically C sharp, the major third of A, with which key the song originally began. In this way, by this extraordinary route, Bowie brings us back full circle, but the journey is far from over. The bass reinforces F natural so that we know that the ultimate key cannot be A; merely the starting point. As A is revealed for the third time (after the third incomplete verse) by the same process, the absence of either C sharp or D flat makes a bare fifth, the dominant D minor, into which key the coda settles, but not without passing references to F major as well. The disembodied voice vocalises from dominant to dominant (E to A) and then, as if by magic, takes F as the starting-point and gently floats down the minor third to D.

So it is D minor after all, revealed naturally without tension or intemperance, but surprisingly, as "The Man Who Sold The World" has come to earth to show us new ways of looking at familiar things, to stretch our experience and to reveal, as only true artists can, the inherent fascination and logic of art. The words of this masterly composition match the astonishingly formal cohesion of the music, for the singer, as hinted at earlier, describes to us a (non-) communication he has had with himself, an alter ego (not necessarily the only one) who can be viewed in several ways, for it matters not what he represents in a moral sense; the important thing is that we recognise the opposite's existence.

"Supermen" steps back a little from the personalised anguish of the earlier "The Man Who Sold The World" material. The gods are revealed as being mortal, and the song – not, it must be admitted, of the highest quality – fulfills many functions, not least that of a simple message to the listener. As the gods have mortal feelings, we should not trust them too much. The salvation and self-realisation must come from within, and not from any form of external grafting. But a veritable Pandora's Box of experience has been opened by the symphonic scope and manner of the subterranean first side, musically by "Supermen" beginning with the same tonic and dominant timpani which closed "The Width Of A Circle". This gentle warning will, perforce, go largely unheeded. The story is just beginning.

1971

"HUNKY DORY"
Side 1: Changes/Oh! You Pretty Things/Eight Line Poem/Life On Mars?/ Kooks/Quicksand
Side 2: Fill Your Heart/Andy Warhol/Song For Bob Dylan/Queen Bitch/ The Bewlay Brothers
The album title, of the second LP from Bowie within a year, is mildly reassuring after the black travels of "The Man Who Sold The World", and the sound image is likewise, being more consistent, generally balanced with all the multifarious sounds standing in clear relief from each other. This clarity is obviously deliberate, initially focusing attention on the lyrics and the music as against the overall musical impressionism that was a feature of the previous album. In one sense, "Hunky Dory" is Bowie's Ravel to the Debussy of "The Man . . ." but we know enough by now not to take things either at imagined or face values. The album reveals a less obsessed artist, and possibly a less profoundly moving one, with one or two exceptions, but the lighter touch, and the greater reliance on keyboard texture we encounter on this album are new features in his work.

The first song, "Changes", implies many things, not least the influence of the previous album, although this remains much more in the background, dimly perceived but present, nonetheless. The opening immediately takes the harmonic discoveries of "The Man . . ." and presents them as gently coalescing changes, rising by semitones (of course) from C (major 7th) to D flat to D (minor) and E flat (7th – implying both major and minor). This upward movement omits E before landing on F, from which key the tempo quickens (doppio movimento – doubling the speed), reinforcing it by way of D to fall as the sub-dominant to C major in which key Bowie enters "I Still Don't Know What I Was Waiting For . . ." and the recollected uncertainty is itself viewed from a position of relative calm and sanity, aided by softly upholstered string chords and a florid, expansive piano part from Rick Wakeman. The hook "ch – ch – ch – changes – Turn and face the stranger" is hammered home by constantly chugging quaver chords, but the metrical outline of the song carries Bowie's creativity in this regard several cubits further; the fingerprint of the 2/4 bar in a 4/4 bar context again throws the rhythm out of true, but no sooner is it put back than a massive 4-bar phrase of 3/4 bars confuses the issue; or does it? The effect can be more properly perceived by counting silently through these bars in the original tempo, when it all clicks back into place like the relief of a whirlygig fairground ride. But Bowie trumps this ace by adding more 3/4 bars at the end, finally restoring the equilibrium in a slower saxophone and piano coda on the rising semitonal chords from the opening, now recollected from the "Changed" distance. The lyrics invite us to consider the impermanence of similar time, beautifully complemented by the subtle changes in the music.

"Oh! You Pretty Things" carries the theme a shade further. The piano now is the only accompanying instrument, a slow steady song, a faint warning to those "Pretty Things" of the dangers of self-satisfaction, but one doubts (as well as the singer does) that the warning will be heeded. Bowie knows it is unlikely, but he is not revelling in the trendiness. On the contrary the astonishingly angular phrase "ma-mas and papas insane", the sudden twist into the melodic minor after the uncertain D major of the opening, has a knowing sympathy which is quite exceptional. The most important pair of lines come from the first and second verses: "Let me make it plain, you've got to make way for the Homo Superior" and the third: "Homo Sapiens have outgrown their use" (i.e., "our news" – today's fashions). The important thing is that the warning is directed against Man as a species. The converse implication is also clear; it is as individuals that we are judged.

This segues immediately into "Eight Line Poem" which after the variety of changes of the previous two songs emerges as a brown-study, calm and unhurried, gradually unfolding as Palestrina counterpoint or the opening of Sibelius's Sixth Symphony. The tape-editing between the songs is primitive; no cross-fading here, just a simple splice, but it is easy to perceive a different pair of hands on the keyboard. These are of Bowie himself, against faintly hesitant and almost stuttering Ronson guitar-work. The song makes a relaxed intermezzo before "Life On

Mars?", a much better and more famous piece. The words of "Life On Mars?" are faintly obscure, not at all obvious, but the girl, in the song unfairly asked to leave home, wanders into a cinema where she watches a film about her own situation. This constant kaleidoscopic reflection is expressed in music that mirrors itself again with what we might be forgiven for thinking of as typical Bowie falling semitones, were it not for the fact that the harmonies of the first eight bars are identical to those of the Paul Anka number, adapted from the French, sung by Sinatra: "My Way". It is a nice touch.

For all its initial use of other material, it is one of Bowie's best songs, certain in its expression, sympathetic to the subject, hauntingly memorable in itself and with a superb sense of harmonic growth (it does not follow "My Way" too closely) culminating in the clear B flat major of "Sailors Fighting In The Dance Hall" (a scene from the film) "Changes", indeed!

"Kooks", which follows, is a delightful song to the new-born Zowie Bowie, the title describing his parents. Several popular song performers of the time wrote songs for their children and the change in Bowie's life, with the arrival of, as he put it on the album sleeve, "small Z", can be well imagined by any parent. This intimate song, of no great importance, leads to the final "Quicksand" which begins innocently enough with a gentle acoustic guitar floating between G and A minor. With the entry of the singer the harmonies become more adventurous, but the colouring of the song remains in monochrome. This reinforces the words; the singer, watching silent footage of Himmler, is "frightened by the total goal": What may not be fully appreciated is that he is "immersed in Crowley's uniform", in that curous pre-dawn time, deep in the night, the depths of consciousness.

One assumes this is Aleister Crowley, the extraordinary pantheistic, pansexual, pannarcotic figure who visualised himself as being the Great Beast 666, warned of in the Book of Revelation. We know that the ultimate expression of free will is suicide, and that the irrationality of unbridled freedom leads invariably to sterility and death, especially when one is in the minority. But, assuming for the moment that Bowie (or his performing, evolving character) has tasted such fruits, he is intelligent and sensitive enough to ponder on where they might lead. Hence the "Quicksand" of the title; the true realisation of the result of "changes", too soon, too many, too awesome as "The Man Who Sold The World" told us.

The song is peopled by figures of the thirties and forties; Crowley, Himmler, Garbo, Churchill – all past figures who exerted enormous power and influence, and still do. Ominously enough, the essential tonality, at the point – "I'm the twisted man of Garbo's eyes" – when all the other instruments join in, is really A major, but delayed almost for ever. Yet the music moves to D major for the main second part of the song with Wakeman's florid piano work. The orchestration is remakably rich and powerful; a solo cello here, a woodwind phrase there, a fat rising violin line, against which Bowie's voice appears faintly disembodied, not much like any other we have encountered him using before. He is here a little way back from the microphone, ensuring we catch the consonants in context, but, as often before, the dying coda (echoing the wordless "death" phrases of the closing words of the song) lead us to ponder the clarity and importance of the message.

In many ways, "Quicksand" marks a watershed in this album: not least for the physical fact of it ending the first side. It is the most profound song on the disc so far and after this high point the rest of the album is very much an appendix. Bowie appears anxious not to dwell too much on the darker side, as "Quicksand" has more than hinted, and the succession of songs on side two changes the locale to the USA. "Fill Your Heart", a song by Paul Williams and Biff Rose brings another change, but the arrangement has to be heard to be believed. The song is innocuous, and almost sent up by the singer, against a wall of sound with a yomping piano within a manic orchestra. It is almost put there to leave us with a smile on our faces, at least we assume we must smile, if a trifle wanly, but the album would have been much better without this unnecessary performance.

This audibly segues (courtesy of some silly studio chat which adds nothing to our perception of the song,) into "Andy Warhol" about its homonymous subject. One cannot describe this as a tribute to the astonishing artist, for that implies a sycophancy to which Bowie would never subscribe (or which, if he did, would be unworthy of his stature). Rather it is an attempt – in this guise brilliantly successful – to put Warhol's artistic ethos into music. In that light it then becomes a marvellous piece, serious and witty by turns, picking essentially non-musical objects as sound and turning them, "changes" again, into new objects of fascination and musical expression. Bowie does this with his usual creative legerdemain, faintly tongue-in-cheek, almost uncommuni-cative in its self-conscious nervousness and inherent shyness, absorbed with insignificant details – for all the world as a third rate follower of the Second Viennese School. But the real achievement of this song is that the fascination it exerts is just so, and no more. It lacks profundity and depth and possibly meaning in a transcendental sense; in other words, a perfect Andy Warhol song.

From Warhol to Bob Dylan: the "Song For Bob Dylan" is rather more of a tribute, for elements of Dylan's laser-vision of urban frailty have long been apparent in Bowie's work, but without the obsessive self-regard that so often flaws Dylan; the feeling of self-righteousness. In this regard, Bowie is the more complete artist; but this is like saying that Dvořak was a more complete artist than Verdi for he succeeded in symphony, concerto, chamber music and opera whereas Verdi concentrated almost exclusively on opera. Both composers are equally great, but different. The Dylan song has the greater musical validity than the Warhol, being first unencumbered by the vapid studio noises that surrounded its predecessor, and secondly by evincing a finer musical intent, from the broadly expanding chordal basis on which it is founded to the tighter vocal line, an echo (not a parody) of Dylan. One should remember, however, that whatever subsequent careers Dylan and Bowie have had, in 1971 there was no question as to who was the more important. But in retrospect this is another pro-American song, as though the impact and influence of David's first visit to the country had been so vivid for him not to be a little overawed by it, which a later, more detached view, would have mellowed. Both "Andy Warhol" and "Song For Bob Dylan" need not have been written, for they contribute little to the Bowie oeuvre.

"Queen Bitch" is still American; more likely New York although the locale is not explicitly stated. As the singer is on the 11th floor and scraps in the text are more than likely American in intent, it is safe to assume that this is another American song. "Queen Bitch" paints the impudent picture of the observer from the eleventh floor of the activities going on amongst the cruisers and pullers below on the street, and how he feels he could have done a lot better than they. Bowie's sexual ambiguity is here, but it is still ambiguous: is the queen bitch he, or the bitch the queen of the streets below? Is his song bitchy, in a gay sense? Is the queen below in fact a transvestite hustler, the "her" pronoun referring in a gay-speak to both sexes, but more properly to the male? Or does the "I Can Do Better Than That" both refer to the quality of cruiser the singer could have picked up, or vice versa, criticising his friend's choice? Is the fantasy about the friend that which dreams about a homosexual relationship between them which can never be initiated by the singer? Or does one exist already and the singer is angry at seeing his friend ready to be picked up? All of these conflicting questions can be legitimately asked as a result of this song; it is up to the listener to make his own evaluation of the situation. Such choices, however, do not blur the point. It is an unusual, if not unique, subject for a song, but the tempo and character are not morbid. The tempo of the song is fast, and the tonality a bland C major, breathed into life by Bowie's rhythmic mouth noises, and the result is a hard driving number with little respite. The atmosphere, the raw energy and the breathtaking subject matter are handled with consummate aplomb, making this one of the most remarkable songs of the decade.

The final song on the album, "The Bewlay Brothers" is equally remarkable but for rather different reasons. The title is obscure and the text even more so, to the extent that it is virtually impenetrable. The composer is himself unforthcoming on the subject but probably for very personal reasons. Most people have had their guesses as to what "The Bewlay Brothers" refer to and the present writer feels they are Bowie himself and his older brother Terry, the Bewlay being a private word recalling perhaps a place in Yorkshire or just possibly a mispronunciation of Bowie. There are other factors of this song which ought to be borne in mind. In the first place, the song's pure impressionism; and secondly the inscrutability of it as the singer reveals in the course of the number that "he can't sing about that". It is also likely that the song is a personal one because of the intimate noises we hear as the backing musicians play their introduction; the stool on which Bowie is perched creaks slightly and one feels that he lights a cigarette before starting to sing. A further very remarkable feature is the startling cockney loudness of the descending scale towards the end of the song, another image, seemingly quite unconnected with those of the earlier parts, suddenly tacked on, quite different to that which we have heard before, and causing a slightly worrying effect. Not for the first time, and certainly not for the last, was David Bowie to bring an album to its conclusion with a question mark. Looking back over "Hunky Dory" it is difficult not to be profoundly impressed by the range and depth of Bowie's achievement. But in spite of this achievement, remarkable in itself, it was in some ways nothing more than a prelude to the most sensational and vividly remembered creation of Bowie's from the early 1970s.

1972

"THE RISE AND FALL OF ZIGGY STARDUST AND THE SPIDERS FROM MARS"

Side 1: Five Years/Soul Love/Moonage Daydream/Starman/It Ain't Easy
Side 2: Lady Stardust/Star/Hang On To Yourself/Ziggy Stardust /Suffragette City/Rock 'n' Roll Suicide

This astounding album, Bowie's greatest work as a creative musician up to that period, begins with such certainty and such manifest self-confidence that one is immediately captivated by the brilliant recording of a brilliant conception, a dazzling sound-world of fiction.

In the opening song, "Five Years", the world has that period left to run (which would take us to 1977, the year of Bowie's thirtieth birthday, which just possibly might have been significant). The planet Earth is therefore doomed, though from exactly what threat is not revealed, and the drama of the song and ultimately of the album is played out against this immediately disclosed threat. "Five Years" is an extraordinary song for many reasons. First, it is a waltz, a strict 3/4 number, although Bowie's sub-division of the pulse — which is in itself alien to rock 'n roll — makes the triple-time appear incidental. In one way, the four-bar groupings make massive 12/8 bars, and this probably is the best way to appreciate the song's rhythmic construction. Secondly, the song's message of doom is shot through with a tenderness and sympathy which reveal Bowie's sensitivity and profound humanity. For example the locale, the "market square", immediately provides a broad mass of humanity from which he can observe and draw his examples. "A girl my age went off her head"; suddenly the strings enter for the first time at this point, warm and comforting in their long-sustained chords. In this instance the musical expression grows directly out of the text, but as each character – the cop, the queer, the black, the soldier with a broken arm, and so on – is mentioned, we glimpse that the album (for the album's title clearly tells us that this is to be a concept LP) is concerned with people and human relationships under threat. And so it proves.

But finally, one must note the amazing sound-world of this song, its inexorable growth and power, and the nicely-timed drum segue into "Soul Love", a restrained and surprisingly gentle song with a fascinating beat. This beat is a mixture of two basic pulses, producing a solo bass note on the seventh half-beat of each bar, a characteristic of slow-paced black soul music of the time and highly significant in view of Bowie's later work. Already, aspects of the Thin White Duke are here but this is to anticipate things; as in "Five Years" the rhythmic construction of this song is its most startling musical characteristic. Another, a slight variation on this, is the reasonably familiar Bowie fingerprint – the slipping of a two-beat bar within a four-beat bar sequence, balanced by another such event a few seconds later. The effect, especially on the melodic outline of the song, one of long notes against the chiaroscuro of the accompanying rhythms, is to produce a fascinating pattern of music, all carefully intertwined like the threads of a lace curtain, and as gentle and softly expressive. Against all this as Bowie sings with a reversion to his quasi-nasal Anthony Newley voice, exaggerating the theatricality of the concept, one is forced into a corner. Is this a real hymn to love, almost as an abstract concept? If it is, what is this vocal fly doing in this particular ointment? The answer is surely given in the text; "All I have is my love of love, and love is not loving". This has to be the answer, for it comes at the farthest-removed harmonic point from the song's basic key (in this case C minor within G major); not so very far removed from each other, but sufficiently strange to reinforce the point. The placing of this song about love (one could hardly call it a "love song") also demonstrates its importance in the scheme of things. Its faint similarity to the construction of "Five Years", particularly the gradually expanding instrumentation, reminds us (albeit subconsciously) that it is to be heard in context.

At such a comparatively early stage in this album, one can already sense that the symphonic nature of the first side of "The Man Who Sold The World" is to be refined further here. And so it proves. The next song, "Moonage Daydream", carries earlier points further in their development. It is the most strongly rock-based song so far, but shot through with touches of non-rock material, particularly the oscillating treble chords in the first extended instrumental break, although based on a slight variation of the multi-layered rhythm of "Soul Love". The concept of voices echoing, repeating and seeming to attack and fly away from the main fabric of the vocal line is not new, but is used with a

As Paul von Przygodsky in the Leguan film production 'Just a Gigolo' (1978).

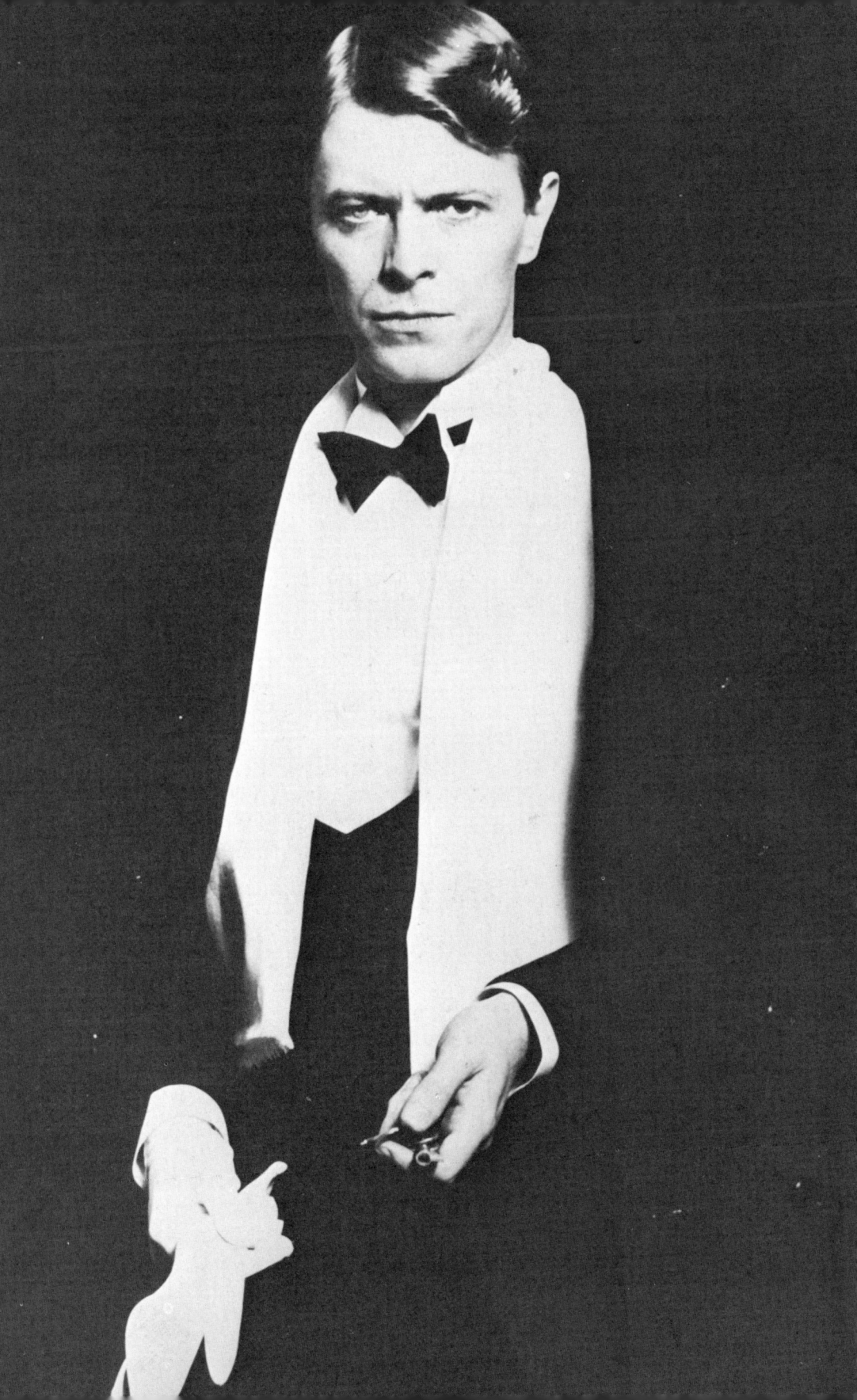

brilliance verging on genius here, for the effect is beautifully dovetailed into an extended but not lengthy Mick Ronson solo, way up in the guitar's highest register, carrying itself and us with it ever higher, climbing surely and effectively into an ethereal sky from which it finally fades.

It follows naturally that "Starman" should be next, a pure science-fiction popular song. Continuing from "Soul Love" the rhythm of "Starman" is a variation on the bassline of the previous number. Melodically, "Starman" takes two quite different entities, "Somewhere Over The Rainbow" and "You Keep Me Hanging On", although the octave leap that characterises the initial vocal music of "Somewhere Over The Rainbow" is the stronger influence. "Starman" has the most clearly-defined and complete story-line of any of the songs on this album. The singer has heard a cosmic voice interrupting his radio listening; on telephoning his friend he discovers he is not alone in hearing it, but the galactic message is one of reassurance. This remarkable concept, which, as has been pointed out by others, shows a startling premonition of the story-line of *Close Encounters Of The Third Kind*, is expressed through an impressively non-fantastical musical manner.

With such an original conception as this album is proving to be, we almost expect a continuous viewpoint on events; the Alien perhaps, the personification of the interrupting voice on the radio of "Starman"? What we get is another voice (almost literally), but in the shape of another writer, the song "It Ain't Easy" by Ray Davies. Bowie's amazing repertoire of vocal tricks is here demonstrated further by his use, or rather our hearing, a tiny distanced voice, the whole concept a stage removed from our previous aural experience. This may indeed be the voice on the radio. It is a remarkable choice and a revealing one, but the effect of this performance is myriad. At a deeper level, it reminds us of Bowie's own performances, not necessarily of his own music; more importantly it throws into relief the other songs we have heard, bringing side one to an end with an unanswered question. Tiny phrases, words, even syllables are momentarily emphasised in an astonishing vocal display by Bowie, becoming almost a disembodied soul singer of outstanding quality, but all put at the service of a higher concept – that of the unfolding drama of the album.

Thus does the brilliant first side of "Ziggy Stardust" end, an incomparable procession of personal brilliance, staggering in its expressive scope and virtually flawless in its realisation. This is a major artistic statement of the highest calibre within its own field, and like all such statements, it enlarges and develops our own experiences. Side two begins with "Lady Stardust", an original Bowie song, introduced by solo piano (Mick Ronson displaying an outstanding ability on this instrument – although he had been heard in this role on side one). The song is told from the viewpoint of a boy who is in love with a rock and roll singer on stage. We hear of his fantasies, but there is no ambiguity here as there was in "Queen Bitch". The "Lady Stardust" in question is almost certainly Marc Bolan (indeed Bowie has indicated as much on several occasions), but that is ultimately irrelevant. The important point is that, for all the adoring description of the singer, this is not a sexual song – although doubtless the singer in this instance would not have minded the opportunity – and the love remains unrequited, distanced. We do not know if the object of the love either knew or cared about the existence of his admirer. The song can be seen to be concerned with all such yearnings, translated into a gay setting not for sensationalism but because a straight song on the subject would not have had the effect of other-worldliness, as of seeming to care for the minority, or of focusing our attention on the sadness of the situation, with all its implications, which the "five year" life of this particular sound world forces us to consider when time has a definite limit imposed upon it. The song is shot through with masterly touches: at the phrase "out of sight" Bowie's voice suddenly leaps skywards, but quietly, the musical equivalent of the words, and retained as part of the melodic line. When this phrase returns with the word "paradise" the ecstasy and heavenwards-thought also fit the rising rapture of his voice like a glove. One final small point; the piano introduction and coda quote (doubtless unconsciously) "Maria" from "West Side Story", for the second time in Bowie's writing career.

The second side is as complete a collection as the first, on which the parameters had been faintly drawn; now, they are to be explored, but within the context of music theatre. As we have heard, the first song, "Lady Stardust", is about performance, seen from the adoring fan's viewpoint. Now, a succession of songs, a mini-gig, almost as a multi-movement cantata within the album side, refracts the image. The next three songs, vastly different though they be, nevertheless make the collective viewpoint. "Star" takes the solo singer, whom we know is called Ziggy Stardust, and reveals his plans for personal world stardom.

But we also know, as he does not, that in this context the Earth's life is a mere five years more. His, therefore, cannot be longer. Furthermore, the pansexuality which pervades these songs is nothing more than Ziggy's desire to appeal at every level to the widest possible audience. "Star" is a remarkable song. It is based on old rock formulae, confirming the dramatic background, but handled with considerable ingenuity, not least with regard to its rhythmic construction and the malleability with which Bowie uses backing voices. The song's seriousness is reinforced by the sudden unexpected change to a slow tempo towards the end, as though a frown has passed across the mind, unbidden, revealing an aspect of stardom which it is probably better not to contemplate.

This new aspect might just possibly be referred to in the next song "Hang On To Yourself" a piece of surprising originality. This is sung to a fast-medium soft-rock tempo and is an overt invitation, if not more than that, to sex, but sung in an insidious half-whipped voice that seems all the more dangerous because it appears plainly determined to get what it wants. "Ziggy Stardust" is a portrait of the star, not of Bowie himself. It is essentially descriptive of the performer at work, seen this time from on stage.

So we have three interlinked songs, related by their harmonies, and rhythmic subtleties, concerned variously with the star's ambition, his influence and his appearance. Now Ziggy himself, fully revealed by this process, sings "Suffragette City", full of those sexual ambiguities noted earlier. In one sense the star realises the helplessness of the situation he has created; as a leader he has his followers, but they are suffocating him and he cannot control them. They, lacking his original certainty of purpose, threaten to overwhelm him and very nearly do; the suffragette, the willingly-led seeker after personal freedom, is both man and woman. It is likely that the seeker is the orginal innocent distant lover of the first song on this side; Ziggy's increasing exasperation finds its outlet initially in the frantic tempo that towards the end freezes into repeated notes with an obsessive disregard for everything. The words tumble beneath a seemingly chaotic spray, as the speeding mind races through a whole kaleidoscope of imagery. The result is a colossal shock, both for the listener and for Ziggy himself, for we never thought it would come to this. And this, the self-created, self-destructive situation can only go in one direction, at least in this frame of mind.

"Rock 'n' Roll Suicide" concludes this amazing piece of work, a slow, beaten, broken song beginning in the depths of despair. The image of a worn-out youth at the end of his imagination is brilliantly drawn; but he is both Ziggy and Ziggy's follower. As Ziggy he cannot escape, as the previous song clearly indicated, and as his followers have no-one to lead them, they drift aimlessly, within a world of finite temporality. But this is reduced to the personal, to the singular; here the suicide – both the person and the act – is that of one individual who is led towards his inevitable suicide. Together, however, Ziggy and his followers might just achieve something. "You're not alone," sings Bowie to himself and to his followers, calling "love" to anyone who wants to hear. It is both a plea for his fans to follow him and to himself to go on to new things, and although this arises from the depths of despair, the music manages, in spite of the slow and doom-laden tread, to heave itself upwards, groaning and protesting the while, from the simplistic C major, the chord reinforced right at the very end of the record. The opening song of the album was in G major; now, at the end, we have harmonically speaking traversed the universe to end on the farthest possible key away – the tritone D flat. Clearly Bowie has a great deal more left in him to say, although whether it will be Ziggy who says it is another matter.

1973

"ALADDIN SANE"
Side 1: Watch That Man (New York)/Aladdin Sane (1913–1938–197?) (R.H.M.S. "Ellinis")/Drive-In Saturday (Seattle–Phoenix)/Panic In Detroit (Detroit)/Cracked Actor (Los Angeles)
Side 2: Time (New Orleans)/The Prettiest Star (Gloucester Road)/Let's Spend The Night Together/The Jean Genie (Detroit and New York)/Lady Grinning Soul (London)
"Ziggy Stardust" was the album by which Bowie became a major international force: "Aladdin Sane" was the first album to come from the top; and so the title – at least that which we hear when the words are spoken, rather than the pantomime aspect we get when the words are read – has to be taken seriously. Even before a note of the music on the album has been heard, we are confronted with another Bowie paradox. On the one hand, we hear "a lad insane" meaning quite clearly a mad young man; on the other hand read of a pantomime figure – Aladdin – who is perfectly sane. The startling artwork on the cover of

the album shows Bowie made up with digonal blue, black and red colouring searing across his face in a figure which could variously be described as a flash of lightning or a stylised Z or S. If the latter interpretation is valid then Ziggy Stardust is here raised to an altogether different level.

Another significant aspect of the album, and one which is apparent before we place the record on the turntable, is the mainly American locale for the majority of the songs. Clearly, if Ziggy as a character is to be taken seriously – and all the indications are that he should be – then it is incumbent on him, in pursuit of his international stardom, to travel; especially in the United States. The theme of this album, at one level, can therefore be seen to be Ziggy on tour, but we must not forget that the original Ziggy album ended in suicide; we were not entirely sure, even at the end of that album, whether the suicide attempt was successful or not. This is another paradox, for, if it was, the action of the new album takes place outside earthly experience; but if it was not, then in some ways, the subject is a fight back from despair. The latter explanation is more likely although the first cannot entirely be ruled out. Assuming for the moment that it is a fight back from the depths of despair, we must expect it to begin in an atmosphere of deranged foreboding and high manic energy. If these two states seem incompatible, the practice of treating potential suicides with drugs has to be borne in mind. In view of the fact that by this time (1973) drugs had become an almost essential part of popular music, this would tend to reinforce the second explanation.

But our initial observations have to be confirmed by the music itself, although it is better to be as well prepared as one can, in order to appreciate this album at its best. The last song we heard from Bowie on an album was "Rock 'n' Roll Suicide" and derangement had been a feature of his work from time to time in the past, often submerged beneath a layer of alter ego. The concepts of his last three albums had given Bowie plenty of scope for the expression of, to put it mildly; extreme uncertainty; the " Aladdin Sane" album takes up this theme but looks at it more objectively. There are plenty of examples in art of the depiction of chaotic states, but they all have one thing in common – chaotic expression. Therefore when the "Aladdin Sane" album is criticised, as it can be, for its more than occasional rough edges, it should be remembered that these crudities are brought into play to express precisely those things.

In essence, the album is a fusion of two states. The first is that of derangement, and the second that of discovery, in this case that of America. When this album was conceived and released, Richard Nixon was still President of the U.S.A. The rumblings of Watergate and the other unsavoury aspects of his administration had already begun to appear, and the country, in its immediate post-Vietnam phase, was collectively at a very low psychological ebb. The combination of these apparently disparate factors may have helped to produce, in this extraordinary album, one of the most astonishing rock statements ever. Worlds away from "popularity", and not much concerned with original rock 'n' roll, the album is a kind of symphonic song-cycle about America, years in advance of Leonard Bernstein's "Songfest" for six singers and orchestra. But – as should always be remembered – this is America seen from Bowie's European eyes. It is difficult, especially from the distance of more than a decade, to appreciate the cumulative effect upon the American collective consciousness of the rise of the Black Power movement, the riots of the 1960s in many American cities, the assassinations of several of the country's more enlightened leaders, the continuing quagmire of the Vietnam War, and the ultimate corruption of Watergate. These influences combined to deliver a collective culture-shock which ran through every stratum of American society. One must not look to Bowie's music to resolve American problems. Rather one must take America as the starting-point, as a peg on which Bowie has hung his ideas.

The first song "Watch That Man" immediately declares this to be a different album from "Ziggy Stardust". Whereas that album was distinguished by a stereo recording of incomparable technical beauty, richness and creativity, "Aladdin Sane" begins with the sound-image of any old badly-balanced, technically crude, poorly realised album – in other words like hundreds of inferior "rock" albums of the time produced all over the world by people who had no right to be in a recording studio.

As has been demonstrated many times before, such is Bowie's fastidiousness that to dismiss this song's technical shortcomings as being a result of pressure of time is less than sympathetic to his creativity. It is a hard, raucous, pushing, shoving, driving, loud, impacted number, with the words largely inaudible apart from the title which manages to force its way through the blanket wall of rhythm and echo. We listen amazed at this musical primitivism, wondering what on earth is to come. After the impact of the first song, which is rather like that of waking up suddenly after a long flight almost as the plane is touching down on the runway, one being momentarily disoriented by the unexpected surroundings. The result, as far as the second song, the title track of the album, is concerned is a complete surprise; yet another sound-world, this time dominated by an unamplified grand piano, outstandingly well played by Mike Garson which, like a Greek chorus, comments upon the song which it introduces and frames like a protective cover. As "Aladdin Sane" progresses, held by a simple base rhythm, the piano becomes ever more startlingly aleatory cutting right across the texture, lacerating the mind with its frenzied and seemingly uncontrolled power, for all the world like a Peter Maxwell Davies piano part infected by Archie Shepp. These characteristics produce hypnotic, obsessive music that eventually subsides, the piano now calmed, but – amazingly – not fading, remaining at the same volume while the singer and the rest of the instruments fade into the distance, the piano recorded with an incredible use of stereo: nothing less than the left hand on the left hand channel and the right hand on the right. A tiny, smiling cadence tosses the song away, a trick ending like that of Rachmaninoff's Paganini Rhapsody. The words are largely irrelevant, not in themselves but because they are largely inaudible, being merely another part of the total aural mix.

"Drive-In Saturday", which follows, is an astonishing glimpse into the future, a time when sexual technique has become a lost art and has to be relearned with porn videos, at drive-in Saturdays. Such a remarkable concept is treated equally remarkably by the music, whi;ch almost demands a chapter to itself. The song begins not on the tonic A (the home key) but in the dominant (a fifth above) and moves to the home key when Bowie enters, sliding to the minor mediant for a colossal change of harmony, and then using this new key as a fresh starting-point, returning eventually not to the home key but almost to it, falling again and again in insistent pulses, but never finding the fleetingly-glimpsed home tonality. In this way, Bowie brilliantly delineates the image of a lost, partly understood art. The end, with its constant repetition of the main extended final phrase, is a massive glimpse into the future.

"Panic In Detroit" returns us to the present-day, the panic referring to political turmoil in Motown (the city, not the record company). It is a splendid song in the best rock traditions, a powerful use of rock idioms to make a liberal political point. This, surely, is the proof – if it be needed – that the creator's attitude is essentially that of the detached sympathetic observer. The song is not therefore concerned with "sanity" as such; more with the manifestation of it in others. The only breath of criticism that could be levelled against it is the balance of Bowie's voice with the backing musicians; once again, he is set a little too far back for the listener to catch the lyric without strain, and while this may induce the "so-what" diathesis, it is nonetheless a failure in communication.

The concluding song of side one, "Cracked Actor", is concerned with the concept of the damaged artist – one which was doubtless appealing to Bowie, especially in the context of this album. Although "Cracked Actor" is not quite from Bowie's top artistic drawer, it is nevertheless a good song, full of admirably tight and chunky rhythmic solidity, especially the "Crack, baby, crack" break. The feeling of Los Angeles in the early 1970s is marvellously created here through a remarkable synthesis, although the subject of the song gets somewhat submerged in the process.

A glance at the titles on this album reveals the locations either to which the songs are intended to refer or the places in which they were written. In either event, the result is like a kind of travelogue diary, although in essence – with one or two notable exceptions – the songs could be interchangeable. From Los Angeles to New Orleans, "Time" opens side two with a greater distanced piano, now at first a weird echoing instrument way on the right hand channel, but Bowie takes the centre stage with another piano just behind him in perspective. Bowie uses a very wide tonal spectrum, but the song tends ultimately to fail, being less coherent than one feels it deserves to be. The tidal waves of repetition do not redeem it, for all its surprising verbal imagery. To be fair, it may be that the general shambles that often passes for tourist music in New Orleans may have had some influence on the presentation here, but it still leaves something to be desired.

"The Prettiest Star" resurrects a number from Bowie's Mercury period. It is not at all a bad song by itself, but it is unusual for Bowie to have picked on material from several years earlier for an album which is in general so far in advance of his work. On the other hand, it may well have been that Bowie felt this song had lasting qualities and deserved a fresh approach. Even without knowing that it comes from an earlier period, there is a different air to this piece, a greater sense of easily definable melody, compared with the angular and harmonically much more daring current material of "Aladdin Sane". In either form, "The Prettiest Star" is not one of Bowie's better efforts; the performance which follows, unquestionably is.

This is a drastic recomposition in performance terms of the classic song by Mick Jagger and Keith Richard, "Let's Spend The Night Together". Bowie turns in an electrifying performance, from the grabbing, absurdly flak-ridden piano introduction – as though Jerry Lee Lewis had been taking lessons from Barraqúe – to the fiercely independent yet rhythmic vocal line against the irresistable driving Chicago-originated urban blues pulse, transformed by the paradoxically disintegrating diallage of the concluding sexual thrusts into an astonishing performance which will never lose its power. A barely-audible taradiddle floats the song off into the right hand channel, from which direction "Jean Genie" bursts into life.

This is so familiar to the Bowie enthusiast that any description of it might appear superfluous, but it is important to bear several factors in mind. The first concerns the title – said to be a homonym of the French writer Jean Genet with whose adventurous spirit Bowie probably found he had much in common. If so, Genet himself does not appear even remotely in the song's lyrics. It is far easier to take the title at sound-face value; that of a small jean-clad boy, in which case it makes far greater sense. The sexual nature of the boy's street activities are broadly hinted at and the music is deliberately primitive – almost provocative. The stomping tonic in the bass, thumped out incessantly on the first three of each group of four beats transfers to the dominant for the chorus, with no let up of the driving pulse, and this main line throb in the artery which feeds the vocal line is so overpowering that it forces the melody into a straight-jacket from which there appears to be no escape. Nor is there. The object of the song is indeed trapped, for all his pathetic and manifestly unsuccessful attempts to seek pleasure. He "loves to be loved", this "poor little greenie" (and in this context one assumes that green equals unsophisticated) and will do anything to get it. As a young man, he has the energy and sexual power, but the ambiguity of the final phrase "Let yourself go" would appear to be taken only one way. Over and above the basic musical construction of this remarkable song, whose essential simplicity is akin to folk music, the sheer impact and power, which are almost physical in their effect, are vivid in the extreme, making a thrilling, totally original and unforgetable piece of music.

A florid dramatic piano recitative, with a faint Spanish influence, introduces "Lady Grinning Soul", a remarkably different song from the previous material. This final number on the album is outstandingly well sung, with superb breath control – a result, no doubt, of Bowie's early experiences as a choir boy. There are sudden changes of image, with the guitar and piano especially brought to the foreground, to showcase Bowie's voice. The lady in question is the American singer Claudia Linnear who had also inspired the Rolling Stones' "Brown Sugar", and she must have been a woman of remarkable personal magnetism. In "Lady Grinning Soul" the intimate nature of Bowie's description has the ring of truth to it; but the moment the song tends to go into highly personal matters the vocal line changes into a florid multi-instrumental coda of upward-rising ecstasy.

One final point concerns the dates (1913, 1938, 197?) after the title song on the album. Like most of Bowie's enigmatic titles (and subtitles), these dates appear to have a purely personal significance, although one can never be certain. It may well be that the dates refer to the first years of life of his father (who was born in 1912) and his half-brother Terry (who was born in 1937) and of his son Zowie (who was born in 1971). If this is the case, then the missing year is 1972, but the years in question also predate those of the first two world wars by one year. Bowie, in his guise as Ziggy Stardust, predicted that the five-year span of time left to Planet Earth in that album expired in 1977, which would mean that the missing year is 1976. A simple numerate solution of the enigma would be 1975 but whatever the correct answer, it is nothing more than a tantalising adjunct to the "Aladdin Sane" concept. The album ends with Bowie back in London and once again he concludes an album with a song slightly out of place with the rest of the material on the LP, as though he was throwing out a new idea, to be taken up at some point in the future. As we shall see this last song throws out several: London, the city to which Bowie belongs and which constituted his musical roots; and black soul music which, as time progressed, was to exert a great pull on his creative faculties. Both of these ideas were to be taken up in his immediately succeeding work, but "Aladdin Sane" brings to an end a truly extraordinary period of Bowie's creativity, and one which over a decade after it was concluded still exerts the most potent influence on a variety of practitioners of popular music all over the world.

CHAPTER NINE

After Stardust: 1973-1976

As we saw in the first part of this book, Bowie 'killed off' Ziggy Stardust in public on the stage of the Hammersmith Odeon in July 1973. As so often with this artist, his pronouncements often have a double meaning. Was this retirement from the performing stage to be that of Bowie himself, or of his character Ziggy? The album "Aladdin Sane" had given, as we saw when considering it, an indication that Bowie was preparing to travel along new paths. It was also clear, although not blindingly obvious, that he had gone just about as far as he could go in exploring the nature of Ziggy. Also the American experience had been profound, through Bowie's personal travels throughout that country and in the influence of current American music – not necessarily that which was the most popular – experienced at grass-roots level. Bowie had travelled far in a very few years and he doubtless felt the need to return to his roots.

As was indicated in discussing "Lady Grinning Soul", with the enigmatic inclusion of London in the title, it did not require much imagination to feel that Bowie's next album, "Pin-Ups", although it came for many people as a surprising statement from him, was the logical continuation of one of the future routes he had mapped out at the end of "Aladdin Sane". Few could have predicted exactly what form this would take. Once again Bowie's creativity was working overtime: all art, in any art form of any worth contains the element of surprise. This is not surprise for surprise's sake; this is the surprise of encountering an original mind which does not do what we expect. If all our expectations are met then we lose interest, realising – albeit subjectively on occasion – that the mind which has created this can only tell us what we want to know. Even the most cursory reader must realise that in David Bowie we encounter an artist who resolutely refuses to supply us with what he thinks (and therefore what we think) we expect. The next stage of his artistic journey was fraught with as many problems as those which marked out his earlier stages. But he arrives at the end with a new and absorbing synthesis of his talents, creating music at least as good as the best he had given us before and in some cases even better.

1973

"PIN-UPS"
Side 1: Rosalyn/Here Comes The Night/I Wish You Would/See Emily Play/Everthing's Alright/I Can't Explain
Side 2: Friday On My Mind/Sorrow/Don't Bring Me Down/Shapes Of Things/Anyway, Anyhow/Where Have All The Good Times Gone?
Bowie's return to his roots was made through this album, a collection of his favourite songs from the period 1964 to 1967, as he says "of London". It was in London, basically, that Bowie served his musical apprenticeship; an apprenticeship longer than that of any other British artist of comparable stature. He had suffered many disappointments and frustrations and had been given chances which he resolutely refused to take simply for commercial reasons. While many people might have thrown in their hands and given up, Bowie's inner certainty of purpose sustained him through these long apprenticeship years. Now, he could play an affectionate and personally needed tribute to his more famous contemporaries of the 1960's. In some ways, this album can be seen to be of greater interest to the students of rock music than to the Bowie enthusiast, and although Bowie probably needed to get this music back into his system in an attempt to get other music out of it, there are no original songs by him on "Pin-Ups" and consequently the album is of little significance in charting his own creative development other than affording him the opportunity of rediscovering himself. Roy Carr and Charles Shaar Murray have valuably compared Bowie's performances with the original. In terms of Bowie's performing ability, little need be said about these songs, for they are not intended to be some kind of nostalgic recreation or pathetic attempt at creating identical versions for a later generation. It is probably true to say that one of the characteristics of popular music which makes it important for the individual is that certain songs and performances are forever bound up with an individual's personal experiences. To hear the song again brings

back the experience, and this must be just as true for David Bowie as it is for any of his listners.

Of the six songs on side one the most remarkable performance of all is the last, of The Who's "I Can't Explain". This is not fit to be compared to the original classic recording and Bowie's adoption of a funeral tempo loses the essential nature of the original. Nor is this replaced by any redeeming feature. Curiously enough, if this track is played at 45 rpm, with the bass boosted to its fullest power, the treble cut to nothing, and the left hand channel trimmed to centralise the stereo image, the result is quite exciting, especially Mick Ronson's guitar breaks, making a refracted piece of early moddery. But at Bowie's tempo the song comes over as a slug of grease.

Among performances on the album's second side that of The Mersey's "Sorrow" has come in for considerable criticism from the writers mentioned above, but it is certainly a quite original and hypnotic performance, detached, with the proper element of wounded pride. In "Shapes of Things" Bowie reverts to his Newley voice that sounds as though it has been drenched in whisky; however, this unusual vocal timbre is redeemed by some outstanding phrasing. The next song is the greatest performance of the album. All the elements on "Anyway, Anyhow, Anywhere" are truly superb and magisterially cohesive. This is an absolutely stunning performance which demonstrates Bowie's generous character in putting his own considerable talents at the disposal of music written many years before by someone else. "Where Have All The Good Times Gone?" is a pleasant enough performance, but perhaps the most significant thing about this track is the title. Once again, Bowie has to look to the future.

1974

"DIAMOND DOGS"
Side 1: Future Legend/Bewitched, Bothered and Bewildered/Diamond Dogs/Sweet Thing/Candidate/Sweet Thing – Reprise/Rebel Rebel
Side 2: Rock 'n' Roll With Me/We Are The Dead/1984/Big Brother /Chant Of The Ever-Circling Skeletal Family
Following the cosmopolitan contemporaneity of "Aladdin Sane" and the backward-looking nature of "Pin-Ups" Bowie clearly took note of his own sense of direction, shown in his previous album, to build on

the rediscovered beginnings of his own art. In "Diamond Dogs" Bowie gives full rein – with a vengeance – to his own considerable creativity, and his own sense of theatrical fantasy and imagination.

The opening track, "Future Legend", immediately plunges the listener into yet another extraordinary sound world, big and vivid and peopled with amazing thoughts and projections of the future. This seems to be a return to Bowie's earlier futurism which is reinforced by the inset provided with the album containing a startling pictorial vision of a future desolate city against which is printed a piece of doom-laden prose, which Bowie interns at the beginning against a mêlée of sound, through which bizarrely and not entirely incongruously one can perceive the chorus of the 1940 Rodgers and Hart classic song "Bewitched, Bothered and Bewildered" from the show "Pal Joey". Here we have "Pins-Ups" with a vengeance. Eventually, this leads to the song itself (Bowie's not Rodgers') in which a new Bowie character is introduced, Hallowe'en Jack. This is a powerful hard rocking number, closer perhaps in character to the Rolling Stones of 1967 to 1969 than anything else, although Bowie's originality is never in doubt. Indeed, in some ways this may be Bowie's own answer to his selection of "Pin-Ups" on the previous album. It is a question of degree, but his song has a greater sense of urgency because it is ostensibly set in the future, a time which Bowie has harrowingly explored before, and his message has little hope. Nor is this a euphemism for despair, which is also largely absent from Bowie's essential sanity (as an artist, not necessarily from his subject-matter). Whatever the reasons, we are on this journey whether we like it or not so we had better settle down and observe it. The music of this first song is the essence of rock: urban, driving, occasionally shot through with the most spectacular musical changes – not for shock or effect, just to keep the imagination working overtime, and leading after a staggering chordal close on guitar (with Bowie himself playing, showing a raw primitivism immediately reducing everything to basics), to the remaining songs on the side which form a massive thirteen-minute tetralogy. Although the first three are banded together, the ear perceives the rest of the first side of this album as in one continuous sweep, and as such – for we are dealing with music, not print – it must be considered.

The immediate impact of the title track has prepared us for some frightening things; the opening sounds of the tetralogy are of some futuristic world (achieved by reasonably simple electronic methods), but suddenly, Bowie enters, intoning an anthem of vividly descriptive power in a voice never before heard from him on disc, as a morbid low bass singer. His voice ranges, like that of no other singer, ever upwards over virtually three octaves and the timbre suggests he is singing at the top of his range – not falsetto – although one can never be sure, because there may be electronic gadgetry at work here. His vocalising is, like just about everything else he does, of such singular originality that he could be doing either or both. The important thing is that he has the manifest ability with which to express his extraordinary vision.

"Sweet Thing", the first of the songs of this section, is an amazing hymn to loveless future sex, loveless in terms of our own time. Whether in the future of Orwell's *Nineteen Eighty-Four*, of Aldous Huxley's *Brave New World* or any one of a hundred other less literary, more popular influences from the culture of the time, future love often appears like that. The music is absolutely astounding, it is among Bowie's richest and densest creations, far removed from the basic rock music of the title track, and teeming with invention. The places of habitation are ruined in the future, one assumes as a result of a nuclear holocaust, with the supposed mutational changes implied on the front cover of the album (in Guy Peellaert's "manimal" embodiment). Such love as Hallowe'en Jack searches for can only take place within the relics of the building, at least in a metropolitan environment. In spite of all the doom and pessimism of Bowie's vision of the future, shared by his illustrious predecessors, the fact that his central character still seeks for love is important in itself, and is the only positive, optimistic aspect of his future existence.

The next song, "Rock 'n' Roll With Me" is a tender love song within a massively chordal, heavily instrumented and slow rock idiom. The genuine tenderness Bowie expresses within such an idiom is most extraordinary especially as there is a wierd Nashville flavour in his voice during the first verse and the succeeding instrumental break, but not in the second. It may be that this is a very subtle reference to the roots of rock 'n' roll that arose in the city of Memphis in the early 1950's. Bowie has made it plain that certain parts of this album are taken from an incompleted project based on George Orwell's *Nineteen Eighty-Four*. While this may be of passing interest, it is largely irrelevant. Bowie's music here, as in all other instances, has to be taken on its own terms.

Curiously enough, the next song is clearly suggested by Orwell's novel. This is "We Are The Dead" and the sound-world is initially very different; a few instruments, stammering in their uncertainty, which feeling remains throughout the piece. The sensitive, introverted yet ultimately insignificant character reduces the relationship to an earthly level for all the intrasigence of the words. The world thus populated is essentially alien, frightening and forever disconcerting. The soul yearns for that which it can never obtain, and this is the future we are invited to contemplate. The most interesting aspect of this song is Bowie's control of time. For example, the basic pulse is maintained throughout, but fading echoes die at a different rate, producing an underlying sense of musical uncertainty which brilliantly exemplifies the words. In addition, the song has an irregular ostinato of falling chords. The use of ostinato produces a static feeling which signifies that the singer cannot escape. His own vocal line, in spite of its occasional rise, is always underpinned by the harmonies and where they are absent, the line falls also. This constant pulling downwards is the most vivid musical ingredient in the song and when combined with the rhythmic subleties noted earlier produces a creation of hypnotic hopelessness.

"1984", the succeeding song is here: a brilliant, shining opening, teeming with glistening hard light ricocheting from one note to the next (yet another oscillation) which flashes across the image throughout the song at intervals, as though we were travelling on a futuristic land-cruiser at speed. The song thus illuminated is another fine achievement. Bowie's performance is strong and certain and there can be no doubt as to his single-mindedness. His voice is a myriad experience of a half-dozen different timbres, echoing and overdubbing with itself and recalling the ending of "The Man Who Sold The World" but the oscillation at the beginning now tintinnabulates as the music, slowly revolving like a sparkling globe, comes to its end.

The next song "Big Brother", the most obviously *Nineteen Eighty-Four*-related song, should have been faded up at the beginning as the ethereal choral voices are cut in a fraction too late. They act as an upholstered cushion for a high instrumental recitative; suddenly, as Bowie emerges – the music plummets basswards, the choral texture occasionally recalled and leads to a powerful rising solo line, framed by a curious halo, the solo line masculine and strong but succeeded by a strangulated imagery as the voices out-manoeuvre Giles Swayne's CRY in their astonishing demands and startling yet entirely musical effects.

This song segues into "Chant of The Ever-Circling Skeletal Family", a modern, if not futuristic, piece. The voices here are wordless and the rhythm – an irregluar 6 plus 5 – is intoned with ever-proliferating sub-rhythms of increasing power inducing a terrifying feeling of trapped horror. In this despairing mood "Diamond Dogs" is brought to a disconcerting end.

"DAVID LIVE"
Side 1: 1984/Rebel Rebel/Moonage Daydream/Sweet Thing
Side 2: Changes/Suffragette City/Aladdin Sane/All The Young Dudes/ Cracked Actor
Side 3: When You Rock 'n' Roll With Me/Watch That Man/Knock On Wood/Diamond Dogs
Side 4: Big Brother/Width Of A Circle/Jean Genie/Rock 'n' Roll Suicide
In the first part of this book we learned the circumstances surrounding the recording of this live double album. The tapings were made on 12th and 13th July, 1974 at the Tower Theatre in Philadelphia. The album cover says, "It is complete and exact. No studio overdubs or re-recording of voices, instruments or audience have been added with the exception of several backing vocals due to loss of theatre mike contact." With a few exceptions all the songs on this album have been discussed on their respective studio albums, so the interest for the student of Bowie's creativity is considerably reduced. One justification for issuing a live album is that the performances are of sufficient stature to warrant such action. However, RCA, with their troubled super-star Elvis Presley, had, by 1974, been forced into the position of issuing live albums of his performances, in an attempt to keep his name before the record buying public. In marketing terms, the idea of a Bowie live double album was an excellent one. His stage shows were just as enthralling spectacles visually as they were musically and frequently, because of the added visual content, inspired him and his backing musicians to considerable heights. It must be admitted, however, that for all the excellence of the technical recording on this double album, Bowie's performances remain less than compelling. Without other aids, which we now thankfully possess, a future generation might very well ask what all the fuss was about on hearing this set. Bowie's voice here is still a multi-faceted instrument, with a strong jazz influence in "Changes". But "All The Young Dudes", the hit he wrote and produced for Mott the Hoople, lacks the one thing which above all it

As 'The Shark' in 'Yellowbeard' (1983). Photograph: Rank Films.

should possess – power – and possesses the one instrument – piano – which above all it should lack. The great "Knock On Wood" by Eddie Floyd and Steve Cropper is fractionally too slow for the thrills it should engender. For all his admirable efforts with this number it is not really Bowie material. Another interesting point about this double album is the performance of "Jean Genie". This is one of the best, possibly *the* best, performance here. It is outstandingly electrifying and the dirty sleaziness of Bowie's altered text makes the sexuality ever more explicit. The one fly in the ointment is the presence of the piano but mercifully there is little of it and it is more than compensated for by the brilliant guitar solo. As a memento of David's live performances of the time this album has some interest, but it is in reality little more than a mildly interesting epicycle to the main orbit of his work. The same comments apply with equal force to Bowie's second live album, "Stage", which appeared in 1978.

1975

"YOUNG AMERICANS"
Side 1: Young Americans/Win/Fascination/Right
Side 2: Somebody Up There Likes Me/Across The Universe/Can You Hear Me/Fame
Bowie's massive transcontinental American tour had inevitably produced a whole succession of extraordinary experiences and influences upon him. In this album, "Young Americans", he returns again to the theme of the United States, which he had touched upon in earlier albums, but this time seen from a closer, more immediate viewpoint. The opening song, the title track on the album, beigns with a light beat that becomes more concerned with the tonic and dominant as Bowie himself enters. The song has a narrative ballad lyric and although its atmosphere reeks of the mid-1970s, the instrumentation has a hypnotic easy-beat which is quite marvellous and timeless. Bowie's breathless voice introduces each of the young characters with which the song is peopled. They have possibly been chosen for their shallowness; the song is all lightness and artifice, worlds apart from the committed profundity of Bowie's earlier work. But the detailed observer – the singer of this particular song – appears disillusioned by what he sees. The quotation from the Beatles' "Sergeant Pepper"

David Bowie with Catherine Deneuve in 'The Hunger' (1983).
Photograph: MGM/UA Entertainment Co.

album "I heard the news today, oh boy" echoes the sympathetic despair, and the final line just before the song fades reveals the barrenness of the panorama.

A superbly upholstered orchestral-style introduction begins "Win" which mixes electronic and natural sounds with an ease that many a contemporary classical composer would envy. The certainty, expertise, and scope of this song are impressive in themselves and the inspired manner in which the voices (Bowie and his backing musicians) fade in and out of the fabric is fascinating. This is the essence of sophisticated seventies rock/popular music. We are in a different world; Sundridge Park is light-years away now as Bowie moves within his creation with the ease and assurance of a great architect showing us around his vast new building of stunning originality and beauty. We listen, wide-eyed, at the tumbling sound-images. Faster but here musically much less interesting is a delayed (seemingly by milliseconds) entry, just keeping the music on flow.

For all this, the third song "Fascination" is musically less interesting than the first two. Bowie indulges in a somewhat selfish repitition without any discernible artistic justification for it, and the result is a third-rate MFSB. One is reminded of Lionel Bart's comment, "When you want to do it you do it. And when you *have* to do it you do it. At the moment I don't have to or want to."

In the last song, "Right", there is a similar feeling of exasperation. Nor is this even good parody. The harmony does not change to any interesting degree; there is a sameness which leaves a great deal to be desired. The atmosphere is of a second-rate Philadelphia black night-club with everyone sitting glumly as though they were in church listening to a boring sermon. Even the mildly interesting lyric "Never no turning back" is repeated *ad nauseam* at the end which is a great pity.

The second side begins with "Somebody Up There Likes Me"; this is the third consecutive slow song on the album, producing the equivalent to aural wall paper. There seems to be no redeeming feature at all, just a zonked-up fascination with nothing, creating an impression of self-induced insanity. Finally in the last ninety seconds of the song's 6 minute 36 second duration the music attempts to pull itself together, although by then the damage has been done.

"Across The Universe" is yet another slow song, with a primitive pulse but a more interesting one, for it has no pretension to being fast.

In this connection, Bowie has hit on an interesting musical fact. Fast music demands fast harmonic change; it is not good enough to write fast music on top of something which harmonically is essentially static. Although a little on the long side, this song is very well sung, but the high loud drum beats on the second and fourth beats in each bar become a serious drawback. The negative aspect of this music, reinforced by "Nothing's gonna change my world" repeated *ad infinitum*, particularly in a song entitled "Across The Universe", is likely to induce some confusion in the listener. The slowness continues yet again in "Can You Hear Me", with exactly the same beat as the previous number. As far as the listener is concerned, Bowie's continued fixation with slow tempi on this album stretches one's patience to the limit. This growing feeling of exasperation – together with the sluggish harmonies and a mildly interesting string arrangement – is really not good enough. The spark of genuine feeling is absent here although the influence of Gamble-Huff is more to the fore.

Thus far we have had over sixteen minutes on this side of continuous slow music, and only the *a capella* ending begins to relieve the boredom. The final song on the album, "Fame", is marginally faster but it is much more interesting as Bowie attempts to weld the previously noted ingredients into a coherent whole. John Lennon's backing vocals on this track may have added to the tension so obviously lacking in previous songs on this side. In addition there is a wider stereo image which certainly makes for a marginally more interesting item for the listener.

In this way "Young Americans" ends and one cannot but feel bitterly disappointed by it. It may have been that Bowie wanted to use this as a kind of musical fragment of autobiography, to encapsulate his own feelings of frustration and boredom with the United States. If this is indeed the case then the album works perfectly, but it must be admitted that the listener has to sit through a great deal of less than compelling music in order for Bowie to make his point.

1976

"STATION TO STATION"
Side 1: Station To Station/Golden Years/Word On A Wing
Side 2: TVC 15/Stay/Wild Is The Wind
Having told us in no uncertain musical terms what he thought of

America in "Young Americans" the new album, which was issued in the first weeks of 1976, marked a welcome return to a more interesting aspect of Bowie's creativity. The opening song, the title track on the album, begins with electronic white noise which is soon transformed to stylised train noises including an electronic whistle. As Bowie was against flying at this time his travels by train, often transcontinental, may very well have sparked off the music of this song. There is a definite impression of a train passing through a station by way of the simple expedient of the sound travelling from right to left across the stereo image. But we are on another conveyance. The song starts almost as a train gathers speed with Bowie's typical oscillating notes imparting this time an oriental feeling to the music which gradually increases in volume.

Little by little Bowie's superb control of fantasy-images is placed before us as the "Thin White Duke" appears. The quality of this song suggests it could indeed be based upon material from a much earlier period of Bowie's life, but that is mere conjecture from nothing more than the evidence of our ears. His voice here is weirdly passionate, pinned down by great thuds of drum work impaling the sound image. What cannot be denied, however, is the outstanding sense of cumulative excitement, the long time-span of the song controlled by a masterly hand. By the end the rhythm has become quite infectiously irresistible with a terrific punch and high-octane energy. Here is a composer in full control of himself, blazing with self-confidence and certainty of touch. Such self-confidence manifests itself in coined words such as "kettner" and "malkuth". He cannot avoid a touch of arrogance here but it is forgivable in this context with music of such magnificence. One suspects that there is the proper development of the attitudes lengthily expressed in "Young Americans". In the first part of the song the music is almost modal in essence and slips to C minor with a flat supertonic of D flat, but in the second part there are tiny scraps of melodic phrases, in utter contrast to the long, arching themes of the first part. Note also the rising bass figure and the minor inflection at "European cannon" where an alien F natural brings a frown to the face of the music. Bowie shows himself to be a master of the fade at the end of this song as the music gradually disappears from our hearing.

"Golden Years", the succeeding song, has a marvellously tropical sun-drenched flavour. Once again, the Bowie trademark of oscillating adjacent notes – in this case F sharp major and E (his semi-tonal fall now stretched to a tone) – and his 2/4 bar insertion makes this a superb synthesis of several earlier fingerprints. These are combined with several new ideas and the whole is a fully-integrated song, excellent in all aspects, written in a personal and original style. Bowie's creativity thus far on this album appears to have returned to something like its previous heights and this is continued in "Word On A Wing", a moderately paced song notable in its instrumentation for the use of the piano as a concertante instrument. It is in the unusual key of B major, rare for rock music, and the change to D flat (effectively one tone up from the home key) leads to some remarkable harmonic progressions. One does not have to be a musician to appreciate that something very strange is going on, harmonically speaking, in this song, but this is nothing more than the musical equivalent of the change that seems to be coming over the protagonist, Bowie himself. For what might be the first time in his writing and performing career a spiritual, almost religious feeling enters his music, reinforced by the choral ending and use of an organ within the texture. While it is probably stretching the point to claim that the stations of the cross may have inspired this particular album track, the "Word" from this song's title could also possibly refer to a religious connection. With this artist anything is possible, however unlikely.

But the opening song on side two "TVC 15" returns us to materialism with its faint boogie harmonies making it very much a fun song, albeit with a blues feel. This song is about a piece of electronic equipment (one wonders whether the TVC of the title is a play on JVC, the Japanese Victor Company, which is RCA in Japan, especially with Bowie's use of 'quadraphonic' in the lyric). But the song itself is quite simply constructed, indeed it is almost antique compared with what Bowie has previously being doing on this album. The singer loses his girl over the machine but as the song continues it grows in electronic gadgetry and in volume so that what began as fun comes to an end with the machine possibly in control of the young man's sanity. Such an idea could of course be carried to frightening conclusions but it is merely touched upon here; an idea perhaps to be taken up in Bowie's later work.

The following song, "Stay", the last original composition by Bowie on this album, has a beautifully funky opening *á la* Isaac Hayes. As with "TVC 15" the song is quite simply constructed in broad terms, but its micro-construction is worth the closest study. It has much subdivision of bars, and much over-loaded slow triplet music against the florid funkiness of the beat, with its spasmodic, jarring major 9th chords like bursts of bright light vividly illuminating, if only momentarily, some dark alley of night.

Melodically, "Stay" quotes from each of the previous songs, reinforcing a growing belief in the listener that this is Bowie's symphonic song cycle *par excellence*: the final song is "Wild Is The Wind", by Ned Washington and Dmitri Tiomkin, the Russian/American composer and pianist who gave the European premiére of Gershwin's Piano Concerto. Once again, Bowie closes an album with an unusual song, as a pendant to his thoughts, not the epitome of them – which more properly belongs to "Station To Station". The bitonality of this song (with adjacent chords, F major and G major, and A minor and G major, heard at the same time) would have appealed to Bowie's musicality and the immigrant American's musical character would also provide an attraction, albeit subconsiously. There is some great singing here from Bowie with a beautifully-floated high B and A at the end. Although we have by now become used to Bowie with a question mark, "Wild Is The Wind" is the faintest of these, albeit one which sticks in the mind after the album has ceased to play. Quite how this change of mind was to develop can be examined in the masterly trilogy of albums which was to be his next work, spread over a period of years, which marked the epitome of his creativity in the late 1970s.

As if to reinforce this idea, the next album is effectively a "Greatest Hits" album chosen by Bowie but not titled as such.

"CHANGESONEBOWIE"
Side 1: Space Oddity/John, I'm Only Dancing/Changes/Ziggy Stardust /Suffragette City/The Jean Genie
Side 2: Diamond Dogs/Rebel Rebel/Young Americans/Fame/Golden Years
This is effectively Bowie's first "Greatest Hits" album, a particularly well chosen selection of his finest work up to that time. Few could have realised that this in more than one way marked the end of an important part of his career and was to lead to the trilogy which forms the basis of the next chapter. The most interesting track is 'John, I'm Only Dancing', the first album appearance of one of Bowie's finest hits. The song's gay nature did not preclude popularity; the quality of the music would have guaranteed that. The tonality oscillates between keys a step apart, by a semitone on the melody, a tone in the bass. This sets up a striking but not overpowering tension, pulling like gently stretched

elastic; when the melody jumps a fifth on "dancing" the effect is extraordinary, releasing all tension with an interval that otherwise would seem unremarkable.

CHAPTER TEN

The Trilogy 1977 – 1979

The album, "Low", which was released in the first few weeks of 1977, marked a significant reaction to most of Bowie's recent work. As we have seen, his American-based compositions had been largely bland and unsatisfactory, although redeemed by much of "Station to Station". Having flexed his muscles, so to speak, in music of significant lengths in "Station to Station", Bowie doubtless feels the need to express himself (as part of this reaction) in pieces of much shorter duration. But the development was far deeper than one of timescale.

1977

"LOW"
Side 1: Speed Of Life/Breaking Glass/What In The World/Sound And Vision/Always Crashing In The Same Car/Be My Wife/A New Career In A New Town
Side 2: Warszawa/Art Decade/Weeping Wall/Subterraneans
Apart from the reaction from most of Bowie's earlier work, perhaps the most remarkable thing about this album is the state of mind it almost exclusively depicts. It begins with "Speed of Life", ushered into life through a gentle moderate rock beat. Although we do not realise it at first, this functions as an overture to the album, for it is an extended instrumental piece with a faintly mounting theme. It encapsulates and grows from several of Bowie's compositional fingerprints, particularly the falling tone. The harmonies descend from E flat to D flat and from B flat to A flat; they could not be simpler or more mundane, but they reflect the inocuous little theme that runs on top of them. This theme continuously falls by semitones over an octave. The piece consists of three versions of a sixteen bar theme each of four

four-bar phrases. In turn, each four-bar phrase is a tune in itself. In this piece Bowie uses the simplest and most predictable method of composition, but he slyly interrupts our knowledge by inserting a twelve bar second part – except that it has thirteen bars. This throws everything out of true. The tune is played twice complete and then begins a third time, only to fade out at the second part break. As the piece fades it is as though a big celestial machine has been put into motion and we have observed its remorseless path. "Speed of Life" is an intriguing tune and is flawlessly presented, or very nearly so: the use of white noise in the introduction is largely irrelevant.

From the harmonic ellipse that traversed again and again around "Speed of Life" we move to the harmonic desert of "Breaking Glass". This is another atonal piece and seems to be nothing more than a page from a notebook rather than the extended composition its original opening seemed to demand. The song's harmonic interest is virtually nil and is replaced by a constant contrapuntal texture, but a skinny one and never more than two parts. In spite of the song being more or less in A major the opening guitar solo takes the farthest removed note – D sharp – as its starting point. The resultant linear corkscrew is certainly a new twist in Bowie's compositional career, like a gigantic refraction of the opening instrumental, for it returns again and again to its initial ideas. Bowie's first entry – long delayed, of course, on this album – comes not as a surprise but almost as a pendant to the fascinating instrumental sounds that have beguiled the ear up to now. Out of the 48 bars of the song, Bowie sings in just over a third. The song makes no claim for popularity: this is a personal statement, made from a depressive state; but can we believe him when he claims that he has been "breaking glass in your room again" or that he drew something awful on the carpet? Probably not, for the musical commentary after each claim is exactly the same. This is surely neither the "couldn't care less" attitude of the person being addressed nor the singer's bluff being called. It is a measure of Bowie's genius that he makes even this abstractedly boring attitude interesting.

The next song, "What In The World", is also brief and a faint early Doors influence can be found. The image of the lonely man in the lonely room created in "What In The World" is taken up again in the following song, "Sound and Vision", although the use of the word song in this context is stretching things somewhat. However, "Sound and Vision" begins as a long instrumental before Bowie eventually enters. His vocal line is lower than in that of any of his previous songs. Clearly, this is a depressed psychotic mood; again the room in which he lives is the extent of his world. Withdrawn into himself, he is unable to see further than the walls. He is the only person, not bothering about his own situation and is in a despairingly low state. The music reflects this lethargy but strangely has an attractive beat which ticks over against a mild spectrum of keys, like a constant movement of clouds across the sky; natural phenomena which continue no matter what human drama is played out on the surface of the planet.

The obsessive feeling now begins to flow as "Always Crashing In The Same Car" follows in exactly the same way as "Sound and Vision". This key never leaves the song, for all the surrounding electronic phantasmagoria which circulate behind the fabric of music like aural cobwebs, as it falls to a minor third below and then up to the flat seventh to the main key again. This takes the processes of "Sound and Vision" and reverses them, but the effect is the same. We cannot be sure whether the singer is recalling an actual event or a dream: in any case it is recollected in the song's depressed – almost fatalistic – frame of mind. Musically, the sound suggests an emotionally depressed state deeper than that of "Sound and Vision". The pull of the minor third below is eventually too strong and the music falls, after a series of haphazard almost careless chords, to the close and no less surprising – in this context – change of key to the minor third *above*. For the title line has suddenly thrown a new perspective on things. The combination of these minor thirds (above and below) becomes an augmented fourth – the *diabolus in musica* as the medievalists called it – the forbidden harmony as it was the barest and harshest discord.

"Be My Wife" continues these miniatures (in every sense). This could by no stretch of the imagination be called a love song, but is a pathetic cry from someone who is desparately lonely, reduced immediately to the most basic and unsubtle. The song contracts further – at least with regard to the vocal line, for the entire melody is confined to just five notes, and they are adjacent. "Be My Wife" is also a synthesis of much of the previous material on this side, for the opening of "Speed Of Life" is recalled here, and used as the beginning of a pattern of influence for the entire song. The image is that of a pathetic character, who, for all his fascination, has to be pitied. The only solution it would seem, as doubtless the woman has rejected him, is 'a new career in a new town'. The lyrics of the song have become

more epigrammatic and they are eventually discarded to provide a punchy instrumental track. This is a succession of beautiful ideas, not always expressed in a "beautiful" way, accompanied by a myriad collection of delicate electronic tracery, echoing the strange tonal pulls, and constantly held by a reasonably fast pulse, as that of a heart on mild speed. The music runs around itself again and again; it is getting nowhere, so can we be sure that the new career in a new town will happen?

By the end of this side we have been confronted with a character that is manifestly in a deeply depressed, almost paranoid state, and one who seems unwilling or unable to rid himself of the blackest and most crushing outlook. This is – it hardly goes without saying – a weird subject for a rock star to devote an album to (for, even without turning the record over, we expect the situation to be further explored on side two). It is also an astonishingly brave and courageous thing to do, for whether Bowie himself is writing a chapter of his musical autobiography here or not, we are forced to consider the music and the lyrics on their own terms. It is perfectly possible for anyone to say that they do not subscribe to Bowie's view of the world as shown in "Low", but purely musical qualities declare this album to be the work of a true artist.

"Warszawa" opens the second side but whilst this may be a new town, it is a grim, forbidding place. This is an extraordinary piece of music, a kind of symphonic poem for electronic orchestra, and absolutely nothing whatsoever to do with rock music or pop music or any other kind of music this side of contemporary classical, which it resembles in its expression. The piece is, in fact, by Brian Eno, and only the words (not in English, but a cleverly made-up language) are by Bowie. However, the words are very much an appendage to the thing – in the circumstances they could hardly be otherwise. This deeply impressive and hypnotic piece reveals a tiny melodic germ which is recognisably Russian rather than what we would call Polish. This small theme is akin to Mussorgsky or Shostakovich, the opening of whose Eleventh Symphony could have influenced this piece, for they have certain similarities, not least the tolling chords, the glacial sound-image, the slow-moving pulse, the echoing chords in the distance, the sphinx-like change of harmony and the overall feeling of distance within a threatening, menacing atmosphere. It is a deeply impressive work, and deserves a much wider audience, perhaps through orchestration for symphonic concert use. The sense of finality and futility is strong

Hamlet. Photograph: London Features International.

and the result of all this decaying art? – "Art Decade". Here Bowie is the composer, not Eno, and cut off from one of his greatest assets – his use of words – Bowie contributes an instrumental piece. The decaying, rotting aspect is even more surely invoked as a two-note obsession dies from the promising opening so swiftly that the music sends a shiver through the body, as it ends forever in one "key" – if such primitivism could be so dignified – from which it eventually fades into nothing. "Weeping Wall" begins as a hypnotic germ of Mike Oldfield's "Tubular Bells" distorted almost beyond recognition, but the increasing fragmentation of the suceeding music, against which hypnotic ideas are drawn as though one were entering a deep black tunnel of no escape with a tiny light at the end which never gets bigger. The essence of this piece – if it means anything, which it probably does not – the "wall", is more than likely the Berlin Wall for the album was completed in that city. But it is that of all such "walls" – the walls of barriers of communication and civilisation which receives its finest and most profound utterance in "Subterraneans", a wonderful evocation of deep forces, not necessarily of night, but of eternal, almost natural phenomena, as a strikingly imaginative counterpart to Eno's "Warszawa". In "Young Americans" we complained of a succession of songs in the same tempo: here Bowie has learned this particular lesson, and has cleverly paced the entire rhythmic construction of this side, the unspoken corollary to the despair that gradually overwhelmed the artist on side one. Towards the end, after the only spark of human life – a fine saxophone solo – has introduced voices, Bowie enters, but in chorus with himself, a rising figure related to one of Eno's "Warszawa" themes, but the words, although in English, offer little enlightenment. It is as though the artist is gradually showing the first signs of life after rousing from a deep comatose state. That itself is encouraging and the final words "failing star" may be the summation of the profound psychological message of the album. Another tiny positive idea is that the album ends on a pure major chord, a semitone up from the key which began the album, which now seems an eternity away. Although "Low" was puzzingly received at the time (it could hardly have been otherwise) it remains an incredible achievement, at times infuriating, but mostly very moving and a truly extraordinary artistic statement.

"HEROES"
Side 1: Beauty And The Beast/Joe the Lion/"Heroes"/Sons Of The Silent Age/Blackout
Side 2: V-2 Schneider/Sense Of Doubt/Moss Garden/Neuköln/The Secret Life of Arabia

With this, the second new album from Bowie to be released within ten months, Bowie marks a significant return from the depressed emotional and mental state in which he bade farewell at the end of "Low". It is a revealing experience to play the opening track of this new album, "Beauty And The Beast", immediately after "Subterraneans" – the last track on the previous album. The differences in attitude and approach are amazing. Clearly, this is to be a very dissimilar statement from that which pervaded much of the previous album (or so it would seem), but like all composers, Bowie cannot – nor should he – entirely rid himself of his natural characteristics, those parts of his artistic makeup which demonstrate his unique qualities. In the course of examining his music we have identified several archetypal musical ideas which run like a linking thread through his work, in particular the use of adjacent notes or tonalities. "Beauty And The Beast" begins with the barest, most exposed statement of this, the smallest of all musical ideas, adjacent notes which form a two-note cell and evolve with an outstanding sense of growth to lead to Bowie's first entry, low in his register. Surrounded by weird electronic sounds which make up a fantasy-world not of horror, more of strangeness, Bowie creates a compelling opening to this album which marks an astonishing creative comeback after the depths – in every sense – of "Low". Bowie's growling within a quite fast tempo gives "Beauty And The Beast" its curious, haunting instrumentation, a distinctly European feel to it. This is not being wise after the event: virtually no American singer or band could have created this remarkable track in quite the same way. Although there are faint traces of the influence of the previous album, this is a much more positive statement; for one thing Bowie's thick voice dominates the proceedings and is combined with other singers; he is no longer alone but leading from the front.

The hook line, "You can't say no to the beauty and the beast," means we have not entirely left the imagining world of "Low". Nor would we necessarily want to. But we would want to exorcise much of it, and this is achieved in the next song "Joe The Lion". This is a raucous number teeming with a many-peopled atmosphere but –

wonder of wonders – it is another song in a fast tempo, as was "Beauty And The Beast". It is at the opposite emotional spectrum from "Low" and, although fragments of the musical aspects of that album's songs are employed here, "Joe The Lion" barges its way through without a second thought. The harmonies are not new in Bowie's output, but they are fashioned by a new approach. The vocal line initially falls over a longish period, especially on "It's Monday". This is significant as it is the day on which most suicides are committed all over the world, and with these words we hear Bowie's voice clearly for the only time in this song when he suddenly comes, unaccompanied, to the foreground, only to recede again immediately. The infectious optimism of such a powerful creativity dispels all doubts. There is to be no rock 'n' roll suicide this week – at least, not here.

The title track "Heroes" has music by Bowie and Brian Eno and it is a magnificent achievement, not least for the utter simplicity of its construction and expression, although it is by the same token infinitely subtle. In some ways, it is preferable in the German version, as it tells the story of a young couple who met each day near the Berlin Wall. Their contact had to be – 1984-like – conducted under the gaze and shadow of the East German guards, but just as powerful is Bowie's more familiar English version. The simplicity of the song is the bare chordal background, slightly changing, and then back again, like the permanence of the Wall itself, but it changes from time to time like a great slow pulse against what seems a constant chord played almost without a break throughout. This induces a hypnotic, almost Oriental concept (but not Oriental in expression) to the music, but there is a nicely-based rock drum undercurrent to complement some gentle bass work (although with so few chords there is little a bassplayer can do in this context and a florid bass would be out of place). The song is also essentially positive with Bowie encouraging the girl to join with him to make them "heroes – just for one day". The trauma-like nature of much of the song's vocals and instrumentation might lead some to think that this is still influenced by "Low". They would be right, but the fast tempo, the positive nature of the words, allied to the length of the song and the continuous nature of the singing together with the forward-looking aspect of the message itself declare that such influence is merely incidental.

In "Sons Of The Silent Age" a rising tonal spectrum is quickly revealed to us almost as the sudden glimpse of a vista much bigger than we imagined. In this regard, compared with the simple harmonies of the first three songs of this album, "Sons Of The Silent Age" has a greater connection with "Low". And so it proves, as the people it introduces come to inhabit the same pessimistic world. But this is the objective view of the man looking back at this period, almost describing it for someone else's benefit. The song leaves a disconcerting feeling in the mind, as though the infection of "Low" had not been entirely eradicated, and it raises several questions which are not entirely answered, at least not yet. It remains as a warning, but because of the thrilling re-creativity of the album up to this point, it is not a terribly worrying one. In any event, Bowie does not describe himself, but others – as though he can identify with their current problems, having been through similar situations himself. The underlying harmonies at the end are interrupted deliciously by a built-in groove-jump as the tape is copied and recut to give the impression of a momentarily flawed idea.

Our feelings of goodwill are short-lived: "Blackout" follows and Bowie unleashes another bag of horrors from the recesses of his mind. The result is a masterpiece. Indeed, one suspects that this is the definitive statement of all he was trying to express in "Low" and even before, in parts of "Young Americans" but submerged there beneath a crushing wall of indifference. In "Blackout" Bowie's creation – and, it must be remembered, this takes place exclusively in *sound* – of his particular state of mind, is little short of amazing. The frantically peopled city, the feeling of isolation and the pleas for help, the whole subsumed into an infectious rock beat which is creative in itself and never tiresomely rigid: all this, and more, is handled with consummate art. Apart from anything else, Bowie's performance of this song is outstanding in every regard, fully realising its kaleidoscopic imagery. The song is, as has been hinted at, set to a fast tempo and the occasional use of long arching vocal phrases (for example with "Kiss you in the rain", which is repeated over and over again) recalls his earlier work. The open major thirds in a melodic sense bring the song into life in a bouncy mood of faint optimism. The result is an endlessly fascinating piece of work which reveals something new no matter how many times it is heard. No more convincing demonstration of Bowie's originality, genius and importance as a creative rock artist can be found anywhere in his work. The interested listener, hearing the album in sequence, will probably by now begin to be aware of an extraordinary sleight-of-hand which Bowie has played upon him. After the slow deliberation of "Low" the initial three songs on the first side of "Heroes" will have led him to feel that Bowie's artistic sensibility is here working in a positive and constructive way. And so, up to a point, it proves to be; but the last two songs on the first side introduce doubts again. It is as though the experience, the psychological cul-de-sac by which the singer was trapped in "Low" to the extent that words became almost literally meaningless and were replaced either by nonsense or disjointed phrases or by purely instrumental movements, has to be looked at a second time, but from the viewpoint of having gone through that experience, not from reliving it.

It should therefore come as no surprise, although it may very well do so for some people, to learn that the second side of "Heroes" reflects – in another typically Bowie manner – the construction of the second side of "Low". This is not to say that the music is the same – far from it – but that the outline and the form of the album concept follows the same broad sense of construction. The second side of "Heroes" opens with "V-2 Schneider", another more direct link with the culture in which Bowie had immersed himself while putting the album together. The song is saturated in the city of Berlin, where he had made his home for some considerable period. The track is purely instrumental, but unlike the slow-moving pieces on the previous album, this is fast. It has another unique sound world, almost as if the listener was flying. The musical technique which has produced this effect is wholly original, declaring yet again that Bowie's aural vision is fabulously rich and almost limitless. This track has been described as light-hearted but the use of the V-2 in the title cannot be entirely treated as inconsequential. The numbing fear that ran through Londoners' bodies as they watched, defenceless, the Nazi V-2 rockets rain down on them in the last year of World War II – although Bowie could not have experienced it himself – is, if not exactly created in this track, nonetheless brought to mind by the extraordinary sense of flight. It is true that artists are very often unaware of all the features contained in their own work, and are often surprised when observers point out characteristics of which they may have been ignorant. But there is a difference between musical content and musical meaning. Bowie could very well have intended this to be a light-hearted piece but it is an indication of the quality and fascination of his invention that "V-2 Schneider" can mean different things to different people. The abstract nature of the piece proves it is not "about" anything, but has to be taken on its own terms as a piece of music – neither pure nor simple. The listener, it is suggested, should study this piece closely, not least for the way Bowie has cleverly dove-tailed his various strands of music to create the entire fabric.

This number ends with the sound seeming to speed away, but "Sense of Doubt" follows in utter contrast. Here all is frozen immobility, and expressed through the tiniest scraps of material, never once showing a lighter viewpoint. The adjacent keyboard chords revolve slowly, as in some monstrous subterranean panorama, for ever underpinned by a descending four-note bass phrase dominated by the timbre of the piano. It seems that no matter how hard one might strive to be rid of this feeling of despair, one is always pulled back, downwards, again. The chords manage to rise eventually to the surface, but it is a cold inhospitable world. The wind blows over the bare dehumanised landscape, strongly suggesting the kind of world similarly depicted at the end of Vaughan Williams's "Sinfonia Antartica" or the rarefied atmosphere of the Himalayas.

Far in the distance, almost beyond our experience, music seems to be playing, and we are now in the segued third piece "Moss Garden" another joint composition by Bowie and Eno over which, it seems, distant airplanes fly. The oriental feeling is pervasive and Bowie plays a finely expressive koto line himself, not too florid, but moving gently with the timeless, inscrutable atmosphere at the slowest possible pace. A noise, almost of a small animal, on the left hand channel, the sound akin to falling water, and the continuous slow drifting sense of the earthly passage of time here has taken the slow thoughts endemic in "Low" but turned them outwards, away from the imploding mental state.

"Neuköln", the next track, also follows *attacca*, and evolves from "Moss Garden" but the saxophone solo (Bowie again) has an almost human aspect as the timbre is electronically transmogrified to make almost the musical equivalent of the outsider, the lonely individual in the landscape. The title takes its name from the Turkish quarter of West Berlin. At the end, the saxophone has the last say – or, rather, cry. We have been confronted with, on this virtually all-instrumental side, a whole succession of images of a widely-travelled person. What they have in common, apart from their connecting threads, is an extra-musical rejection of American culture. There is not one bar which could be related to rock 'n' roll or its roots, or indeed much contemporary American popular music – at least that which we more properly define as being essentially American.

"The Secret Life Of Arabia", another amusing and frankly ludicrous title, is also a group composition by Bowie, Brian Eno and Carlos Alomar who plays rhythm guitar on the album. This restores the human voice to the side, but the eastern connection is hard to see and the tone of Bowie's voice implies that we should not try to take this song too seriously. Does he mean it, or does he not? Is this another case of ending an album with a faint pointer to the future, yet again concluding with a song that seems to stand a little to one side of the main thrust of the work? As so often with this composer, only his succeeding output will clarify the point.

1979

"LODGER"

Side 1: Fantastic Voyage/African Night Flight/Move On/Yassassin/Red Sails
Side 2: D. J./Look Back In Anger/Boys Keep Swinging/Repetition/Red Money

As each new album by David Bowie appears, it becomes clearer that his latest work both illuminates the past and points towards new paths which it might take in the future. The astonishing achievement in artistic terms of "Low" – for all its depressed state – was echoed and lightened by "Heroes". "Lodger" is the third album created in collaboration with Brian Eno, but it must be admitted, before anyone runs away with the idea that their collaboration ruled out working with other musicians, that a basic line-up was reasonably common to all three albums. In addition, perhaps the most telling observation is that the producers of all three albums are shown as Bowie and Tony Visconti. Visconti, of course, had worked with Bowie from his earlier periods and had doubtless been a potent creative influence for many years. But it cannot be denied that Bowie's collaboration with Brian Eno on these three albums marked a significant shift in his work. Indeed it is no exaggeration to claim that the three albums: "Low", "Heroes" and "Lodger" form what might be regarded as the third main period of Bowie's maturity as a creative artist. One thing that emerges quite clearly from a study of Bowie's work is that he is unwilling to be tied down to any particular artistic approach for too long. It is as a wanderer that "Lodger" picks up the germinal ideas of travel on the second side of "Heroes" and turns them into a detached yet sympathetic overview of a variety of conceptual expressions. One of the most remarkable aspects of "Lodger" is its experimental nature, at least with regard to the music. It is one thing to pick chords at random as though one were playing a musical game of chance. But it is quite another to have used this random method of composition (used by certain European classical composers for the previous thirty years) and to create something meaningful and lasting from it. That Bowie does this on this album is another of his extraordinary creative achievements.

The album begins with "Fantastic Voyage", a remarkable song with music by Bowie and Brian Eno. If the music did not tell us, we could guess from the lyrics that it is part of the previous two albums' Ethos when Bowie sings, "We're learning to live with somebody's depression" and "I don't want to live with somebody's depression/we'll get by, I suppose." Having looked at the black despair of suicide, Bowie has come through it in this song, caring for human life, and introducing a more overtly political element into his lyrics. Taking a hint perhaps from the contemporary German composer, Hans Werner Henze, "Fantastic Voyage" is scored for a small band with the additional instrumentation of two pianos and three mandolins. This immediately expands the aural perception of the song onto an all together different plane. The sound-world is almost that of an Eastern European village band, with a fixatious string sound. The song begins with drums flickering from right to left. Bowie's voice has unusual timbre; his voice almost croons, and a remarkable feature of the vocal line is the way in which it rises suddenly at the end of a long fixed harmonic passage like the sudden release of tension. The music of the song *per se* is not out of Bowie's top drawer, but it remains in one's consciousness long after it has ended. The harmonic drops, the languid voice and the emphasis given to certain phrases impart a feeling of flickering images which suddenly loom out of the haze, as on a slow trip. There is a kind of abstract quality about this song; no feelings from another specific person. "Somebody's depression" could be the singer's, but it is unlikely to be that of a definite individual. If it is, then the experience must have been so searing in its intensity as to make any direct or distinct reference unbearable. The song is musically distant, and distanced, as though viewing a scene from a window. We are certainly on a fantastic voyage, but we are almost unwilling participants on the journey.

The "Voyage" theme (if it is so) is carried a stage further in "African Night Flight". Now the drums that almost desultorily flickered the first song into life are teeming with tropical activity. These are not the traditional drums of the standard rock kit – or if they are, they certainly do not sound like it. This is an essential stylisation of ethnic African rhythms (with a steady rock bounce underneath the fabric of the music). As with "Fantastic Voyage", phrases suddenly loom large from Bowie's vocal line. The most remarkable feature is the apparent sound of insects, of an African forest in the dead of a hot night, whilst the observer, the terrain flashing beneath him at terrific speed (a superb piece of *musical* imagery, here) sees with a detached, yet fascinated aspect. The reference to "Elizabeth's father" could be to anyone, and there is an element of coined words which flash with scraps of material producing a constant flickering of images before our astonished mental state. The fade at the end of the song over "African" words is beautifully managed, as the listener reluctantly takes leave of this remarkable song.

No sooner has "African Night Flight" disappeared into the distance than "Move On" continues as the title suggests and the lyrics confirm the 'travel' aspect of this collection. Musically, in a sense, "Move On" is the weakest of the three songs so far, for it is a combination of the driving rhythms of the previous song and the languorous, "seen-it-all" attitude of the experienced traveller on the first song. However, as we have learned by now, not all is as it seems at first or even fiftieth hearing of a piece by this composer. Underneath the faintly predictable texture, the dim memory of another person drags itself momentarily to the forefront of consciousness: "Can't forget you" – who, in this context, is "you"? Does it matter? Not, apparently, particularly so, but it is a new element, as the only other reference to "You" on the album was a throw-away in the previous song – "Sick of you" – and the implications of flight from the hated one. There is a less frenetic quality in "Move On", almost as though sanity is beginning to return, or a more recognisable state of consciousness.

As if to answer these imaginings, "Yassassin" begins. The first three songs, for all their different characters and shared experiences, demand a settling at some point. The fleeting references to Africa, Kyoto, Cyprus (surely a reference to his ex-wife Angie – is this the unmentioned character being fled from?) have one thing in common: their vast distances from each other. If the character, presumably Bowie himself, is to resolve the prolems that presently beset him, then he has to find a place of rest, and preferably also one of anonymity. On "Heroes" Bowie makes several specific references to Berlin. Neuköln, as already noted, is the name of the Turkish quarter of that city and "Yassassin" (a Turkish word meaning long live, as the record insert thoughtfully translates it) must have been inspired by the same suburb. Doubtless Bowie had heard Turkish musicians in Neuköln street cafes, and in "Yassassin", apart from the inherent qualities of the song, he recreates the essential sound-world of Turkish folk music. It is the theme of a stranger in a strange land, and Bowie must have felt attracted to the immigrants in Berlin because he was in a sense one himself. The words reflect the natural fears experienced by any outsider within a large group. The individual in this song has come far – he is not identified as having come from a particular foreign country – "to live in this city", and has come in peace. Apparently the indigenous population resents this, for as Bowie sings "You want to fight/But I don't want to leave/Or drift away", and such is the fascinating sound-world and the hypnotically easy-paced beat of the song, with the title repeated over and over again by the backing voices that, even without reading the lyrics, one instinctively sympathises with the outsider. Hardly a hit record, but an admirable one in many ways. The side ends with "Red Sails" (one is almost tempted to add "in the sunset") and the theme of travel is continued, but as from a distance once again, and with a specifically oriental, almost Japanese flavour to the melodic line (as well as by the vocal quality Bowie imparts), but beneath the incessant din through which the song is communicated, there is a definite sexual hint in the lyrics, as though "Red Sails" actually stood for something else, although quite what remains uncertain.

A rather more familiar sound-world is created in "D.J." – up to a point, for it seems at times to foreshadow the "scratch" techniques of third generation punk recording engineers. The D.J. in question is trapped by his profession, and realises that "I am what I play, can't turn around, no," – for all his claims that he has an audience that believes in him. The music, however, retains traces of the oriental melodies that closed side one, but the song is too long for its purpose. It also lacks the cutting edge of consistently telling observation, and has also been criticised for a lack of power, a comment with which it is difficult not to agree.

"Look Back In Anger" has also been subjected to criticism, although the song is not entirely hopeless: by the end of it, however one might be forgiven for thinking that it should be called "Waiting So Long" as it is this line that is repeated almost *ad nauseam* towards the end. But the driving beat is maintained with impressive consistency to underline the urgent nature of the music: the words, however, are obscure in the extreme and permit a wide spectrum of interpretation, including, naturally, a sexual one. But this uncertainty of knowing exactly what the song is about is the main contributory feature in regarding it as ultimately insignificant.

"Boys Keep Swinging", the next track, is a very different matter – a faintly hedonistic hymn to male youth. But it does not have, as might be supposed, a too-adoring gleam about it; far from it, it starts, in no uncertain terms, with a feeling of immortality, that "anything is possible", and depicted with startling imagery, in the promotional video with Bowie adopting a wide variety of styles and genders not imagined by merely hearing the music. Or so it would seem, but, as has been pointed out by Roy Carr and Charles Shaar Murray, the chordal basis for this song is virtually identical to that of the opening song on the album, "Fantastic Voyage": the deeper imagery might just possibly have a greater influence here, and give the justification for Bowie's extraordinary visual depiction of "Boys Keep Swinging". Without the video's images, the song constitutes a fluent rock bass line in reasonably close proximity to Bowie's comparatively low voacal line. The lengthy coda is a searing, raunchy affair, raucous and brash – the epitom of power.

"Reptition" is a haunting, lurid song about a man called Johnny who beats his wife. Bowie intones this despairing state of affairs with all the passion he would normally bring to reading a railway time-table, the song oscillating between adjacent keys a tone apart (the bass hypnotically plucking away at low A's and B's). It is almost as though the story is told from the viewpoint of a no-longer concerned neighbour, describing events to a policeman, called to sort out the pieces of a domestic disaster. This is nonetheless a superb song – taken on its own terms, without trying to force it to conform to artistic values which the critic has just dreamed up.

This very impressive album ends with "Red Money", a song recomposed with music written by Bowie and Carlos Alomar for "Sister Midnight", a song that began Iggy Pop's "The Idiot" album. In this new guise, the song continues a theme of "Lodger", that of taking a tiny idea from one song and exploring it in the next; but exactly what red money is remains guesswork. Could it simply be bloodmoney? or money that is paid for in blood? Sometimes it is the most obvious which is the correct interpretation and the title "Red Money" clearly echoes that of "Red Sails" that ended side one, but it seems that the object in question is the talisman of the loss of innocence, of the acquisition of responsibility – and, to judge from the song, responsibility that was not sought. An interesting aspect of this side of "Lodger" is the linking verbal thread that the listener can trace through the five songs that make up side two. The reader is well advised to trace this aspect of the album's organic qualities for himself.

CHAPTER ELEVEN

Into the Eighties

1980

"SCARY MONSTERS (AND SUPER-CREEPS)"
Side 1: It's No Game (No.1)/Up the Hill Backwards/Scary Monsters (And Super-Creeps)/Ashes to Ashes/Fashion
Side 2: Teenage Wildlife/Scream Like a Baby/Kingdom Come/Because your Young/It's No Game (No.2)
Noises, as in musique concréte, precede an extraordinary, pulsating, dragging, solid "song". "Song" has to be in inverted commas for this opening track. It is a unique example of a song being sung in two languages simultaneously – Japanese and English. Occasionally one predominates over the other but the effect is startling, and completely disconcerting, for no album in the history of popular music could ever have begun in this manner. Apart from the effect it produces, the song – even to those who speak both languages – is of immense seriousness. "It's No Game" refers to a bleak and serious view of life, and, as at the beginning of "Lodger" there is the element of trying to escape. One suspects the desire to escape is itself fading for the protagonist comes to this new album with a greater degree of experience, the stark realisation of hard practicality and of a sobering certainty that comes from the realisation of the particular desperate situation. How is such a view formed by listening to this music? This extraordinary opening provides us with several clues. The first is the strange non-vocal soundworld that oozes from the loudspeakers; the second is the juxtaposition of Japanese and English, especially with fleeting scraps of the latter language. There is also the collapse of everything at the end into an illtempered outburst, spoken not sung, as though the artist is too

impatient even to think of music with which to express his words. The earliest part of the song, the actual vocal line, is constantly straining upwards, the Japanese voice light and eunuch-like and Bowie's voice desperate and, if not insistent, then hypnotic. A final feature of the song is the slow blues of the instrumental melodic line, and the way that this is bent slowly, tortuously, against the music underneath. On such remarkable characteristics is this quite extraordinary song built and "Up The Hill Backwards" is initially faster than "It's No Game". This second song appears as a less frenetic, less scary experience, but it is not long before we realise that this is illusory reassurance. Bowie's voice is placed far back in the stereo image, so that we are forced to strain to catch his words. Even then, his voice is over-dubbed, so that the effect on the part of the listener is that of an active participator in the song itself, rather than as a passive witness to an event which mildly interests him.

By far the more vivid impressions from this song are the tempo, the deliberate South London voice of Bowie, the legibility of the words, and the staggering display of instrumental virtuosity which at last gives this song the musical personification of the frightening images of the title. Musically, the song is held by a five-note riff which rises and falls like the pulse of some low-speed drug experience.

One can make too much of Bowie's choice of singing timbre, but it demands some explanation. Notice also the easily overlooked descending bass-line at the beginning, as we enter a subterranean experience. Significantly, this figure does not reappear in the song; one of the images that replaces it is the constant light flashing effect of a hypnotic stylisation in the left hand channel, like a soft beckoning pulse, reinforcing the strange sibilants of Bowie's consonants, and the destruction of our expectations. We expect a guitar break, and largely get one, but it becomes another instrument. This is out of our experience and draws us, fascinated, into its own world. Do we resist or submit to this fascination?

With "Ashes To Ashes" we are already following the artist. The question is answered for us, for we are now certainly in a different world. It is strange, lighter, and airily fascinating. "Ashes to Ashes" is an interlude in the proceedings, occupying the region of the mind that is concerned with relative temporal recollections of the past, at least in the context of continuous album listening. All kinds of earlier images float by, almost as a corollary of suggestions that "she" in "Scary

Monsters" is Bowie's *alter ego*. Meanwhile, the singer leaps backwards in time to the point where he imagines things were a lot better than they actually were, and certainly are now. The very title, "Ashes to Ashes", suggests temporality, a life, and the music for all its fascination as an upholstered backing for the vocal line has an intermittent fluttering, like a weird and ghostly heartbeat, for the voice, when Bowie enters, is thicker, more immediate and impacted and the thickness is more like a wide poster brush of sound. This forces itself a few inches almost from our senses, obliterating most other things. But there is no brazen earnestness here, just (just!) the vivid imagery of a sympathetic yet detached view of the past and present at the same time. The words recall "Major Tom" and a succession of tiny fleeting images mirror personal aspects of Bowie's own collapse and upward striving again. The druggy, speed-vividness of shattering, splintering images of the racing mind and heart-beat is trapped within a body that is trying to evade the disastrous disorder of "Free Will". All this is startling to the observer and almost frightening. The music is hypnotic in its tonal fastness; the ritornellos and ostinatos fix it like a nailed picture, the constantly-changing chiaroscuro on the top has the icy detachment of a large impersonal diamond. Yet the words are shot through with a subliminal emotion that is deeply effecting.

As an antidote to the power of "Ashes to Ashes", "Fashion" returns us to the world of the distanced character, so overloaded with layers of psychological protection from the world that it becomes almost impossible to recognise the real person cowering behind them. "Fashion" is the reversal to Bowie's public persona after the glimpse of the real, almost pathetic, central character of the previous song. Paradoxically, the song can be taken to express a variety of conflicting ideas. On the one hand the epitome of fashion, or rather of how "fashion" has become, where anything fashionable is immediately made unfashionable by attracting vulgar favour. This applies most clearly to dress, rather than to popular music, although the incidence of "one-hit bands" constantly seems to increase with a greater rapidity, as the life of a hit grows commensurately shorter. But it is the heart-beat, almost literally, that pulses this song into life, as its insistent pumping on the left hand channel has us a-tapping as another chameleon-like succession of sounds, acoustic and electronic, mixed almost as an absurd subtle jumble, blazes across our consciousness. But the basic inhumanity and emptiness of the intended message is chillingly clear. It is the "nothing matters" state of mental inertia, from which anything can happen.

This may seem a somewhat flowery way to discuss what is, after all, meant to be music in a popular idiom, but it is the overall conception, the impact of each song, which matters more here than the music alone. Bowie's compositional skill does not need elaboration at this point; we have had enough demonstrations of his ability to know what he is capable of. It is when the music is not such an important ingredient and the words have an apparent unimportance that the combination, the total effect, has to be seen in expressive, almost in impressionistic terms. It is an extraordinary way to end a record side. Is this, Bowie seems to be saying, really what it is all about? Is it purely fashion? Do we leave it at that or do we endeavour to find something within the continuous fascination of the work of this extraordinry artist, a more permanent and telling observation upon our human condition? Or do we, by so encompassing popular music, make this "fashionable"?

It is in such a puzzled frame of mind that we turn the album over, almost daring to wonder what new experience Bowie has in store for us. But even the most committed Bowie enthusiast could hardly be prepared for the astounding achievement of "Teenage Wildlife", which is the first song that assaults our ears on the second side of this album. This is one of Bowie's longest songs for some years, and it is an immensely powerful number of massive impact and strength. It almost literally hits one with the force of physical impact. Taking "teenage" as a starting point, Bowie does not philosophise upon the state. He sees it as it really is: as a time of life with blank pages yet to be written upon. Having made a number of mistakes in his own life, Bowie, knowing full well his own fashionable position in the world of popular music, can offer not so much advice as descriptive experience. But the power and impact of the music are such that one can be in no doubt that this, for Bowie, is a deadly serious proposition. "Teenage Wildlife" begins innocently enough, without startling sounds to grab the attention at first. The stage is clearly set for Bowie's entry, as the words are to be the most important part of the song – at least, at first. Bowie intones his first quatrain, and a lengthy instrumental episode lets us muse over his words. His voice gets deliberately more incoherent; not from anger, but from that aspect which demands us to follow it where it will. There is a constant beat, a thump-thump which we feel is permanent, but it also has an organic use when the rhythm suddenly chunks out, the surrounding time clean as a whistle. Against this, the imagery of the instrumental backing to Bowie's words is amazingly appropriate and larded over with layer upon layer like a rich tapestry. There are so many features of this song that it is difficult to list them all, but note particularly the brilliant occasional use of the piano, and the masterly slow fade, one of the most purely *musical* uses of this hoary old trick in the whole of Bowie's recorded repertoire. This then is the sound that hits us from the loadspeakers but the listener should pay close attention to the words. Without actually being the longest song in terms of lyrics on the album, "Teenage Wildlife" demands that its words receive their due. Although there is often a case to be made out for not listening to a song with the words at one's side, in this instance it is an urgent necessity. For all the "advice" that one might think is being imparted to the younger generation by the more experienced Bowie, there is a searing intensity and committed concern in both his voice and the words he sings that make "Teenage Wildlife" one of Bowie's most serious and compelling creations.

Bowie has set himself a considerable challenge in attempting to follow that overwhelming first song but "Scream Like A Baby" takes us back almost to pre-teen life, at least in terms of the title. But the song has not quite the same effect of its predecessor. It is, however, no less fascinating; the curling downward bass-line and the soft rise and fall of the voice coupled with the droid-like noise on the right-hand channel for all the world like a refugee from a group of space-movie extras. The major achievement of "Scream Like A Baby" is the mixture of scraps of half-remembered songs from Bowie and others of the 1960s woven into an unusual patchwork to illustrate the "old songs we loved" in the lyric – however, the character had previously jumped into the furnace. The protagonist is in a desperate state still – but not of despair, almost of physical and mental exhaustion causing him to scream like a baby. The music cannot be overlooked here; Bowie's own performance is, as usual, full of the power of the creator and the driving urgency of his message keeps the pressure very much on.

In "Kingdom Come" (the only song on the album not written by Bowie; it is by Tom Verlaine), which follows almost immediately, the pressure is only marginally relaxed. It fits the mood of *angst* perfectly; and because it is not by Bowie, it offers the relief of a distanced observer. The same frightening aspects of music that have characterised this album are here used in a brilliantly disturbing arrangement, and Bowie's vocal work is little short of amazing, approaching pure insanity at times although finally settling to a reiterated last line to offer a glimpse of hope and possible salvation.

"Because You're Young" brings Bowie back as composer and returns also to the "youth" theme. Or so it would appear from a superficial reading of the title, for the music yawns with great gaping harmonic chasms, vast leaps in the bass line disorienting any remaining feelings of well-being we might have. The rhythm of the vocal line is similarly deliberately out of synchronisation. We have no personal choices here, being taken, willy-nilly, by this extraordinarily creative artist into further reaches of a demon-filled mind. The corruption of innocence is here, the devastating loss of virginity at every level, the pure corruption that runs rife through major areas of our lives, all these things are laid out before us with the certainty of a man who knows *exactly* what he is doing. He is making us think, hard, about what he wants us to consider, as he wanders off on an upholstered cloud of sound.

Bowie has one more message to impart to us: "It's No Game (No.2)". After the searing experiences of this album it almost comes as a relief to return to the opening message of the entire concept. But here the relief is genuine. Discarding the Japanese element and with it all traces of bitterness, Bowie has come full circle. But this is not a convenient tying up of loose ends, it is a coda of grim fatalism that ends this astonishing piece of work on the same level that began it – that of deadly seriousness.

1983

"LET'S DANCE"
Side 1: Modern Love/China Girl/Let's Dance/Without You
Side 2: Ricochet/Criminal World/Cat People (Putting Out Fire)
/Shake It.
The biographical section of this book has outlined Bowie's activities between the effective cessation of his association with RCA and his move to EMI Records. Although the astounding "Scary Monsters" album was followed by the "Changestwobowie" album and an interesting compilation emanating from RCA Italiana entitled "Bowie Rare", there was nothing new musically to give any indication of how

Bowie was to recover from the state of mind in which he'd left the music world at the end of "Sacry Monsters".

After a break of almost three years, the previous doubts and uncertainties are here triumphantly swept aside in a mood of joyous optimism. "Modern Love" is a marvellous fast, driving rocker of the sort that had not been heard from David Bowie for many a day. Closer inspection reveals many of this artist's fingerprints: the unusual use of chords even within a song of such straightforward message as this; the high vocal line meandering around notes a semitone apart; and the unusual structure of the verses. But all this is not meant to give an air of spurious seriousness to a song which is in essence happy and joyous. It is merely to show that Bowie has lost none of his artistry.

Bowie's utterly original approach to harmony, for example, gives the song its driving tension. Listen to how he prepares for the first entry of the voice; the harmonies fall in the bass against sly movements upwards in the treble and almost before we know it, we have been conned into a perfectly straightforward major key. One can search the words, too, for clues as to Bowie's frame of mind but such a course of action is largely irrelevant. The important thing to remember is the initial impact of the music and the character of the song itself rather than any hidden message which may be contained within its lyrics. It is an irresistible opening to a very fine album; utterly different from his previous work but no less important or excellent for being somewhat lighter and deliberately more optimistic in tone. A glance at the cover shows that the singer has come out fighting.

However, not everything is hunky-dory. On this first track does not the song itself seem a little too long for the material? Is there not a trace of self indulgence already to be discerned in this opening number? Perhaps not, but it is an aspect that one should keep at the back of one's mind as the album progresses.

The second song "China Girl" is a joint composition by Bowie and Iggy Pop, and had been heard before on the latter's "Idiot" album. Compared with the rather despairing nature of the performance of the song at its first appearance on disc, on "Let's Dance" it is here transformed into a dynamic and very positive creation. It is not so important to discuss the different performances of "China Girl" as to assess the song's impact in the context of the "Let's Dance" album. The first thing to note is the continuation of the opening buoyant mood. Bowie appears to be in great shape here, mentally and musically, with all fears, real or imaginary, banished. It is indeed a very positive statement, and perhaps rather too much so – not for any reasons of wanting contrast of emotion, but because of the length of the song. The optimism is not forced, but it is a little thinly spread. However attractive and appealing this album is so far, one gets the impression that it might not have any lasting significance other than that of a quick pick-me-up. But even at this level, there is a lot to be said for such an outlook.

Immediately, at the beginning of this song, Japanese-type music fixes an oriental background. The atmosphere is striking and Bowie's quietly confessional tone of voice is as warm and inviting as a recently slept-in bed. Notice also the staccato, yet well-phrased bass line, suggesting the quick movement of tiny bound feet.

With the title track "Let's Dance" the outward-going aspects of Bowie's creativity reach their zenith. This magnificent song, a major international hit for the artist, barges its way through the stream of consciousness and, almost taking us by the scruff of the neck, presents us with an unmistakeable vision of sheer enjoyment and happiness. The words are deliberately basic and unsubtle, but the music is much more than that. At the second "hide" in "If you say hide, we'll hide", the chords clash a tone apart, like the powerful strokes of Japanese Samurai. Sparks fly from this musical collision, and give the song tremendous inner tension. This means that when Bowie expands the number into a fast movement of over seven minutes' duration, the music, for the first time on the album, can stand such treatment. The bitonal potency urges the song on.

The influence of Nile Rodgers (co-producer of the album, contributing musician, and the producer of the then current Paul Simon album "Hearts And Bones") is apparent at the percussive opening of this song after the stylised Beatles' "Twist and Shout" overlapping chords: the clean-cutting image of the first bars, calling us on to the dance floor (the musical manner in which this is done is quite exceptional), if not suggested by Rodgers, at least bear his stamp. The rejection of the oriental spices from the previous song gives "Let's Dance" an international appeal. This is deliberate on Bowie's part for his own languorous manner is set off against the solidly tapping background, itself full of scraps of ideas flying from right to left as material borne on a high wind. The beat becomes insistent, the harmonies more demanding, the compulsion to get up and dance as the track progresses more irresistible, especially as little by little the layers are eventually stripped from the fabric of the music until at one point we are confronted by the bare-boned beat alone, before the process is reversed.

After this exhausting experience, as the music fades from our hearing, a gentle beat, less heavily-scored, ushers in "Without You", a quiet corollary to the first side. On one level this is a gentle love song, but one whose gentleness is contained within the words and Bowie's consistently high falsetto voice, his phrases being interrupted by the comparatively lengthy instrumental breaks. A song such as this can frequently get overlooked, but it is best appreciated after repeated hearings, and not least for purely musical qualities. These include the subtle three-against-two within a medium-slow tempo, and the fact that no phrase actually starts on the first beat of a bar, and Bowie's habit of lazily sliding down a tone, like a car running down, with just a touch of fuel to bring it back up again.

"Ricochet", which opens side two, is another enormously impressive song. The variety of rhythmic life which grows and flowers from the basic pulse is little short of amazing, and the growth of the falling triplet figure after the opening lines to assume the greatest importance is a marvellous experience. This is suddenly interrupted in its path by a four-square figure, a simple diatonic falling phrase reminiscent of a nursery song, but only just enough to disconcert matters before the pulsating rhythm surges back in full power. The use of spoken texts in a constricted, barely audible voice brings another element to our experience, as do the more coherent phrases of the text. But it is the sheer power of the music that creates the most stunning and lasting experience. Anyone who had harboured doubts as to the quality of Bowie's creativity at that time would have been utterly silenced by this thrilling achievement.

Any relevance the old song "Criminal World", written by three members of the band Metro, might possess in the context of the album under discussion is hard to see. From time to time Bowie has cast a backward glance during his career, but the necessity for picking this song from 1978 is obscure. "Criminal World" has some redeeming features, and is well enough arranged and performed, but it leaves a possibly intentional "so what?" response from the listener. Perhaps Bowie is trying to get us not to take things *too* seriously. The opening bars of the next song "Cat People", immediately declare that we are in a different artistic league. The music, however, is not by Bowie but by Giorgio Moroder, who has a considerable reputation as a record producer. Moroder produced most of Donna Summer's albums, as well as having had some success with his own recorded performances. Moroder has also written film music, notably for *American Gigolo*, *Flashdance* and *Metropolis* as well as for *Cat People* from which this song, with words by Bowie, is taken. Although it might be an odd parallel to make, there is a distinct flavour of The Doors and especially Jim Morrison in this performance. One can hardly call it influence to any marked degree, just a question of refinement. Those who are able to pick out a tune from a printed top line will get a considerable shock by comparing the music printed in the "Let's Dance" sheet music album with what Bowie actually sings. He alters the vocal line so much that it is difficult to believe he is singing the same song. "Cat People" is the most serious track on the album so far; it is encouraging to see Bowie extending the range of this album by the use of such material, but for all its excellence and admirable qualities in the last anlysis this is not one of his most memorable tracks.

A bar of "Shake It" is all the listener needs to tell him that it is heavy funk time; a very solid funky beat, beautifully programmed, and the song is bursting with life and raw energy, running figures cascading against the stylisation of powerful funk. Bowie's vocal line is relaxed, as of yore, and it is refreshing to hear him close an album in such a mood of mental and physical well-being. Our old friend has come through it, and seems to have triumphed over previous adversaries. The use of adjacent thirds in the vocal line gives the song an additional bounce, boppy and airy, punctuated by a succession of short chords and a deliberately inane female-sounding chorus which is pure showbiz. It is impossible not to respond to such healthy hedonism as Bowie displays here, and the consistent solid funkiness will have everyone within earshot tapping along. On such a joyous note does this remarkable, yet overall ultimately light-weight, album end. But the opening chords on the album, and the title track among others, remain sensational; almost as if the artist was trying to make some kind of political point.

1984

"TONIGHT"
Side 1: Loving The Alien/Don't Look Down/God Only Knows/Tonight
Side 2: Neighbourhood Threat/Blue Jean/Tumble and Twirl/I Keep Forgettin'/Dancing With The Big Boys

As we have seen, Bowie's ideas of what are referred to as "concept" albums are often, as is only to be expected, quite unlike those of other recording artists. Running through the "Tonight" album there appear to be two parallel themes, one a purely musical atmosphere and the second a wider concept of love. "Loving The Alien" sets out both. One of the most striking and immediately obvious aspects of the musical concept is the large-scale orchestral backing which is employed. It is rich, upholstered sound, a deep cushion of music. Once again, Bowie enthusiasts may be disconcerted by the beginning of this particular album, as the sound is little to do with driving rock music: it would appear to have more in common with ballads and commercial love songs of a type familiar from popular music of several generations earlier. We ought to know David Bowie by now. If he is to use this kind of stylisation, then we should pay attention to the words by which the message is conveyed.

"Loving The Alien" begins orchestrally with a bland middle-of-the-road squash, but the words of the song give it away, a message of love between enemies, and immediately Bowie puts this on an impersonal level. There are references to Palestine, Christians and unbelievers, "hanging by the cross and nail". The puzzling thing is that the music appears completely at odds with such a subject: or does it? Our expectations, as hinted at earlier, are once again utterly frustrated by the artist and the creamy off-centre string line acts as balm to our intermittent frowns. The lengthy orchestral music appears almost as the development section of a symphony, although there is no recapitulation; once again, what we expect is not there. Whether or not this is the musical personification of "alien" is open to question, but it is certainly unpredictable.

"Don't Look Down" which follows is a magnificent song co-written by Iggy Pop and recorded by him on the largely underrated 1979 album "New Values". It is treated as a Caribbean slow shuffle, and the effect is hypnotic and, in a very real sense, beautiful. The upholstered sound, the warm harmonies lazy and rich, barely moving in the tropical breeze,

Live in the Eighties. Photograph: David Redfern.

provide a marvellous background and, as in the first song, the words are startlingly at variance with the musical arrangement. The impressionistic musical haze is fine as far as it goes, but it is not difficult to imagine that the song could be about almost anything, for Bowie appears here as a somewhat indifferent character. It is, without doubt, a song of genuine and gentle optimism – "don't look down" is good advice on many levels – and, as such, the West Indian shuffle with which it is treated, reflects this optimism in a purely musical manner. Once again, Bowie's subtlety is demonstrated, but the level is such that a knowing smile will forgive, as well as signifying the understanding.

Bowie's recurring fascination (it is not an obsession) with popular music of the 1960s, from his own first faltering years, is well known, and one of the most lasting of all the great successful records of that decade was "God Only Knows" by the Beach Boys. Their original recording was perfect with overlapping voices taking each phrase and weaving extraordinary melismata around the musical line. Whatever Bowie thinks of the song – and it is difficult to imagine that he dislikes it – his performance of "God Only Knows" which follows "Don't Look Down" on this album is nothing if not unique. He turns it into something one would not have thought possible; a passionate affair, not hectoring or exaggerated but with an inner tensile strength that the pink fondant Beach Boys never had. It is a truly remarkable and not particularly attractive version, and as one imagines the original recording would be unknown to the majority of the audience at which presumably this arrangement would be aimed, it demands to be taken on its own terms. Bowie's version is at the opposite end of the vocal spectrum from "Don't Look Down"; it is deeply vibrant, throbbing with an intensity that might just possibly be parody. But of what? And what purpose would be served by such a strategy in this context?

No: curiously enough, this apparently disparate collection of material begins to exhibit the other linking thread: that of love, pure and simple, and this theme is confirmed, again at something less than full power, in the final track on the first side – "Tonight", another Bowie/Pop song originally written for Iggy's "Lust for Life" album of 1981. The words are very simple and to the point; but the less than full power referred to earlier does not apply to artistic intensity: it applies to volume. There is little point in comparing this version with that on the Pop album where the song originally appeared, suffice it to say that the versions are utterly different. On the one hand, in the earlier manifes-

David Bowie as Colin Morris and Michelle Pfeiffer as Diana in Universal Pictures' 'Into the Night (1985). Photograph: Universal City Studios.

tation, the song was little more than an emotional outburst, but here it is drastically reorganised. Bowie enlists the aid of the great rhythm and blues singer Tina Turner and the emotion is held firmly in control although it can be perceived as throbbing dangerously below the surface. The rhythm in which this song is now expressed is that of strolling West Indian reggae, and Bowie's vocal performance here is one of his most classic. It may be that in the presence of such a great singer Bowie was spurred on to excel himself. This is likely, but if it is the case, then we are the better for it. One should savour again and again the extraordinary artistic chemistry that comes from the mixture of David Bowie and Tina Turner and the way in which they impart a whole succession of meanings to such simple words: the song is of one person reassuring a partner that their love will be consummated in purely physical terms, rightly intimately and without any musical pseudo-voyeurism.

With this beautiful track the first side ends, and, different though these four songs have been, it is possible to feel that there is not sufficient contrast between them. A more wide-ranging choice would have thrown each song more sharply into relief. The second side opens with "Neighbourhood Threat", another Bowie/Pop song from the 1977 "Lust For Life" album. The dance-like rhythms with which this opens betoken it to be the David Bowie of recent vintage. The vocal line is more immediately recognisable and here upholstered by a truly symphonic sound. This is not the slow-moving orchestration of early 1970s self-indulgence but a richly varied and massive sound, used with a genuine perception of large-scale orchestral forces, allied to an urgent rock-based secondary backing band. The wordsmith will find much to fascinate, comparing the "look down your back stairs . . ." in this song to the "Don't Look Down" on side one. It is clear that the obverse of the situation has been reached. With our seatbelts judiciously in place, we start a heavier trip. The "Neighbourhood Threat" is not particularly important as a statement *per se*; it gains immeasurably from its place in the album's sequence and the effect of the totality. In this regard the words are of secondary importance; listen to how they are threatened and finally crushed by the inexorable tread of the impacting stereo orchestras towards the end.

"Blue Jean" confirms this heavier and more urgent expression: a hard-driving rhythm bursts the song into life with considerable verve but it is a more intimate sound (although loud and full from the orchestra) that emanates from Bowie's voice. Immediately, one realises that his tone is more conspiratorial. Yet a detailed examination of the words brings us face to face with an almost totally forgotten situation from the past. "Blue Jean" can mean several things, and, in spite of the "girl" in the first line, "she" has a "camouflaged face" and a "police bike". In other words, the sexual gender is blurred, and this pansexuality (long-since forgotten memories of Ziggy notwithstanding) is echoed in the next song "Tumble and Twirl" with the reference to "that dusky mulatto in nylons and tattoos" (one assumes the male gender is the starting-point; mulatto is male, although frequently it is incorrectly applied to women of mixed race).

"Tumble and Twirl" is absolutely stunning; a fabulous achievement, and one of Bowie's greatest-ever performances. The impact and sheer vividness of the performance are astounding at every level. In the first place the full and rich orchestral tapestry which drives this song onwards has an animal magnetism which is quite compelling. Indeed, it is difficult not to feel that the musicians were more and more excited by their own virtuosity as the performance continued, but over and above this powerful musical engine rides Bowie's incandescent vocal line. This has to be, by any artistic standards, one of the greatest tracks this artist has ever committed to disc. The faintly surreal nature of the lyrics (it is another song co-written with Iggy) add a faintly otherwordly quality to the instantaneous experience. Such a juxtaposition of musical fact with verbal fantasy heightens the tension. Bowie, clearly sensing the nature of this excitement, makes the most of his opportunity. He takes from the words just about everything he possibly can, but over and above the verbal implications, he *sings* with considerable skill. There can be few other popular musicians, in the widest sense, who would be capable of matching Bowie's performance on this track. Once again, it is a lengthy song, but one's excitement grows as it progresses, and the ending is as breathless as it is pleasurable.

After this astonishing track almost anything would seem to be an anti-climax. As if to take us completely away, Bowie echoes an aspect of planning on side one (of using the 1960s Beach Boys song) by going back to 1962 for the little known Chuck Jackson's early rhythm and blues hit, "I Keep Forgettin'", by the legendary Jerry Leiber and Mike Stroller. This song-writing duo contributed much to early rock 'n' roll, and thirty years later have developed into writers whose recent work appears in classical song recitals. Just why this particular song (which is not particularly outstanding) should have been chosen or placed here on the album, is difficult to ascertain. Perhaps Bowie was trying to demonstrate a return to one aspect of his (and by implication our) musical roots. If that is so, and it is a plausible explanation, then it succeeds, but only up to a point. After the overwhelming experience of "Tumble and Twirl" the shadow of the previous track is still cast across its sucessor. It may be also that the song has some personal significance for Bowie, but if it does, it remains personal.

The final track is "Dancing With The Big Boys", another surrealistic Bowie-Pop collaboration. Here the surrealism is much more prominent than on "Tumble and Twirl"; by all accounts, the song's lyrics are a collage of various phrases, chosen at random and disjointed, and held together by a gradually reducing vocal riff ending with the words "big boys". It should not be imagined, however, that this is some kind of spontaneous improvisation, for the effects are too impressive, too closely worked, for them to have been purely the result of random choice. If it is the result of pure chance, then one can only urge the people concerned to return to the recording studios as soon as possible. Exactly how a song is put together is of marginal interest to most listeners; the specialist might very well wish to know how something came to be written, but it is the results which have to stand or fall through their own merits and not because they were arrived at in a particular way. In this respect "Dancing With The Big Boys" is a very impressive achievement. The song imparts an atmosphere of pleasurable enjoyment and good humour, and with the important proviso that the words have no significance, the music can be enjoyed on its own level. It imparts a wonderful feeling of good-natured satisfaction, the kind that comes from knowing one has done something particularly well. For Bowie it is an unique way to end an album; it is the most positive and encouraging sign for his future development.

PART THREE
THE ARTIST

CHAPTER TWELVE

Bowie as producer

It was in 1877 that the first patent for recorded sound was taken out by Thomas Alva Edison, in the United States. Later innovations such as the development of the flat disc by Emile Berliner in the 1890s and the discovery of electrical recording in 1925 were significant improvements in terms of sound fidelity. But it was not until after World War II, during the late 1940s, that tape recording came to be exclusively utilised in the recording profession. This coincided with the invention of the $33\frac{1}{3}$ rpm long playing record, developed in America by CBS and first released in that country in 1948. For the next dozen years or so, popular albums tended to be collections of singles (songs lasting little more than two or three minutes) which could have been made in a variety of studios, at different times, and frequently were.

The development of stereo recording in the early 1950s (essentially a development by RCA) made its greatest impact in the field of classical music. The advantages of stereo over conventional mono channel recording were obvious: instead of the sound being captured on one channel, it was captured on two and the placement of the playback loudspeakers meant that the resultant mix was a significant improvement in terms of fidelity. Of course, classical music, frequently using many more musicians than the average rock or pop vocalist, benefitted initially from this advance. But it did not take long for the advantages of stereo recording to become apparent in the pop field. By about 1962 or 1963 almost every popular album was being recorded in stereo, whereas the same had been true of virtually every classical recording for the previous three or four years. Few people need reminding that it was in 1962 that the Beatles spearheaded a world revolution in rock music. What is not so generally well appreciated is that their initial album was not released until seven months after their first hit single. Nowadays, of course, such a situation would be regarded as wholly exceptional (or at least until a few years ago), for it is as a direct result of the influence of the Beatles and a great many other bands of importance that the album came to be regarded as a more important statement than the single.

The reasons for this are obvious: in terms of playing-time, the album can run from 30 to 50 minutes or more, but whereas in the 50s and to a large extent up to the mid-60s, popular albums were collections of songs often of no more than two or three minute's duration, it soon became apparent that as the album assumed greater importance in record sales terms, it offered the creative artist a much broader canvas on which to work. Whereas a classical musician will find nothing unusual in listening to a movement from a work lasting five, ten or fifteen minutes, it was exceptional for a rock musician to think in terms of more than five minutes at most. Suddenly, with the importance of the album concept, he was able to work in the same time-span as any classical symphonic writer had done. By no means all of the rock artists who took advantage of this were up to the mark. Music, of course, exists in time, and has to be created and perceived in that medium. The longer the amount of time something takes, the greater the attention both to detail and to the time-span which is being encompassed.

In 1967 the Beatles "Sergeant Pepper's Lonely Hearts Club Band" was the high water mark of their mid career. Not only that, of course; it was one of the most important albums that had ever been issued in rock music up to that time, and still retains the power to thrill and move the committed listener almost twenty years after it first appeared. By 1967 the importance of the man who had produced the Beatles recordings had become much more marked. He was George Martin. Curiously enough, he had begun his career as a classical producer. He therefore brought to the Beatles the experience both of a professional musician and of a man totally at home in the recording studio. George Martin was not alone; throughout the record industry in Europe and America, a large number of very gifted men were applying their experience and refining their craft as record producers. The creative use of new technological developments meant that the link man between the artists and the technicians assumed greater importance.

It is only during the last twenty years that the record producer has come to assume the dominant and important position he now holds. Many people would regard this as a mixed blessing. After, artists are signed to record companies on the basis of their own music-making, and not for what might be brought to them by an employee of the company, or another outsider, at some future date. In addition, it is important that the artist should retain final control over what is put down and issued in his name. It must be obvious therefore that the record producer should possess a number of special qualities. In the first place he has to be completely sympathetic with the musicians whose work he is entrusted to supervise. At the very least he has to be able to get on with them as individuals and to understand fully what it is they are trying to express. Secondly, he must have a thorough understanding (if not knowledge) of the technical aspects of recording. He has to know what is possible and what is not. Last, and by no means least, he ought to be able to ensure that costs for a recording do not get out of hand. It does not require much imagination to see that such men are comparatively rare, and not even the most successful producers have been able to combine these attributes to the same degree. But it must equally be apparent that the record producer is now an important and indispensable part of the recording process.

In what way are David Bowie's productions of other artists significant, and in what way is he fitted to be a record producer? Apart from the obvious cachet of engaging a famous musician to produce a record, it is clear from the albums Bowie has produced for other artists that he possesses the qualities we have identified as making a good record producer. He is an experienced recording artist in his own right. Exceptional among great popular musicians, Bowie's career has taken him to many studios for many companies. He has also worked with some outstanding producers and could hardly fail to have learned something from them. On the other hand, however, there is all the difference in the world between being a significant recording artist and the faintly anonymous character that a record producer must be. We know, from the variety of Bowie's own performance and his occasional desire for anonymity, that he is perfectly capable of subjugating his own personality in adopting a variety of roles. As he is clearly able to do this in a recording studio one does not get the impression from listening to a Bowie-produced album that he has paraded his own musical personality to the detriment of the artists for whom he is responsible.

One of the more common features of modern pop and rock musicians is that as the overwhelming majority of such artists do not read music. Their state of preparedness on arrival at the recording studio can range from having a song complete in their minds, to having very little idea of what is going to happen. Bowie has sometimes been reported as coming to a recording session, with a variety of musicians he has gathered, not possessing anything concrete with which they could work. Without terms of reference, the producer's role is made doubly difficult. It is therefore much more important that he fully understands the artistic ethos of the musicians. It is a measure of Bowie's success in this connection that the majority of the records he has produced for other people have remained in the catalogues for years, not necessarily due entirely to him, although his contribution was never less than significant.

Although Bowie had produced a couple of singles in 1971 and 1972 featuring Freddie Burretti under the name of Arnold Corns, these are of marginal historical importance. It was, however, in 1972 that Bowie produced two albums which did a very great deal for his career in general. The first was for CBS, with the British band Mott the Hoople; the album was "All The Young Dudes". The title track was written by Bowie and became Mott's biggest hit up to that time. It is a remarkable song in itself, slow and powerful, perhaps showing the musical influence of the Beatles' "Hey Jude", but Bowie's ability in the studio to draw from this band an album of such incomparable power and energy declares him to be a producer of great significance. This is not necessarily the ability to oversee the safe taping of music; Mott's career had not been going as it should. It required considerable imagination and skill on Bowie's part to take the material and produce an album of this quality. It is fascinating to examine each track and see the effects slight touches of emphasis here, of balance there, of coloration and of the intelligent use of time. It is most instructive to compare this album with the second of 1972, Lou Reed's "Transformer" for RCA. One listens in vain for fragments of Bowie himself on the Mott album, but Bowie is more to the fore on the Lou Reed album. Perhaps Lou Reed had more in common with Bowie at that time than did the members of Mott, but what is wholly admirable about Bowie's production of the Reed album is the way in which he has created a sound through which Reed himself comes across as a performer and not because of the efforts of other people. With creative input coming from a variety of sources it is virtually impossible to give credit to any one individual for particular felicitous touches of production, but one would not be surprised to learn that it was Bowie's idea to have the high string held note like a constant telephone wire on the most famous track, "Walk On The Wild Side" which ends side one.

With Bowie's work with Iggy Pop, we come to his most important work as a producer. It is reasonably common knowledge that Bowie considered Pop to be an important artist from very early on. What is also unfortunately common knowledge is that Pop was not always able to cope with the pressures of the music business. Pop's one album for CBS was issued in 1973. He had been responsible for overseeing the production himself, but it was clearly beyond him. Bowie was brought in after the tracks had been laid down to try and make the best of some technically inexpert work. Consequently, without having heard the original material, one cannot blame Bowie for any technical flaws in the resultant album. It is unlikely, however, that had Bowie been brought in at the start, the album would have taken the aural shape it did. During the succeeding two or three years, Iggy's career seemed aimless until Bowie, on hearing of Pop's self-admission to a mental hospital in Los Angeles, decided to take him in hand and do all he could to further his friend's career. Within a little over a year RCA had issued three albums by Iggy: "The Idiot", "Lust For Life" and "T.V. Eye", the first of which was completely produced and arranged by Bowie. In addition, Bowie had a hand in each of the album's eight songs.

"The Idiot" is a magnificent album, of such importance that in purely musical terms it may well be shown in the future to have had a greater influence than is generally supposed. Although one can detect Bowie's presence, it is an entirely selfless one; he puts himself utterly at the service of his friend, dedicating his own extraordinary talents to the realisation of Iggy's disconcerting vision. "Lust For Life", which followed six month's later, shows Pop in a rather more appealing vein. The touch is certainly lighter than on the previous album, and it must have given Bowie a great deal of satisaction to see the emergence of this new facet of his friend's musical character. Bowie appeared as a backing musician on the Pop tour arranged to promote the "Lust For Life" album. Several of the appearances were recorded and "T.V. Eye" is a mixture of live material and studio work. This is almost always an unsatisfactory combination, for the producer has no real control over what happens at live concerts – at least with regard to the sound. When one considers that Bowie's live albums leave a great deal to be desired, it is obvious that Bowie, in the recording world, is – like almost all artists – at his best in the studio. It is there that his considerable imagination and creative skills can be realised to the best, whether it be for his own recorded work or for those other artists for whom from time to time he has produced albums. Bowie has so much to say himself, in his own music, that he is unlikely to return to the studio in the producer's role other than on very few occasions, but he has already achieved enough in this regard, certainly in the rescuing of various careers, that his contribution to the craft of producer, although small, is highly significant and should not be overlooked by any future historian.

CHAPTER THIRTEEN

Bowie as Actor

by Curtis Hutchinson

David Bowie's film début was in a fourteen-minute X-certificate, black and white short made in 1967. *The Image*, directed by Michael Armstrong and financed by Border Film Productions, was shot in just three days. Its first public showing was not until 1969, the year of Bowie's first hit single *Space Oddity*.

An artist, played by Michael Byrne, becomes haunted by the subject of his painting – a boy portrayed by Bowie – who appears out of the blue at a rain-splattered window. The artist then tries to kill the boy in a series of violent scenes, ending with him falling destructively on his painting.

The director's description of the film was "a study of the illusionary reality world within the schizophrenic mind of the artist at his point of creativity". Brian Murphy, reviewing *The Image* in *Films & Filming*, was quite favourable, describing Bowie's role as "well played". He also sheds some light on the apparent need of an X-certificate by remarking that the "film has its crudities, certainly both technical and conceptional, much of the editing is ragged, without suggesting violence, and the Lady Macbeth cleanliness business really ought to be banned from the cinema for at least fifty years."

Bowie had no dialogue in *The Image*, which precludes any assessment of his acting, rather than his mime, as far as this particular film is concerned. It is, perhaps, best described as a piece of best forgotton sixties paranoia, which aroused little interest when it was first released and has rarely been screened since. Now it is just an item of Bowie folklore.

The mime artist Lindsay Kemp came to Bowie's attention when he learned that Kemp was using excerpts from the '"*David Bowie*" Deram LP as a backdrop for some of his performances. Bowie was obviously flattered that an artist of Kemp's calibre should use his music and lost no time in making himself known to Kemp, eventually enrolling at his mime school (mime was later to play a major part in his stage appearances as Ziggy Stardust and was used to great effect in a scene in *Merry Christmas Mr Lawrence* in which Bowie mimes the last ritual acts of a condemned man before a mock execution). Bowie was not forgetful of his debt to Kemp, who was invited to perform a piece of mime at a lavish Ziggy concert at the Rainbow in 1972.

Pierrot in Turquoise was the title of the Lindsay Kemp Company production in which Bowie played a character called Cloud, who was used as a feed-man for Kemp as Pierrot and Jack Birkett as Harlequin. By performing a number of songs, which helped explain the action on stage, Bowie provided the necessary link between the audience and the performers, a not too dissimilar role to that of *Baal*, which he would play fourteen years later.

During the last two years of the swinging sixties, Bowie drifted in and out of work. His manager, Kenneth Pitt, was uncertain as to whether Bowie's future lay in acting or singing, which, coupled with his desperate financial situation, explains the diversity of his career at that time. On 30th January, 1968, a brief appearance in a BBC 2 play saw Bowie dance a short minuet with his girlfriend Hermione Farthingale, also a student of Lindsay Kemp. But no dialogue: that would not follow for another six years. An audition for John Dexter's screen version of Leslie Thomas' story of a group of British army recruits in Singapore in 1960, *Virgin Soldiers*, brought Bowie a bit-part in a crowd scene: his first real big-screen appearance in a commercially distributed film, almost unrecognisable with regulation short-back-and-sides.

The next screen appearance was longer and certainly more bizarre. A new ice-cream, with the very sixties-sounding name of *Luv*, was launched with a thirty-second commercial in which Bowie runs up the stairs of a London double-decker bus brandishing no less than three ice-lollies, wearing a wider than wide smile. The year did get better for him! Towards the end of January, Bowie starred in his own film *Love You Till Tuesday*, which was financed by Kenneth Pitt and directed by Malcolm J. Thomson with a view to submitting it to either the BBC or ITV as a showcase for Bowie's writing, singing and acting. It featured him performing tracks from his Deram LP as well as the unreleased tracks "When I'm Five", "Ching-A-Ling" and a song he wrote specially for the film, "Space Oddity". Stylistically the film is comparable to present day promotional videos made by pop groups to promote their latest singles, a medium of which Bowie subsequently made more imaginative use than most, in the videos *Boys Keep Swinging*, *Ashes to Ashes*, *Let's Dance*, *China Girl* and the mini film *Jazzin' For Blue Jean*, which received a theatrical release in 1984 as the supporting feature to *The Company of Wolves*.

In *Love You Till Tuesday* Bowie walks across Hampstead Heath to the accompaniment of "When I Live My Dream" and dons a Major Tom space-suit, complete with psychedelic boots, for "Space Oddity". There is also an interesting piece of mime called "The Mask", in which Bowie steals a mask from a junk shop, takes it home and entertains his parents with it and eventually becomes a celebrity, only to be smothered onstage at the London Palladium by the character he has created. With this character Bowie had unwittingly created a poignant predecessor to Ziggy Stardust. Apart from the excursion to Hampstead, the film is studio-based with Bowie working in front of a white backdrop with occasional props — a model guitar for "Let Me Sleep Beside You", a row of chairs for "Rubber Band" and a giant birthday cake for "When I'm Five" — and quite suprisingly, in this age of hi-tech videos, the film is very professional, with all concerned making the most of what was a very tight budget. Although snatches of "Love You Till Tuesday" have been shown on British television, after Bowie's rise to fame, it was never publicly shown in its entirety and looked destined to collect dust in a private archive for the foreseeable future, that is until its release on video in 1984.

During this period, there were a number of unsuccessful auditions: for a small part in the West End production of *Hair*; as the bi-sexual lover of Glenda Jackson and Peter Finch in John Schlesinger's sublime melodrama *Sunday Bloody Sunday* and a supporting role in Frank Nesbit's story of a lecherous, rural miser, *Dulcima*. A stage play of Sir Walter Scott's *The Fair Maid of Perth* and a couple of documentaries by Tony Palmer were projects with which Bowie was involved, but never materialised. With the exception of his "stage personas", Ziggy Stardust and Aladdin Sane, Bowie's next appearance as an actor was in 1976 as *The Man Who Fell to Earth*.

After the false starts of his early years, Bowie's film career began in earnest with Nicolas Roeg's film *The Man Who Fell to Earth*, closely based on an obscure science fiction novel written by Walter Trevis in 1963 about an alien stranded on Earth in the 1980s. This precursor of

E.T. is a benevolent creature who travels to Earth to save his dying planet. After splashdown in a lake outside a small Kentucky town, he adopts the personality of Thomas Jerome Newton and, armed only with a British passport, single-handedly revolutionises the electronic and communication systems of America. By using the advanced scientific know-how of his home planet, he is able to patent nine key inventions that eventually make him a billionaire, which incurs the jealousy and mistrust of the business community. Newton ploughs his millions into the first private enterprise space programme to transport the surviving inhabitants of planet Athena to Earth. Human emotions – and the alien's inability to cope with them – thwart his master plan and reduce him to an alcoholic. The space mission is aborted minutes before blast-off by government agents and the inter-galactic Noah's Ark is destroyed, leaving Newton stranded on Earth.

The Man Who Fell to Earth has the distinction of being the first British film to be made entirely in America, shot during the summer of 1975 on location in New York and New Mexico, with a predominantly British crew, a British director and, of course, a British star. *British Lion Films* raised the £1 million budget, without, as the trade paper *Variety* commented, "an upfront coin from the USA".

The film's director Nicolas Roeg first gained attention with his beautiful camera work as the photographer on *Far From the Madding Crowd* and later cemented his reputation as a director with *Performance*, *Walkabout*, *Don't Look Back* and, more recently, *Bad Timing Eureka* and *Insignificance*. His use of fast editing and flashbacks, closely juxtaposing past and present, give his films a distinctive flair. For the most part, Roeg faithfully adhered to Trevis' original story, but expanded its imagery, creating a quasi-surrealist work.

The Man Who Fell to Earth is replete with startling images: Bowie, stripped of his contact lenses, hair, ears and genitals, confronting his petrified lover; repeated images of Newton's dying family on their stricken planet; his lawyer thrown against a window and apologising to his assailants for it not breaking. Perhaps most evocative of all, a glazed Bowie sitting in front of twelve television sets, simultaneously absorbing the programmes on all of them.

Bowie's frail, skeletal frame, his androgynous features and anaemic colouring with oddly matched eyes, were perfect for his debut role. If anyone could play an alien from outer space, it was Bowie, who had, after all, successfully assumed the strange and esoteric personas of

Ziggy Stardust and Aladdin Sane. There was something absolutely *right* about Bowie as the benevolent extra-terrestrial. Curiously, Trevis' description of his character – written when Bowie was still David Jones at Bromley Technical High School – was "tall, thin, with fine delecate bone structure . . . smooth skin and a boyish face, but the eyes were very strange as though they were over-sensitive".

What appealed to Bowie about the script was that it did not call on him to sing or play a pop star, but was well suited to a non-professional actor, since the character was cold and unexpressive. Moreover, he had long been fascinated by science fiction, a recurring theme in his compositions "The Man Who Sold the World", "Space Oddity" and "Starman", as well as in his stage personas of Ziggy Stardust and Aladdin Sane, so that the role of Thomas Jerome Newton was one which his fans would readily identify with him: after all Newton might be the new persona to replace Ziggy and Aladdin Sane.

There was never any doubt as to who was the focal character in the film. Roeg structured *The Man Who Fell to Earth* around Bowie in much the same way as he had Mick Jagger in *Performance*. The director first discovered Bowie through Alan Yentob's documentary for BBC television, *Cracked Actor*, which brilliantly captured Bowie's enigmatic character and convinced Roeg that Bowie playing Bowie was perfect for Thomas Jerome Newton. It is hard to determine where in the film, Bowie stops and Newton begins; the audience is presented with yet another alter-ego of the star, who has since admitted that part of the role's appeal lay in the degree of "non-acting" it called for.

It is therefore hardly suprising that Bowie's performance was original and relaxed throughout. Rip Torn, as the libidinous professor, and Candy Clark, as Newton's lover, acquitted themselves equally well. The picture was both a critical and commercial success, with many critics agreeing that the film was not only a remarkable technical achievement, but one of the most daring British films of recent years. Some felt that it overplayed its sexual angle – Roeg had added a sexual dimension to Trevis' story by making Newton and Mary Lou lovers – but there was unanimity as far as Bowie's casting was concerned: it was faultless. They would not be so generous with his next film.

Bowie, the critics and cinema-going public all accept that his next film, *Just a Gigolo*, was not a good film. Bowie was later to disown it as his "thirty-two Elvis Presley movies rolled into one", although he enjoyed working with David Hemmings more than with Nicolas Roeg.

Bowie's comment is too harsh a criticism, for *Just a Gigolo* does have a few saving graces: well crafted opening scenes, a sometimes witty and perceptive script and good performances by Marlene Dietrich, Kim Novak, Curt Jürgens and Sydne Rome.

Set in Berlin between 1918 and 1928, the film is the story of a young Prussian officer's attempt to establish himself in post-war society. It begins in the trenches on the last day of the First World War, where Paul von Przygodski (Bowie) reports for duty to Captain Kraft (Hemmings). From the outset, Bowie is 'different'; he wears an immaculate new uniform. The captain asks him what he wants, to which the lieutenant replies, "Fame and glory, of course, I'm a Prussian. Heriosm is my destiny". Prepared for a glorious death in action, von Przygodski follows his captain in a last-ditch attempt to win the war after the German surrender had been announced, only to be blown up by a stray British shell.

Von Przygodski awakes in hospital only to discover that he has been mistaken for a French hero; his heroism is therefore achieved by proxy. Returning to Berlin with his only possession, a pig, he finds his family home turned into a boarding house with some very strange tenants. His father is a motionless figure in a wheelchair and his mother reduced to an assistant in a Turkish bath. Shocked by his family's downfall, he realises that he too must adapt to the harsh reality of a defeated country. He swallows his pride and tries to find employment and, after drifting in and out of work, meets his former captain, who is in the process of starting a right-wing paramilitary movement dedicated to the reversal of the Versailles Treaty. Paul is not interested and finally, after being spotted by Dietrich as the Baroness von Semering, ends up as just a gigolo.

Later, walking along an apparently deserted street, Paul is killed in the cross-fire between communists and brownshirts. Von Przygodski is made into a martyr of the Right by the unscrupulous Captain Kraft. Paul thus achieved the heroism, albeit by accident, he regarded as his destiny.

At first sight, the story sounds an interesting one, but the final released version is disappointing and suffered on two major counts: its rushed editing (the film was originally released in Europe with a running time of 147 minutes only to be withdrawn after bad reviews and cut to 105 minutes) and Bowie's miscasting. In *The Man Who Fell To Earth*, Bowie *was* Newton, but not even his most ardent fan could claim that he gave a good performance as a Prussian officer, a role better suited to Helmut Berger or Michael York. Bowie was not able to breath life into Paul von Przygodski.

David Hemmings had made his name as an actor in *Blow Up*, a film almost synonymous with the London of the swinging sixties, and *Just a Gigolo* was his first – and to date, apart from the as yet unreleased documentary of Bowie's 1978 tour, last – project as a director. The film was ambitiously conceived: not only was it to be the most expensive film shot in Germany, but Hemmings had assembled a star-studded cast. The opening sequence suggests a witty period piece and the first few minutes are beautifully shot in sepia, with a spendidly speeded up title sequence, shot in twenties style, which charts the return to Berlin of Bowie and his pig.

Just a Gigolo did nothing to further David Bowie's acting career. After the favourable reviews of *The Man Who Fell To Earth*, Bowie was now accused of being a charlatan. The film was also a commercial failure, but Bowie played bravely against type and learned from his mistakes.

The lead in the American stage production of Bernard Pomerance's *The Elephant Man* was instrumental in helping to establish Bowie as a serious actor. His sympathetic portrayal of the hideously deformed John Merrick won praise even from the notoriously difficult to please American critics. Bowie appeared in this production across the United States, playing at: The Denver Center of the Performing Arts, 29th July - 3rd August, 1980; Chicago Blackstone Theatre, 5th - 31st August, 1980; ending with a run on Broadway at the Booth Theatre, 23rd September 1980 - January 1981.

Unlike the film version, the stage production could not rely so heavily on the elaborate make-up that transformed John Hurt into Merrick. Bowie drew on his experience as a mime artist to convey Merrick's deformity, naked, except for a loin cloth, standing centre-stage and contorting his body according to a narration describing Merrick's physique.

This portrayal was not exploitative or sensational in any way; Bowie brought a totally unexpected degree of compassion and warmth to the role and had learnt how to project and vary his voice, something that the critics were quick to spot. *Variety* remaked that "he has a strong stage voice and a relaxed manner" and that "judging from his projection of this part, Bowie has the chance to achieve legitimate stardom". Praise indeed, and in view of what was to come, quite prophetic.

With the success of *The Elephant Man* behind him, Bowie started to look around for a role to widen his repertoire and found it in the work of Bertholt Brecht, one of the most influential playwrights of this century and a key figure in contemporary German literature. A television production, first broadcast on 2nd February 1982, of *Baal*, faithfully translated from the German by John Willett and directed by Alan Clarke, exonerated Bowie for his role in *Just a Gigolo*; his powerful portrayal of Baal, a difficult part for any actor to tackle, was proof that Bowie had once again bounced back.

Retitled *David Bowie in Baal*, it did well in the all important ratings, despite clashing with Sir Laurence Olivier's tour de force *Voyage Around by Father*. The BBC decided to adapt Brecht's re-write of *Baal* for television as it was under half the length of his original version, with a tighter plot and only eleven scenes. The complexities of the piece are all the more astonishing when one takes into account that Brecht was only twenty when he first wrote it in 1918. The re-write was drafted some eight years later, when Brecht could distance himself from the subjective youth who had conceived it. The important differences between the two plays is that the original treats *Baal* more like a hero, whereas the later version is somewhat more objective in its assessment of Baal's character.

The attraction that *Baal* held for Bowie is not surprising: he had always had a fascination for the decadent aspects of Weimar Germany, and though the story is set in the ten years immediately preceding the First World War, it tells the story of an amoral, wandering poet who delights in exploiting those unfortunate enough to come into contact with him. He mistreats his women, ending his life as a fugitive after murdering his only friend in a whiskey bar brawl. Once again, like Thomas Jerome Newton, Paul von Przygodski and John Merrick, Bowie plays the misfit, but this time portraying a complete cynic and one with homicidal tendencies at that! Bowie seemed to revel in his performance of a malevolent character, beyond the pale of social acceptability.

Bowie had to change his physical appearance completely for the role, so the character who appears on the screen is not immediately recognisable as David Bowie. The hair is unkempt and greasy, the chin hidden by stubble, dirty teeth and filthy, ill fitting clothes. But the biggest transformation was Bowie's acting. His voice became charged with a new urgency and he used his face with the agility of a mime artist to produce a demonic, drunken grin, probably the most memorable image of the entire production.

He was supported by an able cast, but, as the central character, Bowie shouldered the responsibility and can therefore take credit for its success. Bowie the actor had found his feet.

To date Bowie had wisely steered away from singing roles, *Baal* at last gave him the perfect opportunity to put his talents as a singer to serious theatrical use, for the part called for a handful of songs, written by Brecht, to illustrate the actions on stage, without detracting from them by the subtle use of the split screen effect to make Bowie a detached, but necessary chronicler, who punctuates each scene.

David Bowie in Baal presented him in a totally different and unexpected guise which showed his public and the critics that his acting career was being pursued with the same versatility as his music and, above all, that he had successfully overcome the restrictive stereotypes of the two films he had made by then. Bowie could now be recognised as a proficient character actor who had taken on one of the most challenging roles of modern German drama.

Bowie's next two films were shot in quick succession. Following the success of *Baal*, he returned to the big screen in a stylish horror film directed by Tony Scott about two vampire lovers set in contemporary New York. For the first time in his film career, Bowie was not the star; that was undeniably the French actress, Catherine Deneuve, as Miriam, born in Egypt 4000 years ago and possessed of the secret of eternal life. Bowie was cast as her lover, John Baylock, an eighteenth-century Englishman of seemingly aristocratic birth.

Miriam carries with her an ankh, a looped cross, which, although a symbol of life, is used to slit her victims' throats to drain their blood. She has the power to offer the the gift of eternal life, but, unlike her, those on whom she bestows it, age with the passing of three centuries. Baylock has a sleepless night; age begins to catch up with him and Miriam's response is to seduce a doctor, who is involved in researching the ageing process, played by Sarah Sarandon, in the hope of finding either a cure for Baylock, or failing that, another companion to replace him.

The film suffers from lapses in plot and lacks the pace of a nail-biting thriller, but is redeemed by excellent visual effects and Bowie's performance as the doomed vampire.

Tony Scott established himself as one of Britain's leading directors of television commercials; *The Hunger* was his first feature film, so, once again, Bowie was in the hands of a relative novice. It is Scott's distinct flair for visual effect that contributes to the film's appeal: the billowing curtains; the subtle use of soft focus and brightly lit sets reminiscent of a lavish commercial for an expensive perfume or jewellery. Bowie's performance as a man doomed to eternal life was captivating; his acting had improved out of all recognition from *Just a Gigolo*. His role comprised two characters: Miriam's young and debonair lover and an ageing old man. As the first, his blond hair, delicate features and clear skin acted as a fine counter balance to Catherine Deneuve's glacial beauty. Despite the reported friction between them and the leading lady's much publicised reluctance to play a nude shower scene with him, on film the couple appear as the epitome of New York chic; they are "the beautiful people" straight from the pages of *Vogue*. Bowie's poise and diction reinforce the suggested nobility of Baylock's background.

The scenes in which he has to age rapidly called for five hours of make up each morning and were the work of a leading make-up artist Dick Smith, who had worked on *The Exorcist*, *The Godfather* and *Altered States*. Baylock ageing fifty years within two hours in a doctor's waiting room is a most memorable scene. Bowie, the perfectionist, insisted on a complete change of voice for his portrayal of the old man, apparently developing his quivering tones by screaming a selection of Little Richard songs at the top of his voice on the banks of the Thames. Whatever the means, the result justified them.

No sooner had he finished *The Hunger* than a telephone call from the Japanese director Nagisa Oshima brought him the offer of a part in Oshima's new film that was to begin shooting in three weeks. Accepting the role, Bowie spent a brief working holiday in Java to familiarise himself with his next working environment before embarking on what was to prove a milestone in his acting career.

Merry Christmas Mr Lawrence presented Bowie with his finest role and best performance to date. Based on the semi-autobiographical book by the South African writer Sir Laurens van der Post, *The Seed and The Sower* (1951), the film follows the novel in that it draws on van der Post's understanding of his captors as a British officer in a Japanese prisoner-of-war camp through living in Japan during the twenties as a reporter for a South African newspaper.

The film reflects the empathy Sir Laurens once felt for the Japanese and his subsequent disillusion through two central characters: Lieutenant Colonel John Lawrence (an obvious pun on the author's name) and Major Jack Celliers, Bowie's role in the film. Lawrence, played by Tom Conti, is the only prisoner who speaks Japanese, which makes him an enigmatic figure to both his fellow prisoners and his captors; his commanding officer sees his understanding of the enemy as bordering on collaboration, while the Japanese regard him as honourable and therefore fail to understand why he surrendered.

The story is seen very much through Lawrence's eyes; how much of the real Sir Laurens is in the character played by Bowie is uncertain, but in both the book and the film, it is Celliers who emerges as the dominant character, the one *who sows the seed*.

Celliers is guilt-ridden by the childhood memory of allowing his deformed younger brother to be the victim of a grossly degrading school-yard initiation ceremony and welcomes the outbreak of war as a means of redemption through an honourable death in action. Fate, however, does not comply with his scheme of things and he is forced to surrender to stop the Japanese massacre of an innocent village. His guilt feelings are reflected in his explanation to Colonel Lawrence that his "expertise lies in the field of human betrayal".

Bowie's role as a New Zealander in a predominantly British prisoner-of-war camp is still that of an outsider, of someone who does not quite fit in: a role with which he seems always ready to identify. His apparent lack of fear for his captors, such as the smuggling of manju cakes into the hospital when the camp commandant has enforced a forty-eight hour fast, both perplexes and heartens his fellow inmates, while the Japanese misconstrue his bravery as that of a malevolent spirit, a concept of which Celliers takes full advantage. When Captain Yanoi asks him directly whether he is an evil spirit, Celliers replies, "Yes, and one of yours I hope". At one point, he successfully halts the execution of the British commanding officer by breaking rank and confronting Captain Yanoi with his latent homosexuality by kissing him on both cheeks.

No one could deny that Bowie's stagecraft had come a long way from his performance as *The Man Who Fell To Earth*. He is relaxed and convincing throughout the film. His experience on the American stage and in the BBC's production of *Baal* had clearly served him well; he makes full use of the soliloquies the script affords him and in a mime routine, of which Lindsay Kemp would have been proud, Bowie shaves, eats his last meal, drinks a cup of tea and smokes an imaginary cigarette to the amazement of his guards. Perhaps his most powerful scene, however, is the recollection of his past to Lawrence: Bowie's distinctive voice narrates, while Oshima illustrates with childhood images of Celliers, from a twelve-year old to a sixth former, showing the visions that have haunted Celliers throughout his adult life. There is no sense of urgency in Bowie's voice: he speaks slowly and makes the most of each word.

His understanding of mime enables Bowie to express himself succinctly through facial expression. It is as though Oshima immediately recognised this quality, for the first camera shots of Bowie concentrate on his face to convey his emotional reaction to the questions fired at him by a Japanese court-martial. He appears to be relaxed and nonchalant, until Captain Yanoi asks him a question in English, prefacing it with a quote from Shakespeare, which momentarily throws Celliers. The instant of confusion is beautifully captured by Bowie.

The casting of a Japanese pop star (Ryuichi Sakamoto) and comedian (Beat Takeshi) reflects Oshima's preference for *performers*, rather than *actors*, who he believes offer a greater purity of performance than trained actors, who can sometime be guided too much by technique and thus sacrifice the 'feel' of a part. Oshima nearly did not use Bowie for this very reason, he thought him 'too good' in *The Elephant Man*.

Casting the occidental and oriental pop stars opposite each other worked well. As a commercial consideration, it might well have enticed their massive followings to see the film, but, even if this were so, they would have been rewarded by two excellent performances and Oshima's superb direction.

Bowie immediately established a rapport with Oshima; both shared a talent for improvisation. Oshima makes films in the same way that Bowie makes records, so that it must have been relatively easy for Bowie to adapt to Oshima's inclination to edit in the camera. Oshima seldom had to do more than two takes of any one scene, he knew exactly what he wanted, which is hardly surprising as the project had been planned for five years and he had probably shot the film in his mind's eye countless times. This working environment, which allowed the actors a degree of improvisation, also exerted its own discipline as well as the necessary pressure to give a perfect performance first time round: a framework ideally suited to Bowie's temperament.

Merry Christmas Mr Lawrence sets the standard by which Bowie's future film performances can be judged. It represents a milestone in his acting career and establishes him once and for all as a serious actor. It is to his credit that he achieved this in a film in which his role was not paramount, but, if anything, helped popularise Nagisa Oshima's work and introduced the Japanese director to an audience outside that of the 'arthouse' cinema.

In the wake of *Merry Christmas Mr Lawrence* came the release of a film shot in 1973, simply, or not so simply, titled *Ziggy Stardust and the Spiders from Mars*, a remarkable documentary account of Bowie's final appearance as Ziggy Stardust, his first, and by far the most popular, of his stage personas. This film, long awaited by his fans – its release had been spasmodically mentioned over ten years – was at last made available to them.

Ten years after the event, Bowie clearly felt himself to be sufficiently distanced from Ziggy to indulge in a little nostalgia and that is precisely what this film is: a trip down Bowie's memory lane. He apparently enjoyed working on *Ziggy Stardust and the Spiders from Mars*; it was Bowie who remixed the soundtrack and the project was blessed with his approval and consent. A record in celluloid of his playing Ziggy for the very last time, the performance came at the end of a particularly gruelling world tour, yet Bowie's performance is sublime on all counts, despite the physical and mental strain the tour must have put on him. To his new generation of fans, too young to remember Ziggy the first time round, the film provides a completely fresh aspect of Bowie as performer, who dominates the stage with animal-like grace. His enthusiasm is evident; a smile is seldom from his lips, in fact he seems to be enjoying the performance as much as the sea of fans in the stalls of the Hammersmith Odeon.

Without question, Ziggy Stardust is Bowie's most successful stage persona; his successors Aladdin Sane and the Thin White Duke were never as clearly defined. Ziggy, the archetypal self-destructive rock star was the seventies version of Jimi Hendrix, Jim Morrison and Janis Joplin, all rolled into one. Any performance Bowie gave of Ziggy was one to which his fans would flock; they were not going to hear Bowie sing a handful of hit songs, they were going to see Bowie act out this role. An easily recognisable figure, Ziggy's rise and fall is chronicled on the album that gave him life. Aladdin Sane and the Thin White Duke were more abstract; the audience, and probably Bowie himself, were uncertain where the singer began and the actor stopped.

Bowie felt the filming of Ziggy's last performance important enough to enlist the aid of the acclaimed American documentary maker D. A. Pennebaker, who, with his team of cameramen, successfully captured the mood and excitement of the performance on a cramped stage under what were clearly difficult technical conditions.

Ziggy Stardust and the Spiders from Mars is essential viewing for any Bowie follower, but it could have added a whole new dimension to Ziggy's character if it had made use of more back-stage footage. In *Don't Look Back*, the same director provided a unique fly-on-the-wall perspective of Bob Dylan's backstage court, but, as it is, this film is enhanced by the imaginative use of a good stereo soundtrack and an excellent performance by Bowie. The all too few glimpses back-stage we are permitted are very revealing: Ziggy's anaemic body helped into another costume, fragments of conversation with Ringo Starr, Twiggy and his wife Angie.

Bowie's mime routine in which Ziggy frantically tries to break out of the bubble imprisoning him is beautifully captured by Pennebaker; a lasting image of a memorable film.

Two "performances" have not been mentioned: his appearance in Ulrich Edel's *Christiane F*, which was not a role as such, but live footage of a concert Bowie gave in Berlin, used as the backdrop of one particular scene and his startlingly bizarre cameo role in Mel Damski's comedy *Yellowbeard*, with which, in a curious way, his career as an actor came full circle, for only secure in the knowledge that he had acquitted himself well in *Baal*, *The Elephant Man* and superbly in *Merry Christmas Mr Lawrence*, could he afford to appear as "The Shark", with a fin inexplicably tied to his back, to deliver just these lines – "I think she might be ready to talk now", "Thank You, Sir" and "Shall I meet you in the pump room, Sir?".

Critical debate as to the quality of his individual performances will, of course, continue. Bowie, like any other actor, will inevitably have his ups and down, but what is certain is that, unlike any other pop star, Bowie has successfully made the difficult transition from musician to film star and his status as a serious actor can no longer be in any doubt.

CHAPTER FOURTEEN

Theatre of Music

Historical study of the arts teaches us that anything is possible creatively given two virtues – imagination and technical ability – which are not invariably found together. On the rare occasions when they combine, artistic creativity becomes possible, an expression of transcendence in artistic terms, or at least an attempt at it.

Art once created (unless it is destroyed by a physical process) remains true for as long as human beings want it. People today can be moved by music written centuries ago and the same is true of works in the other arts. As Lord Clark observed in his masterly study of Leonardo da Vinci, they have to be re-interpreted for each generation.

Another conclusion to be drawn from historical study of the arts is that, apparently without precedent, a group of artists will arise in about the same place and time, all practitioners of the same art. There are many examples, of which only a few will suffice: Florentine art of the quattrocento, Scandinavian drama in the late nineteenth century, Russian literature of the same century and the Flemish school of painters of the sixteenth and seventeenth centuries. There are many more; as far as England is concerned the clutch of artists that produced Tudor choral music and Elizabethan drama, or Restoration Comedy and the rise of the novel in successive centuries are others. A fanciful osberver may believe that these are manifestations of John Wyndham's *Midwich Cuckoos*, but a more practical analysis might conclude that these outbreaks are the result of the removal of previously oppressive circumstances, for such events often follow the freeing of a group or race of people from some form of oppression.

David Bowie was a child at the 'bulge' – a product of the post-war boom in the birth-rate between 1946 and 1949. The generation to which he belonged had been engendered in sacrifice: the effort of the war years, followed by the era of privation and rationing while the

Welfare State was being built. The collective experience of that generation of young people marked a new departure in Britain's cultural history: there were more of them than ever before. And in 1962, the abolition of national service – the compulsory two-year period in the armed forces for men over eighteen – released them all, almost simultaneously, into a new world of freedom from the restrictions of service life and the trauma of foreign conflicts. They were growing up in an increasingly prosperous, free-spending, consumerist society created by the mood of *enrichissez-vous* of the years of Harold Macmillan's governments. The popular arts had the wealth and demographic dynamism to sustain them; a background to react against; and a climate of liberation in which to flourish unfettered.

Other factors combined to turn the London in which Bowie grew up into the most important capital for the creative arts in the 'sixties: the international acceptance of the first generation of rock-and-roll musicians, which started in 1955; the growth of English as an international language; the relative cheapness of the pound sterling; the long period of Labour government under Harold Wilson from 1964. By the time of the election of the first Wilson government the Beatles had experienced their early international success. No artist of the last twenty years can have remained uninfluenced by the Beatles. This exciting environment made London the Mecca for rock musicians from all over the world and spawned a variety of styles.

Although the fact that Bowie was a Londoner might seem to have given him distinct advantages, the nature of his genius nevertheless caused enormous problems early on. It should be remembered that Bowie was no teenage idol. He had to struggle for years against an indifferent, unsympathetic hierarchy and suffer a series of misfortunes and reversals which would have broken many lesser men. It says much for his innate stength of character, to say nothing of his profound belief in his own ability, that he was able to withstand these blows.

It would be quite wrong to assert that he remained unaffected by the myriad styles which were musically fashionable in the mid-1960s. He did affect a number of guises, both with regard to his appearance and with his own music, which demonstrate the influence of these styles. One only has to look at early publicity photographs of Davy Jones and the Lower Third and to hear such early songs as "I'm Not Losing Sleep", "Good Morning Girl", and "I Say To Myself" to realise the truth of this, but the comparative failure of these early songs and the constant state of flux in which Bowie found himself indicate two things, which may or may not be complementary. These are that in this early stage in his career he showed his chameleon-like character, and the other is that he was uncertain of the direction his music should take.

Bowie's underlying strength of character enabled him to persist in his individual way towards the achievement of his first success, "Space Oddity" album. It is misleading to think of this album as something that sprang fully-formed without insemination and fertilisation from outside influences. As has been shown in the main body of this book, influences are present, but all subsumed into a unique document. The influences one ought to emphasise here are those of an other-worldliness derived from U.S. Apollo moonshots of the time, and the phenomenal success established among young people of Stanley Kubrick's film *2001*, with its incredible psychedelic conclusion. The album came at just the right moment and for the first time Bowie's singular genius was demonstrated on an international scale.

The result was a gradually increasing obsession with what might be called a non-human persona in "The Man Who Sold The World". The album title indicates this, and we observe in "Life On Mars?" on the "Hunky Dory" album the continuation of this aspect which reached its fruition in "Ziggy Stardust". By this time Bowie's obsession with the character he had evolved had reached the point where he was in danger of becoming, Frankenstein-like, overwhelmed by his own creation. His ritual "killing-off" of the character, never to reappear, seemed at the time to almost all observers an act of extreme folly. What was not appreciated and could not have been foreseen even by his closest friends and admirers was that Ziggy was but one facet of Bowie's life, which – we have since come to learn – can never be regarded as so important as to obliterate the others.

One aspect of the Ziggy character was his human anonymity, to the extent where, because he was someone from outer space, his sexuality was irrelevant. With Bowie's next albums this fact assumes greater importance; not of course through the now defunct Ziggy but through a series of characters behind whom the true Bowie lurks as a multi-faceted actor fronted by a series of masks. The sexual nature of "Aladdin Sane", "Hunky Dory", and more especially "Diamond Dogs", is perhaps the most striking feature outside of the albums' musical qualities and this sexuality – albeit of an indeterminate nature – can be seen to be a continuiation of the outrageous theatricality of Ziggy Stardust. Bowie's comments on his own sexuality are comparatively unimportant but in his stage performances at the time he hit upon a profound psychological fact. This is that young people at the time of their physical maturity are invariably subjected to a great many pressures both from within and without and in an attempt to rationalise their new-found experience they tend to adopt certain attitudes. Each individual person's sexuality has to be expressed in accordance with the demands of his or her particular psyche. The process of sexual self orientation takes time. The formative years are full of uncertainties. In some cases they are never dispelled. For young people confused by their sexuality, consumed by interest in it and desire to explore it, what Bowie did was to become the personification on stage of a pan-sexual figure. Suddenly his admirers saw a living embodiment of their own innermost fantasies. Here was a person who, being married and with a son, freely admitted to (if not openly advocating) a wide range of concurrent sexual experience.

This honesty (if such it is) can openly have been maintained by someone whose music meant a very great deal, as anyone could have said what Bowie said and dressed up as he did, to no effect. Bowie's effect was reinforced and made more startling by the nature of the musical genius on these albums, even in the case of "Pin-Ups" which is made up of new versions of some favourite songs by other writers from the sixties. With the exception of this album Bowie has almost invariably been a singer-songwriter, but it would be quite wrong to think of him as just such an artist. As we have noted, Bowie, even in his earliest work, possessed the ability to personify on stage the essential character of the particular song or album. Additionally, Bowie becomes this personification in a theatrical manner. This is through a variety of ways but principally includes gesture, costume, lighting and production. Only a very strong inner character can bring this off, probably aided and abetted by theatrical experience, and especially by mastery of mime. In David Bowie, the cement which binds the musician to the theatrical performance is more than technique: his essential character is profoundly charismatic.

Charisma in popular entertainers is a frequently-applied and a much-abused term but there is no doubt that a select number of greatly talented individuals possess it. It is rarely met with but when it is, it is unmistakable. In Bowie's case, for virtually the first time in the history of popular music, it was a natural progression for him to undertake serious acting commitments. If this seems a surprising statement, then one should remember that Curtis Hutchinson has shown that Bowie approached this aspect of his career from a completely different standpoint than that of any other rock star-turned-actor.

It is often maintained that Bowie's frequent change of image is a so far successful attempt to keep one step ahead of his followers and contemporaries. While this may or may not be true (and personally I doubt it) by going through his various music and image changes during the past fifteen years or so Bowie has done no more than reveal different aspects of a multi-faceted musical make-up. While this is exceptional in art and particularly so in music, it is by no means unique. Stravinsky, for example, underwent a number of deliberate changes of style, alarming his most ardent followers, yet remaining at all times true to himself. In pictorial art of the twentieth century the kaleidosopic character of Picasso is an obvious example. It follows that what Bowie exhibits to us at any one time cannot be the complete artistic statement if we go by his previous work.

There are musicians who affect a style in which anything can happen and frequently does. The result is akin to confusion and must necessarily be so if the artist has no overall sense of direction. For it is a sad fact that versatility in an artist can be a curse, especially if he has no clear over-view of his life and is easily persuaded to dissipate his energies on a variety of projects which are outside the main thrust of his life's work. That can never happen to Bowie. For we have seen that he has immense strength of character, sensitivity both as actor and as creative musician and, by all accounts, generosity of spirit. We are confronted, therefore, by an utterly consistent artist. In all his 'changes', he is true to himself.

This book has tried to demonstrate the musical qualities of Bowie's creativity. These would be remarkable in themselves if there were nothing else to consider but of all rock-oriented musicians of the last twenty years it is true to say that hardly any other artist of world stature has had such a far-reaching influence on his own and successive generations as has Bowie. It is a chastening experience to look at the record sleeves of his early albums and to contrast them with those of current artists. There is something timeless about each Bowie album and certainly about his overall achievement. While Bowie was rebelling, through Ziggy and his sexuality, against the apparent complacency of much rock music of the early 1970s the high-energy street revolution of Punk in 1976 and 1977 can be said to have had its roots in 'unwashed and somewhat slightly dazed' of the "Space Oddity" album, together with the rebelliousness of "Ziggy Stardust" 'to be played at maximum volume'. Bowie's influence extends beyond Punk; indeed, it is hard to find any artist of consequence who has not been influenced by him in some way or another.

It nevertheless remains an astonishing fact that Bowie's recent work has been his most phenomenally successful, clear proof – if proof be needed – that his musical creativity is far from finished. But in retrospect the most surprising and almost inexplicable characteristic of this extraordinary man has been his commitment to himself to live out in music the story of his own remarkable life, and to perform the musical equivalent of that life in public appearances. Bowie is entirely unique, totally unafraid, and willing to invite us to share in his theatre of music. Those who admire his work respond to the invitation: that is the final and sufficient proof of his validity and relevance as a creative artist of the highest order.

APPENDIX 1

Select Discography

Of all important musicians of his generation, the recorded legacy of David Bowie is the most puzzling, for by no means all of his work has been invariably issued in album form. The B sides of singles, and sometimes the A sides as well, have occasionally remained the only format for certain material. As the album has now become the most important statement that a musician can make, it follows that material deemed unworthy to appear in album form is of less, often little, significance to the artist. In addition, singles – even hit singles – are almost invariably deleted after a few months, rendering the material unavailable.

This Appendix lists all recordings discussed in Part II, but recouplings and reissues are not listed automatically except where such information would assist, rather than tend to confuse, those anxious to obtain them. Singles subsequently issued from earlier albums are also not normally listed, unless there are good reasons to do so, and occasionally the record in question, if not discussed in Part II, will have a brief comment appended to it.

Record numbers shown are of UK releases; unless otherwise shown, all listings are for 12" (30 cm) long-playing ($33\frac{1}{3}$ rpm) albums); (45) after a record number signifies a 7" 45 rpm 'single' release. EPs, and ten-inch albums are shown where appropriate. Fuller discographical details (of backing artists, producers, recording and technical venues and dates) can often, but not always, be found on the relevant album sleeve. Although issued in several formats, only the album number is given; cassette, 8-track or compact disc release numbers are readily obtainable from record dealers.

1964

Davie Jones with the King Bees
Liza Jane/Louie Louie Go Home
Decca Vocalion-Pop V.9221 (45)

1965

The Manish Boys
I Pity The Fool/Take My Tip
Parlophone R.5250 (45)

Davy Jones (and The Lower Third)
You've Got A Habit Of Leaving/Baby Loves That Way
Parlophone R.5315 (45)

1966

David Bowie and The Lower Third
Can't Help Thinking About Me/And I Say To Myself
Pye 7N 17020 (45)

David Bowie
Do Anything You Say/Good Morning Girl
Pye 7N 17079 (45)

David Bowie
I Dig Everything/I'm Not Losing Sleep
Pye 7N 17157 (45)

David Bowie
Rubber Band/London Boys
Decca Deram DM 107 (45)

1967

From 1967, unless otherwise shown, all releases listed feature David Bowie exclusively.
The Laughing Gnome/The Gospel According to Tony Day
Decca Deram DM 123 (45)

'DAVID BOWIE'
Uncle Arthur; Sell Me A Coat; Rubber Band; Love You Till Tuesday; There Is A Happy Land; We Are Hungry Men; When I Live My Dream/Little Bombardier; Silly Boy Blue; Come And Buy My Toys; Join The Gang; She's Got Medals; Maids of Bond Street; Please Mr Gravedigger
Decca Deram DML 1007

Love You Till Tuesday/Did You Ever Have A Dream
Decca Deram DM 135 (45)
'Love You Till Tuesday' is a different recording from that contained on the album; it is not noticeably different, but is marginally preferable.

1969

Space Oddity/Wild Eyed Boy From Freecloud
Philips BF 1801 (45)
'Wild Eyed Boy From Freecloud' is a different recording from that issued on the subsequent album; arranged here for a tiny chamber group featuring acoustic guitar and a solo cello, this naturally focuses attention upon the linear and harmonic aspects of the song at a basic level, and is without the hefty orchestral feel of the album version. The song, of course, remains the same, but this exceptionally interesting version, of considerable character and fragile beauty, ought quite definitely to be made available again permanently.

'DAVID BOWIE'
Space Oddity; Unwashed and Somewhat Slightly Dazed; Letter to Hermione; Cygnet Committee/Janine; An Occasional Dream; The Wild

Eyed Boy From Freecloud; God Knows I'm Good; Memory of a Free Festival
Philips SBL 7912 Reissued in 1972 on RCA LSP 4813 as 'SPACE ODDITY'

1970

The Prettiest Star/Conversation Piece
Mercury MF 1135 (45)
Both of these original recordings remain otherwise unavailable; 'The Prettiest Star' is not the same version as appeared on the 'Aladdin Sane' album in 1973. The most obvious difference is the tempo, for here it is slower and the mood generally is not as febrile as it subsequently became; the character and gentleness of utterance – comparatively speaking – relate this performance to the musical pacification of 'Wild Eyed Boy From Freecloud' of a year before. 'Conversation Piece' is an interesting song, and it was also re-recorded in 1973 but has never been issued in this new version. The interest lies in the curious mixture of a relatively simple backing, akin to then-current country music, allied to a parlando text of somewhat obscure cast. But the song is not worthless, and certainly – along with much of Bowie's material from this period – deserves preservation in album form.

'THE WORLD OF DAVID BOWIE'
Uncle Arthur; Love You Till Tuesday; There Is A Happy Land; Little Bombardier; Sell Me A Coat; Silly Boy Blue; The London Boys/Karma Man; Rubber Band; Let Me Sleep Beside You; Come And Buy My Toys; She's Got Medals; In The Heat Of The Morning; When I Live My Dream
Decca SPA 58

Memory Of A Free Festival (parts 1/2)
Mercury 6052 026 (45)
As can be gleaned from the format, this is a much longer and extensively treated version of the song that concluded the Philips 'David Bowie'

album. It has little more than historical significance, but – once again – could make an intriguing reissue album track.

1971

Holy, Holy/Black Country Rock
Mercury 6052 049 (45)
'Holy, Holy' has been reissued in album form, on the Italian-originated 'Rare' album (see below).

'THE MAN WHO SOLD THE WORLD'
The Width of A Circle; All The Madmen; Black Country Rock; After All/Running Gun Blues; Saviour Machine; She Shook Me Cold; The Man Who Sold The World; The Supermen
Mercury 6338 041 Reissued in 1972 on RCA LSP 4816 with the same title

'HUNKY DORY'
Changes; Oh! You Pretty Things; Eight Line Poem; Life On Mars?; Kooks; Quicksand/Fill Your Heart; Andy Warhol; Song For Bob Dylan; Queen Bitch; The Bewlay Brothers
RCA SF 8244

1972

'THE RISE AND FALL OF ZIGGY STARDUST AND THE SPIDERS FROM MARS'
Five Years; Soul Love; Moonage Daydream; Starman; It Ain't Easy/ Lady Stardust; Star; Hang On To Yourself; Ziggy Stardust; Suffragette City; Rock 'n' Roll Suicide
RCA SF 8287

'REVELATIONS' A Musical Anthology For Glastonbury Fayre
David Bowie: Supermen; coupled with tracks by *The Grateful Dead, Brinsley Schwarz, Mighty Baby, Marc Bolan, Pete Townshend,*

Hawkwind, Skin Alley, Daevid Allen & Gong, The Pink Fairies, The Edgar Broughton Band
Revelation REV 1-3
A triple album compilation of music performed at the Glastonbury Fayre in 1971. Bowie's track is a studio version of 'Supermen' of considerable power and impact – if this is RCA property, it should certainly be reissued, rather than languish tantalisingly on this somewhat faded and comparatively unknown set.

John, I'm Only Dancing/Hang On To Yourself
RCA 2263 (45)
This is the first of three versions of 'John', all of which have been available at one time or another; it is the version which is apparently on later editions of the 'ChangesOneBowie' album.

1973

Drive-In Saturday/Around And Around
RCA 2352 (45)
'Around And Around' is another track that has never received LP transfer; it most certainly should be so reissued, for although the song is not by Bowie (it is by Chuck Berry), it receives a fabulous performance, one of Bowie's best efforts at interpreting another artist's material, but is – in the nature of things – utterly unknown.

'ALADDIN SANE'
Watch That Man; Aladdin Sane (1913–1938–197?); Drive-In Saturday; Panic in Detroit; Cracked Actor/Time; The Prettiest Star; Let's Spend The Night Together; The Jean Genie; Lady Grinning Soul
RCA RS 1001

Sorrow/Amsterdam
RCA 2424 (45)
'Amsterdam' is little more than an apparent out-take from the then-imminent 'Pin-Ups' album, on which, thankfully, it does not appear. The song, by Jacques Brel, is mildly interesting, but is so distoned and maltreated by Bowie as to make one think one of two things: either he

hates the song so intensely that he feels he has to murder it, or that he felt some good could have come from a completely inside-out view of the material. Such artistic entrails as are picked over in this performance are hardly worth the effort. The song resurfaced on the 'Rare' Italian compilation.

'PIN-UPS'
Rosalyn; Here Comes The Night; I Wish You Would; See Emily Play; Everything's Alright; I Can't Explain/Friday On My Mind; Sorrow; Don't Bring Me Down; Shapes Of Things; Anyway, Anyhow, Anywhere; Where Have All The Good Times Gone?
RCA RS 1003

1974

'DIAMOND DOGS'
Future Legend; Bewitched, Bothered and Bewildered; Diamond Dogs; Sweet Thing; Candidate; Sweet Thing – reprise; Rebel Rebel/Rock 'n' Roll With Me; We Are The Dead; 1984; Big Brother; Chant Of The Ever Circling Skeletal Family
RCA APL1 0576

Knock On Wood/Panic In Detroit
RCA 2466 (45)
These are live recordings, the first included on the "David Live" album listed below, but the version of "Panic In Detroit" has never appeared in album form. It is only for fervid admirers of live recordings.

'DAVID LIVE'
Record 1:
1984; Rebel, Rebel; Moonage Daydream; Sweet Thing/Changes; Suffragette City; Aladdin Sane; All The Young Dudes; Cracked Actor
Record 2:
When You Rock'n'Roll With Me; Watch That Man; Knock On Wood; Diamond Dogs/Big Brother; Width Of A Circle; Jean Genie; Rock'n'Roll Suicide
RCA APL2 0771 (2)

1975

'YOUNG AMERICANS'
Young Americans; Win; Fascination; Right/Somebody Up There Likes Me; Across The Universe; Can You Hear Me; Fame
RCA RS 1006

'IMAGES'
Record 1:
Rubber Band; Maids Of Bond Street; Sell Me A Coat; Love You Till Tuesday; There Is A Happy Land/The Laughing Gnome; The Gospel According To Tony Day; Did You Ever Have A Dream; Uncle Arthur; We Are Hungry Men; When I Live My Dream
Record 2:
Join The Gang; Little Bombardier; Come And Buy My Toys; Silly Boy Blue; She's Got Medals/Please Mr Gravedigger; London Boys; Karma Man; Let Me Sleep Beside You; In The Heat Of The Morning
Decca Deram DPA 3017/8 – 2-record set
Bowie's complete Decca recordings definitively assembled.
Space Oddity/Changes; Velvet Goldmine
RCA 2593 (45)
This was one of a series of 'Maximillion' 45 reissued discs, containing three tracks 'for the price of two'. 'Velvet Goldmine' had not been released before, and resurfaced on the 'Rare' album. It has been suggested that this first release was done without Bowie's approval, which is very surprising if true, but one can understand the star's reluctance to sanction the issue, for it does not reveal him at anything like his best. If it is true, then the chart position achieved by this reissue (No 1 in the UK charts, it's first appearance at the top) would have tended to blunt criticism.

1976

'STATION TO STATION'
Station To Station; Golden Years; Word On A Wing/TVC 15; Stay; Wild Is The Wind
RCA APL1 1327

'CHANGESONEBOWIE'
Space Oddity; John, I'm Only Dancing; Changes; Ziggy Stardust; Suffragette City, The Jean Genie/Diamond Dogs; Rebel Rebel; Young Americans; Fame; Golden Years
RCA RS 1055

1977

'LOW'
Speed Of Life; Breaking Glass; What In The World; Sound And Vision; Always Crashing In The Same Car; Be My Wife; A New Career In A New Town/Warszawa; Art Decade; Weeping Wall; Subterraneans
RCA PL 12030

'HEROES'
Beauty and The Beast; Joe The Lion; "Heroes"; Sons Of The Silent Age; Blackout/V-2 Schneider; Sense Of Doubt; Moss Garden; Neuköln; The Secret Life Of Arabia
RCA PL 12533

1978

PROKOFIEV: PETER AND THE WOLF opus 67
David Bowie, narrator
Philadelphia Orchestra, Eugene Ormandy, conductor
RCA RL 12743
The circumstances surrounding the release of this version of Prokofiev's work are related in the main body of the book; it is an excellent performance, with Bowie adopting just the right youthful avuncular style which shows this fairy-tale in its best light, far removed from the patronising attitude so often adopted. The orchestral playing is first-class, as one would expect, and the balance between Bowie's voice and the Philadelphia Orchestra is beautifully judged. The reverse is a brilliant performance of Britten's 'Young Person's Guide To The Orchestra' (Variations and Fugue on a Theme of Purcell, op 34),

without narration, which is a pity, for in its original form the work had an important part for narrator, with additional music never heard today.

'STAGE'
Record 1:
Hang On To Yourself; Ziggy Stardust; Five Years; Soul Love; Star/Station To Station; Fame; TVC 15
Record 2:
Warszawa; Speed Of Life; Art Decade; Sense Of Doubt; Breaking Glass/"Heroes"; What In The World; Blackout; Beauty And The Beast
RCA PL 02913 (2) – double-album
This album is not commented upon in the main body of this book; it consists of recordings of live versions of material already better performed and recorded, and available, on studio albums. The performances add nothing to our appreciation of the artist, other than his manifest ability to create on stage music previously created in the studio. The only additional ingredient is the noise of the audience, which some may consider a mixed blessing.

1979

'LODGER'
Fantastic Voyage; African Night Flight; Move On; Yassassin; Red Sails/D.J.; Look Back In Anger; Boys Keep Swinging; Repetition; Red Money
RCA BOW LP 1
John, I'm Only Dancing (Again)/John, I'm Only Dancing
RCA BOW 4 (45)
The (Again) version was recorded at the Sigma Sound Studios during the making of the 'Young Americans' album in 1975, and was coupled with the original single version of three years earlier. In many ways, the 1975 edition was a very superior performance to the original, although the melodic qualities of the song tend to get lost, recollected almost as a half-remembered dream.

1980

Alabama Song/Space Oddity
RCA BOW 5 (45)
This version of the 'Alabama Song' from Kurt Weill's 'The Rise And Fall Of The City Of Mahagonny', with a libretto by Bertholt Brecht owes something to Lotte Lenya's original (1930) recording, and her later remake from the late 1950s, but it is an astonishing version, utterly in keeping with the spirit, and almost the letter, of the original English song within the original German. The deliberate confusion of Weill's bitonality is brilliantly caught, the spirit-sodden brain of the desperate alcoholic tending to overtake all, which is not quite what Weill and Brecht intended, but nevertheless a valid and – apart from the unnecessary speeding-up just before the end – impressive version. The recording of 'Space Oddity' was brand new, being made in London in September 1979; it is essentially different from the original, being a cleaner, sparer, and more *musical* performance, showing how significant this song had become for its creator – without becoming too significant.

Crystal Japan/Alabama Song
RCA Japan (RVC) SS-3270 (45)
'Crystal Japan' was released on the 'Rare' album, thereby being the first chance most Europeans had had to hear the music he created for the Japanese television commercial; it is slow, faintly hypnotic, and exudes an atmosphere of heady, relaxed contemplation. However, it hardly has a particularly strong or immediately recognisable character, but it is an interesting chip from the workbench.

'SCARY MONSTERS (AND SUPER CREEPS)'
It's No Game; Up The Hill Backwards; Scary Monsters (And Super Creeps); Ashes to Ashes; Fashion/Teenage Wildlife; Scream Like A Baby; Kingdom Come; Because You're Young; It's No Game (No 2)
RCA BOW LP 2

1981

'DON'T BE FOOLED BY THE NAME'
I'm Not Losing Sleep; I Dig Everything; Can't Help Thinking About Me/Do Anything You Say; Good Morning Girl; And I Say To Myself
PRT DOW 1 – 10" LP
A useful reissue of Bowie's six Pye recordings. Because only six were taped for that company, a 10-inch $33\frac{1}{3}$ rpm LP record (common in the 1950s and early 1960s, but exceptionally rare since) was the most logical, if unusual, format.

'CHRISTIANE F. – WIR KINDER VOM BAHNHOF ZOO'
Original Soundtrack
V-2 Schneider; TVC-15; Heroes-Helden; Boys Keep Swinging; Sense Of Doubt/Station To Station; Look Back In Anger; Stay; Warszawa
RCA (Germany) BL 43606
The songs featured in the film, and an interesting memento of an outstanding landmark in post-war German cinema, as well as offering the German-language version of "Heroes".

David Bowie and Queen
Under Pressure/Soul Brother
EMI 5250 (45)
An interesting admixture of first-class artists combining their talents, and successfully so, for within a short while the single went to number one in the UK singles charts, where it remained for two weeks. The success of this effort might very well have impressed Bowie with EMI's marketing and promotional skills, and could have led to him signing with that company a year later. But musically, it adds little to our knowledge of Bowie's art.

'CHANGESTWOBOWIE'
Aladdin Sane; Oh You Pretty Things; Starman; 1984; Ashes To Ashes/ Sound And Vision; Fashion; Wild Is The Wind; John, I'm Only Dancing (Again) (1975 version); D.J.
RCA BOW LP 3
'Bowie's 'Greatest Hits', Volume 2', the track-listing being all the

prospective purchaser would wish to know. Not discussed in the text, the performances have all been available previously.

1982

'BAAL'
Baal's Hymn; Remembering Marie A/Ballard of the Adventurers; The Drowned Girl; The Dirty Song
RCA (Germany) PG 45092
Released to coincide with the BBC television broadcast of Brecht's *Baal*, these brief songs, an integral part of the play, were written by Brecht and are well performed by Bowie, a fascinating document, as valuable as the earlier 'Alabama Song' performance as evidence of his fascination with the art contemporary with the collapse of the Weimar Republic.

'ANOTHER FACE'
Rubber Band; The London Boys; The Gospel According To Tony Day; There Is A Happy Land; Maids Of Bond Street; When I Live My Dream; Liza Jane/The Laughing Gnome; In The Heat Of The Morning; Did You Ever Have A Dream; Please, Mr Gravedigger; Join The Gang; Love You Till Tuesday; Louie, Louie, Go Home
Decca TAB 17
A good selection from Bowie's early material.

David Bowie and Bing Crosby
Peace On Earth; Little Drummer Boy/Fantastic Voyage
RCA BOW 12 (45)
A piece of history, it has to be listened to with indulgence, in much the same way as the televised duet between Frank Sinatra and Elvis Presley had to be; the voices blend better than might have been expected, but the result is artistically curious rather than valuable.

The Manish Boys/Davy Jones and The Lower Third
I Pity The Fool; Take My Tip/You've Got A Habit Of Leaving; Baby Loves That Way
Charly CYM 1 10" $33\frac{1}{3}$ rpm

This ten-inch album (similar to the PRT issue noted above) conveniently groups Bowie's earliest recordings, and is the second such compilation to be released, the first, in 1979, was on EMI's NUT EP (45) series, EMI 2925.

'BOWIE RARE'
Ragazza Solo, Ragazza Sola; 'Round and 'Round; Amsterdam; Holy, Holy; Panic In Detroit; Young Americans/Velvet Goldmine; Helden; John, I'm Only Dancing (Again) (1975); Moon Of Alabama; Crystal Japan
RCA PL 45406
The Italian-originated valuable collection of earlier, often long-unobtainable, songs including the instrumental 'Crystal Japan'.

1983

'LET'S DANCE'
Modern Love; China Girl; Let's Dance; Without You/Ricochet; Criminal World; Cat People (Putting Out Fire); Shake It
EMI America AML 3029

'A SECOND FACE'
Let Me Sleep Beside You; Sell Me A Coat; She's Got Medals; We Are Hungry Men; In The Heat Of The Morning/Karma Man; Little Bombardier; Love You Till Tuesday; Come And Buy My Toys; Silly Boy Blue; Uncle Arthur; When I Live My Dream
Decca TAP 71
The companion album to 'Another Face', some of whose titles it duplicates.

1984

'TONIGHT'
Loving The Alien; Don't Look Down; God Only Knows; Tonight/Neighbourhood Threat; Blue Jean; Tumble And Twirl; I Keep Forgettin'; Dancing With The Big Boys
EMI America DB 1

1985

David Bowie and Pat Methany
This Is Not America/Instrumental
EMI EA 190 (45)

ALBUMS PRODUCED BY DAVID BOWIE REFERRED TO IN CHAPTER TWELVE

1972

Mott The Hoople
'ALL THE YOUNG DUDES'
Sweet Jane; Momma's Little Jewel; All The Young Dudes; Sucker; Jerkin' Crocus/One Of The Boys; Soft Ground; Ready For Love – After Lights; Sea Diver
CBS 65184

Lou Reed
'TRANSFORMER'
Vicious; Andy's Chest; Perfect Day; Hangin' 'Round; Walk On The Wild Side/Make Up; Satellite Of Love; Wagon Wheel; New York Telephone Conversation; I'm So Fine; Goodnight Ladies
RCA LSP 4807

1973

Iggy And The Stooges
'RAW POWER'
Search And Destroy; Gimme Danger; Your Pretty Face Is Going To Hell; Penetration/Raw Power; I Need Somebody; Shake Appeal; Death Trip
CBS 65586
Although not, strictly speaking, produced by David Bowie in the generally accepted sense of the term, as the text makes clear this album

could not have seen the light of day without Bowie's extensive post-'production' work on the original tapes.

1977

Iggy Pop
'THE IDIOT'
Sister Midnight; Nighclubbing; Funtime; Baby; China Girl/Dum Dum Boys; Tiny Girls; Mass Production
RCA PL 12275

Iggy Pop
'LUST FOR LIFE'
Lust For Life; Sixteen; Some Weird Sin; The Passenger; Tonight/Success; True Blue; Neighbourhood Threat; Fall In Love With Me
RCA PL 12488

1978

Iggy Pop
'T.V. EYE'
T.V. Eye; Funtime; Sixteen; I Got A Right/Lust For Life; Dirt; Nighclubbing; I Wanna Be Your Dog
RCA PL 12796

APPENDIX 2

Filmography

1968

THE VIRGIN SOLDIERS
Columbia Pictures
Director..................................John Dexter
Producer................................Ned Sherrin
Screenplay............................adapted from the novel by Leslie Thomas by John Hopkins
Starring: Hywel Bennet, Nigel Patrick, Lynn Redgrave, Nigel Davenport
David Bowie features as an extra in one scene in a bar-room.

1969

LOVE YOU TILL TUESDAY
Kenneth Pitt
Creative Director......................Malcolm J. Thomson
Producer..................................Kenneth Pitt
Director of Photography............David McDonald
Starring: David Bowie, with Hermione Farthingale, John Hutchinson, and others also featured.

1969

THE IMAGE
Negus-Fancey/Border Films
Director...................................Michael Armstrong
Producer.................................Negus Fancey
Screenplay.............................Michael Armstrong
Starring: David Bowie, Michael Armstrong.

1976

THE MAN WHO FELL TO EARTH
British Lion Films
Director...................................Nicholas Roeg
Producers..............................Michael Deeley, Barry Spikings
Screenplay.............................Paul Mayersberg
Starring: David Bowie, Rip Torn, Candy Clark, Buck Henry, Bernie Casey, Jackson D. Kane, Rick Riccardo, Tony Mascia.

1978

JUST A GIGOLO
Leguan Films
Director...................................David Hemmings
Producer.................................Rolf Thiele
Screenplay.............................Ennio De Conan, Joshua Sinclair
Starring: David Bowie, Sydne Rome, Kim Novak, David Hemmings, Maria Schell, Kurt Jurgens, Marlene Dietrich.

1981

WIR KINDER VOM BAHNHOF ZOO (CHRISTIANE F.)
Solaris Film Productions
Director.....................................Ulrich Edel
Producers.................................Bernd Eichinger
Screenplay...............................Herman Weigel
Starring: Natja Brunckhorst, Thomas Haustein; David Bowie appears as himself.

1983

THE HUNGER
MGM
Director.....................................Tony Scott
Producer..................................Richard Shepherd
Screenplay..............................Ivan Davis and Michael Thomas
Starring: David Bowie, Catherine Deneuve, Susan Sarandon, Beth Ehlers, Graham Jarvis, Zoe Wanamaker, Pete Murphy.

MERRY CHRISTMAS, MR LAWRENCE
Palace Pictures (A UK/Japanese Production)
Director.....................................Nagisa Oshima
Producer..................................Jeremy Thomas
Screenplay..............................Nagisha Oshima and Paul Mayersberg
Starring: David Bowie, Tom Conti, Jack Thomson.

YELLOWBEARD
Orion Pictures
Director.....................................Mel Damski
Producer..................................Carter De Haven
Screenplay..............................Graham Chapman, Peter Cook, Bernard McKenna
Starring: Graham Chapman, Peter Boyle, Peter Cook, Marty Feldman,

Eric Idle, Madeline Kahn, James Mason, John Cleese. David Bowie plays a cameo part.

1984

JAZZIN' FOR BLUE JEAN
Picture Music
Director..................................Julian Temple
Starring: David Bowie, Lorion Scott.

1985

INTO THE NIGHT
Universal
Director..................................John Landis
Producers..............................George Folsey, jr. and Ron Koslow
Screenplay............................Ron Koslow
Starring: Jeff Goldblum, Michelle Pfeiffer, Richard Farnsworth, Irene Papas, Kathryn Harrold and David Bowie.

1986

LABYRINTH
Henson Associates Inc/Lucasfilm
Director..................................Jim Henson
Producer................................Eric Rattray
Screenplay............................Terry Jones, Laura Phillips
Starring: David Bowie.

APPENDIX 3

Select Bibliography

Bowie, Angie: *Free Spirit* Mushroom 1981
Charlesworth, Chris: *David Bowie – A Profile* Proteus 1981
Cann, Kevin: *David Bowie – A Chronology* Vermilion 1983
Carr, Roy and Shaar Murray, Charles: *Bowie – An Illustrated Record* Eel Pie 1981
Douglas, David: *Presenting David Bowie* Pinnacle Books 1975
Miles, Barry: *Bowie In His Own Words* Omnibus Press 1980
Miles, Barry: *David Bowie Black Book* Omnibus Press 1980
Pitt, Kenneth: *David Bowie – The Pitt Report* Design Music 1983
Tremlett, George: *The David Bowie Story* Futura 1974
Various: *David Bowie – A Portrait* Wise Publications 1974

Index of Music and Album Titles

1984 35, 98, 101, 102

A New Career In A New Town 109
Abraham and Isaac (Britten) 67
Across the Universe 103, 104, 105
African Night Flight 119, 121
After All 71, 73, 74
Alabama Song 49
Aladdin Sane 31, 32, 33, 36, 37, 88, 89, 90, 91, 93, 94, 96, 98, 102, 166
All the Madmen 25, 71, 72
All The Young Dudes 30, 102, 146
All You Need Is Love 69
Always Crashing In The Same Car 109, 111
An Occasional Dream 66, 69
And I Say To Myself 10, 60, 165
Andy Warhol 77, 80, 81
Anyway Anyhow 97, 98
Art Decade 109, 113
Ashes to Ashes 50, 125, 126, 127, 151

Baby Loves That Way 8, 59, 60
Beauty and the Beast 114
Because Your Young 125, 130
Be My Wife 109, 111
Best of Bowie, The 51
Bewitched, Bothered and Bewildered 35, 36, 98, 99
Bewlay Brothers, The 77, 82

Big Brother 98, 101, 102
Black Country Rock 71, 73
Blackout 114, 116
Blueberry Hill 4
Blue Jean 135, 137, 138
Bowie Rare 130
Boys Keep Swinging 49, 119, 151
Breaking Glass 109, 110
Brown Sugar 94

Candidate 98
Can't Help Thinking About Me 10, 11, 60
Can You Hear Me 103, 105
Carmina Burana (Carl Orff) 61
Cat People (Putting Out Fire) 130, 133, 134
Changes 77, 79, 102, 108
ChangesoneBowie 43, 108
ChangestwoBowie 51, 130
Chant of the Ever Circling Skeletal Family 98, 101
China Girl 52, 130, 131, 151
Ching-A-Ling 150
Come and Buy my Toys 64
Conversation Piece 23
Cracked Actor 32, 38, 92, 102
Criminal World 130, 133
CRY (Giles Swayne) 101
Crystal Japan 50

191

Dancing With The Big Boys 135, 139
David Live 102
Diamond Dogs 35, 36, 37, 38, 39, 98, 99, 102, 108
Did You Ever Have A Dream? 13, 66
D.J. 119, 122
Do Anything You Say 11, 61
Don't Bring Me Down 97
Don't Look Down 135, 136, 137
Drive-In-Saturday 31, 88, 91

Eight Line Poem 77
Even A Fool Loves To Love 15
Everything's Alright 97

Fame 41, 103, 105, 108
Fantastic Voyage 119, 120, 121
Fascination 103, 104
Fashion 125, 127
Fill Your Heart 77, 80
Five Years 83, 84
Friday on My Mind 97
Future Legend 35, 36, 98, 99

God Knows I'm Good 66, 69
God Only Knows 135, 136
Golden Years 41, 42, 105, 106, 108
Good Morning Girl 11, 61, 165
Gospel According to Tony Day, The 12, 63

Hair 151
Hang on to Yourself 83, 87
Hearts and Bones 132
Here Comes the Night 97
"Heroes" 45, 46, 114, 115, 117, 119, 120, 122
Hey Jude 146
Hound Dog 4
Hunky Dory 27, 82, 166

I Can't Explain 97, 98
I Dig Everything 61
I Keep Forgettin' 135, 138
I Pity the Fool 7, 59
I Was Kaiser Bill's Batman 62
I Wish You Would 97
Idiot The 43, 131, 147
Images 40
I'm Not Losing Sleep 61, 165
In The Heat Of The Morning 65
It Ain't Easy 83, 85
It's No Game (No 1) 125, 126
It's No Game (No 2) 125, 130

Janine 66, 69
Jean Genie 30, 88, 93, 102, 103, 108
Joe The Lion 114, 115
John I'm Only Dancing 30, 40, 108
Join The Gang 64

Karma Man 66
Keep on Running 61
Kingdom Come 125, 129
Knock on Wood 102
Kooks 25, 77, 79

Lady Grinning Soul 88, 94, 96
Lady Stardust 83, 86
Laughing Gnome, The 12, 13, 35, 63, 64, 65, 73
Let Me Sleep Beside You 66, 151
Let's Dance 52, 53, 130, 131, 132, 134, 151
Let's Spend the Night Together 88, 93
Letter to Hermione 66
Life on Mars? 77, 78, 79, 166
Little Bombardier 64
Little Drummer Boy, The 46
Liza Jane 6, 58
Lodger 48, 49, 119, 120, 124, 125
London Boys 12, 62, 63

London Bye Ta-Ta 23
Look Back In Anger 119
Louie, Louie Go Home 6, 58
Love You Till Tuesday 13, 64, 66
Loving The Alien 135
Low 44, 45, 46, 109, 112, 113, 114, 115, 116, 117, 118, 119
Lust for Life 45, 136, 137, 147

Man Who Sold The World, The 24, 25, 26, 31, 37, 46, 71, 75, 76, 77, 78, 79, 84, 101, 153, 166
Maids of Bond Street 13, 64, 65
Maria (West Side Story) 69, 86
Memory of a Free Festival 21, 66, 69, 73
Modern Love 130, 131
Moonage Daydream 83, 84, 102
Moss Garden 114, 118
Move On 119, 121
My Way 16, 79

Neighbourhood Threat 135, 137
Neuköln 114, 118
New Values 135

Oh You Pretty Things 25, 77

Paganini Rhapsody (Rachmaninoff) 91
Pal Joey 99
Panic in Detroit 32, 88, 91
Peter and the Wolf 46
Piano Concerto (Gershwin) 108
Pin-Ups 34, 35, 96, 97, 98, 99, 167
Please Mr Gravedigger 64, 65
Prettiest Star, The 23, 32, 88, 92, 93

Queen Bitch 37, 77, 81, 86
Quicksand 77, 79, 80

Ragazzo Solo, Ragazza Sola 24
Ready Teddy 4
Rebel, Rebel 37, 52, 98, 102, 108
Red Morning 119, 124
Red Sails 119, 122, 124
Repetition 119
Ricochet 130, 133
Right 103, 104
Rip It Up 4
Rise and Fall of the City of Mahagonny 49
Rise and Fall of Ziggy Stardust and the Spiders from Mars 28, 36, 71, 83, 85, 88, 90, 166
Rock 'n' Roll Suicide 83, 87, 89, 102
Rock 'n' Roll With Me 98, 100
Ronnie d'Habitude 15
Rosalyn 97
Rubber Band 12, 62, 64, 151
Running Gun Blues 71, 74

Saviour Machine 71, 74
Scary Monsters 50, 125, 126, 130, 131
Scream Like a Baby 125, 129
See Emily Play 97
Secret Life of Arabia, The 114, 119
Sell Me A Coat 64, 65
Sense of Doubt 114, 118
Sergeant Pepper's Lonely Heart's Club Band 144
Shake It 130, 134
Shakin' All Over 8
Shapes of Things 97, 98
She's Got Medals 64
She Shook Me Cold 71, 75
Silly Boy Blue 64
Sinfonia Antartica (Vaughan Williams) 118
Somebody Up There Likes Me 103, 104

Somewhere Over The Rainbow 85
Songfest (Bernstein) 90
Song For Bob Dylan 25, 77, 81
Sons of the Silent Age 114, 115, 116
Sorrow 35, 97, 98
Soul Love 83, 84, 85
Sound and Vision 109, 110, 111
Space Oddity 16, 19, 20, 21, 22, 23, 24, 41, 49, 66, 67, 68, 71, 108, 149, 150, 151, 153, 166, 169
Speed of Life 109, 110
Stage 47, 48, 103
Star 83, 86, 87
Starlight Express 38
Starman 28, 83, 85, 153
Station to Station 41, 42, 44, 105, 108, 109
Stay 105, 107
Subterraneans 109, 113, 114
Suffragette City 83, 87, 102, 108
Superman 26, 71, 76, 77
Sweet Thing 98, 100, 102
Symphony No 4 (Shostakovitch) 64
Symphony No 11 (Shostakovitch) 112

Take My Tip 7, 59
Teenage Wildlife 125, 128, 129
Tennessee Waltz 63
There is a Happy Land 64
Time 88, 92
Tonight 135, 136
Transformer 146
Tubular Bells (Mike Oldfield) 113
Tumble and Twirl 135, 138, 139
TVC 15 44, 105, 107
TV Eye 147
Twist and Shout 59, 132

Uncle Arthur 64

Unwashed and Somewhat Slightly Dazed 66, 67
Up The Hill Backwards 125, 126

V-2 Schneider 114, 117

Walk on the Wild Side 147
Watch That Man 32, 37, 88, 90, 102
War Requiem (Britten) 62
Warszawa 109, 112, 113
We Are Hungry Men 13, 64
We Are The Dead 98, 100
Weeping Wall 109, 113
West Side Story (Bernstein) 86
What In The World 109, 110
When I Live My Dreams 13, 19, 64, 151
When I'm Five 150, 151
When You Rock 'n' Roll With Me 102
Where Have All The Good Times Gone? 97, 98
Width of a Circle, The 71, 73, 74, 75, 77, 102
Wild-Eyed Boy From Freecloud 19, 66, 69
Wild Is The Wind 105, 106, 108
Win 103
Without You 130, 133
Word on a Wing 105, 107

Yassassin 119, 121, 122
You Keep Me Hanging On 85
Young Americans 39, 40, 41, 103, 105, 106, 108, 113, 116
You've Got A Habit Of Leaving 8, 59

Ziggy Stardust (Album: see 'The Rise and Fall of Ziggy Stardust and the Spiders from Mars')
Ziggy Stardust (song) 83, 87, 108, 169

Index of Persons

Alomar, Carlos 52, 119
Armstrong, Michael 16, 17, 149
Anglim, Philip 50
Anka, Paul 16, 79

Band Seven 7
Barnet, Helena Marie 18
Barnet, Mary-Angela (Angie Bowie) 17, 18, 19, 20, 21, 24, 121, 162
Barnet, Milton John 18
Barraqué, Jean 93
Bart, Lionel 8, 104
Beach Boys The 136, 138
Beatles, The 12, 59, 69, 103, 132, 143, 144, 146, 166
Berger, Helmut 154
Berliner, Emile 143
Bernstein, Leonard 69, 90
Birkett, Jack 150
Bloom, John 6
Bolan, Marc 7, 15, 17, 34, 45, 46, 86
Bolan, Rolan 46
Bowie, Jim 10
Bowie, Zowie (son) 25, 46, 49, 51, 79, 94
Brecht, Berthold 49, 51, 155, 156, 157
Britten, Benjamin 62, 67
Brown, Arthur 9

Buckmaster, Paul 19
Burbeck, Rodney 27, 28
Buretti, Freddi 26, 35, 146
Burns, Margaret (mother): *see* Jones, Margaret
Buzz, The 11
Byrne, Michael 149

Cage, John 44
Cambridge, John 23
Carr, Roy 97
Chaplin, Lady Oona 49
Chopin, Frederic 34
Churchill, Sir Winston 80
Clark, Candy 153
Clark, Lord 165
Clarke, Alan 156
Coltrane, John 5
Conn, Leslie 6, 7, 58
Conti, Tom 52, 159
Corns, Arnold 146
Cropper, Steve 103
Crosby, Bing 46
Crowley, Aleister 79, 80

Damski, Mel 162
Davies, Ray 85
Davis, Spencer 60, 61
Debussy, Claude 77
Defries, Tony 24, 26, 27, 28, 30, 37, 39, 40, 41

195

Deneuve, Catherine 52, 157, 158
Dexter, John 150
Dietrich, Marlene 47, 154
Dolphy, Eric 5
Domino, Fats 4
Doors, The 110, 134
Dvorak, Antonin 81
Dylan, Bob 25, 69, 81, 162

Edel, Ulrich 162
Edinburgh, Duke of 46
Edison, Thomas Alva 143
Eichinger, Bernd 51
Elizabeth, Princess (Queen Elizabeth II) 46
Eno, Brian 44, 46, 48, 50, 112, 113, 115, 118, 119, 120

Fame, Georgie 7
Farlowe, Chris 61
Farthingale, Hermione 15, 16, 150
Finch, Peter 151
Fish, Mr 25
Flowers, Herbie 19
Floyd, Eddie 103
Frampton, Peter 5
François, Claude 15

Gamble and Huff 38, 39, 105
Garbo, Greta 80
Garson, Mike 91
Genet, Jean 93
George and the Dragons 5
Georve VI, King 46
Gerry and the Pacemakers 8
Gershwin, George 107
Glancy, Ken 38, 39, 105

Hall, Tony 13
Hart, Lorenz 35, 99
Harty, Russell 41
Hatch, Tony 8, 10, 60, 61

Hayes, Isaac 107
Hemmings, David 45, 153, 154
Henze, Hans Werner 120
Hilton, Ronnie 13
Himmler, Heinrich 79, 80
Hofsiss, Jack 49
Horton, Ralph 9, 11, 12
Humble Pie 21
Hurt, John 155
Hutchinson, John 16
Huxley, Aldous 100
Hype, The 23

Jackson, Chuck 138
Jackson, Glenda 151
Jagger, Mick 93, 153
Jones, Annette 3
Jones, Davy/Davey/Davie (David Bowie) 7, 8, 9, 166
Jones, Davy (of the Monkees) 10
Jones, Haywood Stenton (father) 5, 20, 94
Jones, Hilda 3, 4
Jones, Margaret (Peggy), (mother) 4, 51
Jones, Terence 4, 32, 82, 94
Junior's Eyes 23
Jürgens, Curt 154

Katz, Dennis 26
Kemp, Lindsay 14, 149, 150, 159
Kemp, William 14
Kidd, Johnny and the Pirates 8
King Bees, The 6, 59
King Crimson 17
Kinks, The 8, 61
Kon-Rads, The 5
Kubrick, Stanley 16, 167

Langford, Barry 7
Lee, Calvin Mark 18, 19
Lee, Peggy 68

Leiber, Jerry 138
Lennon, John 39, 69, 105
Lenya, Lotte 49
Lewis, Jerry Lee 93
Linnear, Claudia 94
Lippman, Michael 41, 44
Little Ravens, The 5
Lloyd Webber, Andrew 38
Lower Third, The 8, 11
Lukan, George 41
Lulu 37

McCartney, Paul 69
Mace, Ralph 26, 46
McEnroe, John 52
Macmillan, Harold 165
Manish Boys, The 7, 59
Margaret, Princess 21
Martin, George 144
Maxwell Davies, Peter 91
Menon, Bhaskar 52
Merrick, John 49, 50, 155
Merseys, The 98
Metro 133
Michelmore, Cliff 7
Miller, Kenny 7
Money, Zoot Big Roll Band 7
Monkees, The 10, 29
Moroder, George 134
Morrison, Jim 134
Most, Micky 25
Mott the Hoople, 30, 102, 146
Murphy, Brian 149
Murray, Charles Shaar 97
Mussorgsky, Modest 112

Nesbit, Frank 151
Newley, Anthony 13, 63, 84, 98
Nixon, President Richard M. 90
Noone, Peter 25
Novak, Kim 154

Oldfield, Mike 113
Oldham, Andrew Loog 21
Olivier, Sir Laurence 156
Orff, Carl 61
Ormandy, Eugene 46
Orwell, George 35, 36, 100
Oshima, Nagisa 158, 160, 161

Palmer, Tony 21, 151
Paramor, Norrie 19
Peel, John 25
Peellaert, Guy 36, 100
Pennebaker, D.A. 162
Picasso, Pablo 168
Pickett, Wilson 64
Pitney, Gene 8
Pitt, Kenneth 9, 10, 11, 12, 13, 14,
    15, 16, 19, 20, 24, 40, 65, 150
Pomerance, Bernard 49, 155
Pop, Iggy 27, 31, 40, 41, 43, 44, 45,
    52, 53, 131, 135, 136, 137, 138,
    139, 147
Presley, Elvis 4, 27, 38, 102, 153
Prokofiev, Serge 46

Queen 51

Rachmaninoff, Serge 91
Ravel, Maurice 77
Reed, Lou 27, 29, 146
Revere, Paul 59
Richard, Keith 41, 93
Richard, Little 4, 5, 158
Rigg, Diana 37
Riviera, Jake 26
Rodgers, Nile 52, 132
Rodgers, Richard 35, 99
Roeg, Nicholas 40, 44, 151, 152,
    153
Rolling Stones, The 12, 21, 58, 59,
    94, 99
Rome, Sydne 45, 154

Ronson, Mick 23, 37, 85, 86, 98
Rose, Biff 80
Ross, Ronnie 5

Sakamoto, Ryuichi 160
Sarandon, Sarah 157
Scaffold, The 18
Schlesinger, John 151
Scott, Tony 52, 157
Scott, Sir Walter 151
Shakespeare, William 160
Shepp, Archie 91
Shostakovitch, Dmitri 64, 112
Simon, Paul 68, 132
Sinatra, Frank 15, 79
Smith, Dick 158
Starr, Ringo 162
Stoller, Mike 138
Stravinsky, Igor 168

Takeshi, Beat 160
Talmy, Shel 7, 8, 59
Thomas, Leslie 16, 150
Thomson, Malcolm J. 150
Three Degrees, The 38
Tiomkin, Dmitri 107
Torn, Rip 153
Trevis, Walter 41, 151, 152, 153
Turner, Tina 137

Twiggy 34, 162

Underwood, George 5, 6, 25

Valentino Rudy 26
van der Post, Sir Laurens 52, 158, 159
Vaughan Williams, Ralph 118
Verdi, Giuseppe 81
Verlaine, Tom 129
Visconti, Tony 13, 14, 23, 44, 47, 119

Wakeman, Rick 19, 80
Warhol, Andy 27, 31, 80, 81
Washington, Ned 108
Wath, Hans 51
Weill, Kurt 49
Who, The 18, 59, 60, 98
Willett, John 156
Williams, Paul 80
Wilson, Harold 165
Woodmanssey, Woody 24
Wyndham, John 164
Wyper, Olav 26

Yentob, Alan 153
York, Michael 154